D0935446

The Yellow Earl

The Yellow Earl

THE LIFE OF HUGH LOWTHER
5TH EARL OF LONSDALE, K.G., G.C.V.O.,
1857-1944

by

Douglas Sutherland

With a Preface by the present Earl

COWARD-McCANN, Inc.

NEW YORK

DA566
.9
.L6S9
1966

COPYRIGHT © 1965 BY DOUGLAS SUTHERLAND
FIRST AMERICAN EDITION 1966

All rights reserved. This book, or parts thereof, may not be reproduced in any form without permission in writing from the Publisher.

Library of Congress Catalog
Card Number: 66-10422

MANUFACTURED IN THE UNITED STATES OF AMERICA

To Muriel, Viscountess Lowther,
with my thanks for all the help
she has given me with this book

223248

Preface

by James Lowther, Rt. Hon. the 7th Earl of Lonsdale

Those of us in the Lowther family who had grown up to know our great-uncle only slightly in the years between the two wars had an image of a person held in great affection in this district where we live, surrounded by legend and spoken of with awe. We knew of his influential life after the first war and were at the receiving end of his great generosity and kindness. We had visited him and our Aunt Gracie in their London house on our way to and from school and watched the processions along The Mall from its windows at the time of the Coronation of George VI. There were stories, of course, that he had been to the North Pole which he used to foster by showing us the snow shoes, stuffed bears, moose heads and so on in Lowther Castle, and that he had been an outstanding Master of the Cottesmore and Quorn Foxhounds, and had performed remarkable feats of horsemanship; but this was not the side of him we knew.

When a boy I remember being taken to Sunday lunch at the Castle and sitting at table on best behaviour from 1.30 to 3.30 p.m. There followed a regular routine of feeding the pigeons and the seemingly endless numbers of ponies, with all the grooms on parade and with the head gardener in attendance in case some detail of the enormous flower-beds or immense lawns should cause comment. Afterwards there would be a visit to the hot-house to inspect the vines or peach trees, or whatever exotic plant should be in bloom. Then we would return to the Castle for tea—which I remember well because of the apple jelly and the minute pieces of very white bread and butter—eaten in the saloon, a room the size of a tennis court with all manner of red plush sofas, chairs and exotic pot-plants growing almost to the height of the room. Uncle Hugh would always give my brother, my sister and myself half-a-crown when we left to go home.

I also remember one never-to-be-forgotten Christmas. My

father's whole family stayed at the Castle and we had a complete wing to ourselves near the stable yard—a wing which still exists and is now occupied as a flat by the family who look after the pig herds and broiler houses on my farm. Whilst there, to the consternation of all, I developed 'flu, and my great-uncle insisted on taking charge. He banished my mother, and personally attended to all that was necessary. He applied his own formula for a cure—a huge blazing coal fire, every window shut, a darkened room, no sheets merely blankets to lie between, poisonous tasting quinine brews to drink, and constant attention. No patient could have had better nursing, and what fun it was to be ill with him throwing strange powders on the fire to produce flames of all the colours of the rainbow. He had a gimmick for every occasion.

I recall a quiet and laughing voice and a person kind and playful but never hearty or boisterous, with side whiskers, a blue pin-striped suit, an ever present smell of cigars, and an endless supply of gadgets in his pockets which seemed to serve every conceivable purpose. Behind all this I remember Aunt Gracie, a quiet elderly person, seemingly always dressed in dark brown and always in the background.

Lowther Castle itself, to a child, was awe-inspiring, with huge and vault-like halls and corridors and passages—warm but airless. Steady streams of hot air rose from the circular grids at intervals in the stone floors, and the miles of corridors and rooms a small boy had to travel to find a lavatory seemed endless. But after Uncle Hugh had left the Castle in 1935 it became our playground, much to the despair of the caretaker who stalked gloomily through the numberless and huge rooms with the furniture, pictures and ornaments still in their places, but all dust-sheeted. Then the military descended, my brother and I went off to the war, and the next time I saw Lowther was in 1946 when my father was selling the furniture and effects. Gathered together for this sale in the main rooms at the Castle was an enormous collection selected from the contents of the Castle itself with 365 rooms, Carlton House Terrace, the house at Newmarket and my great-uncle's house in Rutland.

So ended my direct memories of Uncle Hugh. Since those days a great deal has happened. The estates collected their fullest possible quota of death duties and I had to carry out a comprehensive scheme of modernization to meet them. The Castle itself is now a ruin, but incidental effects of Uncle Hugh's long tenancy have paradoxically made my task much easier in rebuilding the estate's prosperity.

Whilst he had not been interested in posterity and had therefore thwarted attempts to plant trees and modernize farms, in the interests of his own personal activities and predilections he had prevented the felling of trees and plantations. By vastly enlarging his park at the turn of the century, he left a great deal of land which provided the foundation for large scale and economic farming, and a fell he had acquired for its grouse shooting is now a highly productive lime works.

I gave Mr. Sutherland the opportunity to write this biography two years ago, and when I read through the first drafts he had written, I soon realized that I was reading the story of no ordinary life. Mr. Sutherland has successfully managed to compress into 300 pages material which could fill 1,000 and provide inspiration for plays and novels—the extraordinary Wyoming episode, of historical and economic significance in the development of the American West; his relationship with the German Kaiser at the turn of the century (they exchanged Christmas cards right up to the outbreak of the last war); the incredible Violet Cameron affairs; his fight against J. L. Sullivan. Each incident would probably be the highlight of a less adventurous career.

Much of his life seemed unbelievable even to me, yet Mr. Sutherland was able to build the story upon a plethora of factual evidence which had been to hand for years—in the Lowther Estate Office strong room are fifteen crates of letters and papers and many boxes and albums of photographs, quite apart from the usual domestic photograph albums removed from Lowther Castle; all of which had been carefully bundled and put away. Perhaps Uncle Hugh had entertained some hope that his biography would be written, for none of his correspondence appears to have been destroyed (although it was all carefully edited!) and copies were kept of all the letters he wrote. The bundles, too, were all labelled with helpful comments, as if specifically for a biography. All this along with the bric-à-brac of a long, full and adventurous life, culminating with numberless presents large and small, some of great value and some very modest in cost, many very touching, some merely ostentatious, given to them both not only on the occasion of their golden wedding but for their diamond wedding as well.

From all this Mr. Sutherland was able to build up an image of my great-uncle about whom this can be said: As long as boxing is tolerated, so long as the British people enjoy coursing, hunting, shooting and racing, not to forget the circus, show jumping and the more mundane world of agricultural shows, sheep-dog trials and hound trails, his name will live on, and I, and I hope my descendants, will be proud to remember not just his extraordinary life and deeds and his apparent lack of interest in the material development of the family interests, but his drive, energy and belief in the popularizing and welfare of sport in all its forms.

JAMES LONSDALE

Contents

Illustrations

following page 112

ILLUSTRATIONS

following page 208

Unless otherwise stated, all the photographs and paintings are from the collection of James Lowther, 7th Earl of Lonsdale, by whose kind permission they are reproduced in this book.

Lowther, in thy majestic pile are seen
Cathedral pomp and grace in apt accord
With thy baronial castles sterner mien,
Union significant of God's adored
And charters won and gloried by the sword
Of ancient honour whence thy godly state
Of policy which wise men venerate
And will maintain, if God His help afford.
Hourly the democratic current swells
For airy promises and hopes suborned
The strength of backward looking thoughts is scorned.
Fall if ye must, ye Towers and Pinnacles
With what ye symbolize, authentic story
Will say, ye disappeared with England's glory.

William Wordsworth

Introduction

When Hugh Cecil Lowther, 5th Earl of Londsale, was born on 25th January 1857, Abraham Lincoln had not yet become President of the United States of America, the second French Empire was in its infancy and Queen Victoria was to be on the throne for another forty-four years. When he died the Second World War was almost at an end. Russia's tanks were hammering at the gates of Berlin and the Allied forces were pouring in a flood tide through Germany's western defences. Within a year the bomb was to be exploded which, in one fearful moment, was to incinerate a city and usher in the atomic age.

Hugh Lonsdale's life-span covered a period of change unparalleled in the history of the world, but in the middle of the nineteenth century the way of life of the upper classes in Britain could never have seemed more permanent and secure. The rakish extravagance which had typified the Regency era had settled down into the complacency of solid Victorian wealth.

The new industrial age swept away the old feudal system which had united the landowner and his dependants in a common endeavour. Now a great gap yawned between the upper and the lower classes. The royalty-rich squirearchy from whom most of the Victorian aristocracy had sprung had created its own tight, secure little world which had been labelled Society. To be outside Society was to be nothing and no one.

The second Earl of Lonsdale, who was alive when Hugh was born, was very much in Society. His ancient lineage, his high rank and his important political offices, and above all his immense personal fortune made his position secure. He had been Master of the Horse to his close friend George IV. Wearing a vivid red wig in an effort to disguise his age he was to live for another fifteen years after Hugh was born to enjoy his two favourite sports of hunting and entertaining actresses. When he died, in the arms of a well-known opera singer, he was succeeded by his nephew, Hugh Lowther's father—but for Hugh and his two younger brothers Charles and Lancelot the likelihood of their ever succeeding to the spectacular family fortunes remained remote. The third Earl was still in his fifties and his heir was Hugh's elder brother, St. George, who was only two years the senior. St. George had only to marry and produce a son for the younger brother's chance of inheritance to pass away for ever.

So unconsidered was Hugh's chance of succession that his father could not be persuaded to bother to educate him properly. Whilst St. George was being carefully groomed for a gilded future, Hugh spent most of his time in the stable yard at the family home of Asfordby or running wild in the surrounding countryside.

Yet only ten years after the old second Earl had passed away both Hugh's father and elder brother were dead.

St. George held the title for six years and they were six years of misery for Hugh. Condemned to make his way in a money-conscious society on an income which in no way matched his extravagant tastes, his resentment of his immensely rich brother became a dominating passion. Earthy, virile and with an unquenchable zest for living, he longed for the limelight in which the introverted, intellectual St. George moved so uneasily. Desperately he tried to outdo him and to prove to the world that only in the accident of birth was St. George the better man. The effort led him into a series of scandals which caused many of the most desirable doors to be shut in his face and reduced him almost to bankruptcy. At the eleventh hour St. George died and Hugh, spurned by Society and hounded by his creditors, became overnight one of the richest men in England.

In addition to his sonorous titles he inherited a kingdom in Cumberland and Westmorland. Lowther Castle was one of the largest houses in the country. There was an agricultural estate upwards of fifty thousand acres and another fifty thousand of common land, over which he owned the sporting and mineral rights. There were the lakes of Windermere and Grasmere and the ruggedly beautiful Haweswater. In West Cumberland he owned the whole town of Whitehaven, the rich coal fields which stretched far out under the Irish Sea, and another family seat, Whitehaven Castle. In London two of the great mansions in Carlton House Terrace, knocked into one, provided him with a Town house. There was another house at Newmarket and two steam yachts lying at anchor at Cowes. There were rich lands in the heart of the hunting country in Rutland and the magnificent hunting box and stables of Barleythorpe.

Above all, from his own coal fields, iron mines and agricultural lands there flowed a prodigious, tax-free income of almost £4,000 a *week*.

Hugh set about enjoying his good fortune with unsurpassed vigour. Trumpeting like a thirsty bull elephant who suddenly scents water, he cut a swathe through Society—who never quite forgave him for it. His boyhood had made him shy and uneasy with his social equals. His father's grooms, the tenant farmers and their workers he knew and understood. He covered up his shyness in Society with a flamboyance which, even in the ostentatious age of the Edwardians, people found hard to accept. At the same time his passionate devotion to sport, his sure instinct for fair play and his showman's love of the spectacular earned him the adulation of the crowds and a reputation as 'England's Greatest Sportsman' which spread far outside these Islands.

His yellow carriages, his colourful entourage and his feudal style of living made him one of the best-known figures of his time. His big cigars, immaculate clothes and ever-fresh gardenia were the delight of cartoonists. His public appearances at sporting events were acclaimed with as much delight as if he had been Royalty. As he drove down the course at Ascot behind the King, his yellow carriages and liveried postillions making the Royal carriages almost drab by comparison; the cheers for 'Lordy' were at least as loud and prolonged as they were for the Monarch.

He never grew out of the indiscretions of his early youth, but his involvement with beautiful women and unpopular causes added to rather than detracted from his popularity with the public. He never subscribed to the prudery of an age whose motto might have been 'It does not matter how you behave so long as you are not found out.' Instead he nailed his colours to the mast and kept them flying defiantly. In his own often used phrase, life for him was 'lovely fun'.

But behind the glittering façade there was sadness. Even before he had inherited, the doctors decreed that his wife Grace could never have a child. Although, through his younger brother Lancelot, the line of succession was secure, Hugh would never admit to it. When taxed by his Trustees about some new extravagance, he would hunch his shoulders and reply, 'What does it matter. I am the last of the Lowthers.' It was the same spirit as Lord Cardigan had shown as he prepared to gallop at the head of his Light Brigade into the teeth of the Russian batteries at Balaclava. 'Here goes the last of the Brudenells.' Perhaps in Hugh Lonsdale it reflected the same mood of do or die. As the safe world into which he had been born started to crumble about his ears and the noose fashioned by his own extravagance draw tighter and tighter, he did not let his public image suffer by one farthingsworth.

Before he inherited, in a desperate search for money, he had sold his reversion. It had been bought by the estate so that the settled land at Whitehaven and Lowther was managed by Trustees who, in consequence, also controlled the purse-strings. For the whole of the sixty-two years he was the Earl, Hugh fought tooth and nail to extract every penny he could from the Trustees in order to keep up his fantastic scale of living.

His lavish entertainment of the Kaiser and other European royalty, his vast stables of horses, his private orchestra, and even the money he poured into equipping the private battalions he raised to fight in the Boer War and the First World War was only paid for after bitter battles with the Trustees, whom he came to regard as the Great Enemy.

By the time he died the outer defences had been breached. Step by step he had retreated as the lights of his personal empire were snuffed out one by one. Whitehaven Castle was sold, then Barleythorpe. Finally Carlton House Terrace and Lowther had to be closed. Like an old dog fox headed at every turn he went to earth at Stud House in Rutland, near the scenes of his carefree boyhood. He had outlived all his contemporaries but to the end he preserved his own world of fantasy.

Never quite accepted by a Victorian Society, he became, with the public, a legend in his own lifetime. It was their cheers that he sought more than any other thing. Lord Ancaster once described him as 'almost an Emperor and not quite a gentleman'. Perhaps it was an epitaph that he would not finally have objected to.

Part I

The Victorian

Chapter 1

The history of the Lowther family is unique.

Many of the more ancient families of England trace their origins, in one way or another, back to the invasion of William the Conqueror. Not so the Lowthers. Whilst the Conqueror was struggling to establish a beach-head at Hastings, the Lowthers were already ensconced in their wild, mountainous country of Westmorland and Cumberland.

Their ancestors had come over in the Danish longboats, and, having carved out a considerable freeholding for themselves, proceeded to stick to it through thick and thin down the centuries. For over seven hundred years Lowther knight followed Lowther knight in direct succession. From the family archives colourful names gleam through the dust of the centuries: there is Sir Gervase de Lowther who married the beautiful daughter of Lord Ross of Hemlock and, putting duty before beauty, lost his life crusading in the Holy Land; and Sir Hugh de Lowther who was Attorney General to 'The Hammer of the Scots', Edward I. Another Sir Hugh plotted with the Earl of Lancaster to murder Edward II's effeminate favourite Piers Gaveston, and was later pardoned for his part in the crime by a grateful nation. Yet another Sir Hugh fought at the Battle of Agincourt in the reign of Henry V. Sir Richard de Lowther, High Sheriff of Cumberland and Lord Warden of the West Marches, infuriated Queen Elizabeth by harbouring Mary Queen of Scots and allowing the Catholic Duke of Norfolk to visit her at Carlisle Castle. She had him locked up in the Tower.

For generation after generation the family craft survived the turbulent stream of history. It nearly sank forever when the Lancastrians were defeated in the Wars of the Roses and was again in serious danger when Oliver Cromwell defeated Charles I.

In 1689, however, Sir John Lowther of Lowther backed the right horse. He espoused the cause of William of Orange, securing on his behalf the City of Carlisle and the Counties of Westmorland and Cumberland. Sir John was rewarded, on King William's accession, by being made Vice-Chamberlain to the Royal Household, a Privy Councillor and, in 1696, was created Baron Lowther of Lowther and Viscount Lowther.

Perhaps no family in England has continued to produce in each generation so exactly the characteristics of the last. Sagacious, courageous in their judgements and loyal to their friends, they have epitomized the strength and endurance of the dalesmen—clinging to what they own and adding to it at every opportunity.

Where England's great political families point with pride to their record of service in Parliament, none can rival the Lowthers, who count a total of more than a hundred Members of the name of Lowther reaching back to the very beginning of Parliament itself. Some held high office but, for the most part, it was the role of the younger sons to take their seats to protect the Lowther interest rather than to concern themselves with wider causes. 'If I had to choose between betraying my country and betraying my friends, I hope I should have the guts to betray my country,' E. M. Forster once wrote,* and it is a dictum of which a long succession of Lowthers would not altogether have disapproved.

It was the first Viscount Lowther who transformed the family stronghold at Lowther from a keep into a country house—a rather premature move for a Border Lord with the Scottish rebellions of 1715 and 1745 still to come. In fact the lovely Queen Anne house was destroyed not by siege but by an accidental fire, so that only two unconnected wings remained to be infested by Bonnie Prince Charlie's raggle-taggle army.

Although the Lowthers as a family played an important part in Border affairs they were never as important as the great Border Barons of the Middle Ages, like the de Cliffords of Appleby Castle, the Dacres of Naworth or the Lucys of Cockermouth. Rather they allied themselves to one or other of their powerful neighbours to maintain a fragile balance of power on which the safety of their lands depended.

In the peaceful years following the '45 rebellion, the whole picture was dramatically altered. In 1760 Sir James Lowther of Whitehaven on the Cumberland coast discovered that the waste seaboard lands

* *Two Cheers for Democracy* (Arnold, 1951).

which comprised much of his estate were rich in coal with seams reaching far out under the sea. Even more important, deep under the barren fells there were great deposits of iron-ore and other minerals ready to supply the awakening appetite of industrial Britain.

Whilst the old feudal families remained embattled behind their ramparts, Sir James Lowther and the Industrial Revolution took to each other with passionate fervour. Before he died at the turn of the century, the sleepy little collection of fishing huts which he owned on the Whitehaven inlet had grown into a flourishing industrial town and a sea port which rated third in importance in the whole country.

Sir James never married. Whitehaven was his life and his only love. He had the new town laid out by Adam and built factory chimneys in the shape of his favourite silver candlesticks. Looking over the town he created for himself an imposing home surrounded by parkland, which he called Whitehaven Castle. Born a modest squire, when he died in 1775 he was one of the richest men in the country.

Before Sir James's death, the honours of the main branch of the family, in the person of Viscount Lonsdale, had become extinct; but two great estates, one at Maulds Meaburn and the other centred round the burnt-out shell of Lowther Hall, remained. On the death of Viscount Lowther the two estates had been inherited by a boy of fourteen—also called Sir James Lowther, but who was to earn his place in the family history under the name of 'Wicked Jimmy'. The boy had unruly dark hair, smouldering eyes, uncouth manners and a turbulent personality. When at the age of twenty-six he added to his already considerable estates all the West Cumberland lands and the vast wealth of old Sir James, the established aristocracy regarded the whole business as being in the worst possible taste.

Ruthless, able and ambitious, the new Sir James Lowther hankered after more and more power. Determined to make a good marriage and spurned by his envious neighbours, he went to a marriage broker, with the help of whose services he secured the hand of the daughter of the Marquis of Bute, having been rejected by the Duke of Marlborough as being *nouveau riche* and uncouth. Although she made her husband socially more acceptable, the marriage itself was a failure. They had no children and he soon left her to her own devices and consoled himself with his real love, the daughter of one of his tenant farmers. When she died he preserved her body in a glass-lidded

9

coffin, which he left in a cupboard at Maulds Meaburn Hall, so that he could continue to gaze at her beauty.

His tempestuous life was a mixture of arrogant tyranny and real achievement. He spent a fortune improving the harbour at Whitehaven, but he had a Whitehaven shopkeeper who offended him pressed into the Navy and kept at sea for ten years. He bought any land that came on to the market until his estates comprised almost 100,000 acres. He bought the valuable iron-ore deposits at Hodbarrow and Millom which gave him almost a local monopoly in the mining industry, but he never bothered to rebuild Lowther Hall, so that his household eked out a miserable existence in the two smoke-blackened wings.

In politics he showed himself equally greedy for power. At one time, by purchase or political pressure, he controlled, absolutely, nine seats in Parliament, known as 'Lowther's Nine-pins'. He put up his secretary as his nominee for Appleby. The secretary eventually became better known than Sir James himself—as William Pitt. The poet Wordsworth's father was his political agent and was almost ruined through Wicked Jimmy's pathological objection to paying his salary.

Wicked Jimmy was rewarded for this ambivalent record by being created Baron Lowther of Kendal, Baron Burgh and the first Earl of Lonsdale.

So many stories have been told about him that his name has become a legend throughout the North. De Quincey describes how he used to drive at breakneck speed through the villages of his domain where every door and window was shuttered against his evil eye. In his private park droves of wild horses roamed, whilst his own neglected coach and ungroomed horses exhibited his contempt for appearances. On windy nights when the moon is up, it is said he is still to be heard driving furiously in his coach, while, with streaming manes and thundering hooves, the wild horses gallop after him.

Poor Wicked Jimmy. He died in 1802, unloved and unmourned. Yet he did much to bring prosperity to the west coast of Cumberland through his development of the mining industry. Boycotted by his neighbours and distrusted by his political allies, he nevertheless foresaw the years of prosperity through expanding trade and commerce which lay ahead and used his abilities to bring it about.

On the other hand Wicked Jimmy also nearly brought about the end of the Lowther dynasty he had striven so hard to enrich. His sister, whom he dearly loved, and to whom he wrote some untypically tender letters, was married to Lord Darlington. He had promised her that her son* should be his heir, so, when the news of his death was known, the young man travelled confidently to Lowther to take possession of his great heritage. It must have been a bitter disappointment to him to discover that, on a whim, Wicked Jimmy had crossed out his name and substituted the name of a distant cousin in Yorkshire, William Lowther, son of the Rev. Sir William Lowther of Swillington. It was altogether a close shave for the Lowther family.

The Governing Families of England give the following description of William Lowther: 'He seems to have been an amiable man. An amiability not less appreciated from the contrast with his wild predecessor, but he is chiefly remembered as a munificent patron of the arts and the peer who changed Lowther Hall into the magnificent seat styled Lowther Castle. He apparently did not care to struggle after political power as did his predecessor at Lowther. . . .'

His lack of political ambition must have been greatly pleasing to William Pitt after so many years of dealing with his tempestuous forebear. One can almost sense the relief in the note Pitt wrote to him at the time: 'I wished to thank you for the note you sent me with an account of Lord Lonsdale's death, as well as to assure you (what I hope you cannot doubt) how much I partook of the pleasure, which I believe was very generally felt, when the destination of his property was known.'

With the accession of William all the wealth of the Lowthers was gathered back to the main stem, but the relationship was too remote to preserve the title. The joining up of the Yorkshire estates did, however, even further increase the family power in the North. William brought with him such considerable lands of his own that it was said he could walk from the west coast of England to the east without ever setting foot off his own ground.

William was a totally different personality from Wicked Jimmy. Born in the reign of George II he lived on into the first few years of Queen Victoria's reign. With an income of over £200,000 a year he had the means to indulge his own ideas of a spacious life. In restoring Lowther Hall he did not rebuild the house in its old form. Instead he commissioned Smirke, the fashionable architect of the day, to create a vast pseudo-Gothic castle with huge, impersonal reception rooms, cavernous kitchens and over a hundred bedrooms joined by miles of windswept passageways.

It could never, under any circumstances, be described as a home.

* Later the 1st Duke of Cleveland.

Nor was it treated as such by Sir William or his descendants. It was only lived in during the summer months or for short duty visits at other times of the year. As was happening in so many houses, the old furniture was banished to the servants' quarters and good, solid tables and chairs in light oak were made to furnish the main rooms. Leather-bound books were bought by the hundred to fill the shelves in the library. Wine was imported by the cask from France, and great quantities of linen and damask bought from Ireland. When the work was finished the transformation was complete. Not a trace of the old Lowther Hall remained.

With this majestic pile as proof of their importance, Sir William and his wife now held undisputed sway in the two counties of Westmorland and Cumberland. When, in 1807, George III showed his favour by regranting the title, making Sir William first Earl of Lonsdale of the second creation, their position was impregnable.

William extended his patronage to artists and writers on a generous scale. Hogarth, a local boy from nearby Kendal, showed his gratitude by giving his patron a copy in miniature, painted on ivory, of every picture he painted.* Wordsworth, the celebrated son of Wicked Jimmy's impoverished political agent, was now an honoured guest at the Castle. In gratitude to his hostess, Augusta Lonsdale, he wrote in her album:

> High born Augusta,
> Witness towers and groves,
> And thou, wild streams,
> That givest the honoured name
> Of Lowther to this ancient line.
> Bear witness from thy most sacred haunts,
> And ye parterres
> Which she is pleased and proud to call her own,
> Witness how oft upon my noble friend
> Mute offerings, tribute from the inward sense
> Of admiration and respectful love.

Nor could William escape the fulsome praise of the gratified poet.

> Lonsdale, it were unworthy of a guest,
> Whose heart with gratitude to thee inclines,
> If he should speak of fancy touched of signs

---

* Only one survives. Hugh Lowther's mother, considering some of the subjects unsuitable for her children, had them all destroyed.

On thy abode harmoniously imprest
Yet be unmoved with wishes to attest
How thy mind and moral frame agreed
Fortitude, and that Christian Charity
Which, filling, consecrates the human breast.
And if the motto on thy scutcheon teach
With truth, that magistracy shows the man,
That secret test thy public course has stood.
As will be owned alike by bad and good
Soon as the measuring of life's little span
Shall place thy virtues out of envy's reach.

Creevy, the diarist, who stayed at Lowther in 1827, records his impressions of the household in a less formal way. He wrote to Miss Orde:

I think I am settled here for life. I do not know where to begin and before I do I shall have to end, as Lady Caroline and I are going for an airing and at present I am rather boski after luncheon. At five o'clock yesterday evening I thought I had entered on the most formal house in England, and at half-past six dear Lady Lonsdale and I were going in to dinner arm in arm, three boys of Colonel Lowther pulling with all their might and main at my coat flaps to make me stay and play with them, and in the evening, as we could have no cards, from it being Sunday, Lord Pollington was kind enough to entertain us with his excellent imitations of squeaking pigs, guinea fowl, dialogues between crying children and the devil knows what else besides.

In spite of his efforts at Lowther, however, William's heart was not really in Westmorland. Leicestershire was his real love and the new sport of foxhunting was his favourite occupation. He devoted at least seven months in the year to it.

The Lowther connection with foxhunting goes back to Henry, Viscount Lowther who owned what was probably the first pack of foxhounds in this country. In William's time the descendants of the Viscount's pack were owned by Mr. Noel,* who, with Hugh Meynell of Quorndom Hall in Leicestershire, was one of the pioneers of foxhunting as we know it today.

Sir William bought back Old Noel's hounds about three years before he inherited the Lowther estates, and at once set about the scientific study of hound breeding. Practically every hound in England today is descended from this famous pack.

* Generally known as 'Old Noel', he was a relative of Lord Gainsborough.

In those days hunting the fox with hounds was a very different business from foxhunting in its present form. Much of the Leicestershire countryside, which was the cradle of foxhunting, was undrained and unfenced. A fox, once found, was hunted with slow determination. The owner of the pack and his friends jogged stoldily in pursuit, seldom raising better than a trot, and the hunting of one fox might take the whole day.

In order to hunt, Sir William rented Cottesmore House, where he kennelled his hounds and which eventually gave its name to the pack.

Whilst his miners hacked out the rich seams of coal below the Irish Sea and burrowed deep into the fellside for iron ore, producing for him an ever-increasing avalanche of wealth, he set about the business of running his pack with dedicated zeal. He remained as Master of his own pack for fifty years until his death. By then the breeding of foxhounds had become, largely due to Sir William, an exact science, while the rich and the fashionable all over the country vied with each other in the perfection of their horses and the demonstration of their prowess in the hunting-field.

Even during the summer months William could not bear to be parted from his hounds. When the hunting season ended, he trotted them two hundred miles back again to Lowther. The journey each way lasted just under a month.

For his second son Henry, who shared his father's love of hunting, he bought Barleythorpe, a hunting box on a princely scale which was to become the hunting headquarters of later generations of Lowthers. Henry also followed in the family tradition, after a period as Colonel of the Life Guards, by entering Parliament as the Member for Westmorland. He was a Member for fifty-five years. The fact that during the whole of that time he never made a speech must stand near to a record. On one occasion a political opponent, maddened beyond endurance at being beaten once again at the hustings by 'Lowther the Silent', made an impassioned harangue against him from the platform after the result had been declared. Called upon to make some reply the Colonel mildly remarked, 'I point, Gentlemen, to the poll,' and bowing stifly from the waist, withdrew from the field of battle. As Sir James Graham remarked, he was 'a genuine old Tory of the long-horned kind'.

William's long reign did more than inculcate a love of hunting in his successors. It also marked the beginning of a new attitude towards the family estates. Lowther Castle remained the seat of their power and wealth, but the real business of living was now centred around Cottesmore and Barleythorpe. A sense of duty took them back to Lowther out of the hunting season, but for the greater part of the year all the fun was to be had in the south. Wicked Jimmy, Sir James of Whitehaven and a long succession of ancestors would definitely not have approved.

William, perhaps because of his benign absenteeism, earned for himself the title of William the Good. He died in 1844 and was succeeded by his eldest son William who by contrast became known as William the Bad.

The second Earl William never went to Lowther if he could possibly avoid it, although in his lifetime the journey was reduced from an arduous three-day stage to a comfortable train journey. He had inherited a love of politics and he brought to it all the family shrewdness. In addition to his almost automatic election as Lord Lieutenant of Cumberland and Westmorland, he held the posts of Master of Horse to George IV, First Lord of the Admiralty, Commissioner for Indian Affairs, Lord of the Treasury, Chief Commissioner for Woods and Forests, Vice President of the Board of Trade and Treasurer to the Navy, Post-Master-General, Lord President of the Council and permanent Chairman of the Metropolitan Roads Commission. He carried out his multifarious duties with almost casual competence but refused to become completely involved in public affairs. He twice refused the Premiership on the grounds that his duties might interfere too seriously with his private life.

For him London was the only place where life was supportable for any length of time: in spite of his love of hunting, even Leicestershire was too far afield for comfort. From his friend George IV he obtained a lease on two adjoining mansions in Carlton House Terrace which he knocked into one to form his London residence. A great admirer of the Continental way of life, he filled the great rooms with a priceless collection of French furniture collected on his travels abroad. A patron of the opera, he was also a great collector of opera singers whose charms did much to reconcile him to his state of life-long bachelordom.

Second to opera singers, hunting was his great passion in life. He kept a private pack of hounds and a pack of harriers at one of his houses, Tring Park. His attention to the affairs of State depended in the winter to a large extent on the state of the weather. Before breakfast each morning he dug his heel into a plot of grass, grown for the purpose outside the morning-room window at Carlton House Terrace. If the ground proved soft enough he would catch the first train to Tring, gallop furiously all day after a succession of foxes let out of bags at strategic points, returning in time to take his box at the opera to see what further sport the night might provide. Only when the ground was frozen would he concern himself with official matters.

The life seemed to suit him for, apart from recourse to a red wig, he remained in full possession of all his faculties until he died, at the age of eighty-five, in 1872.

He was succeeded by his nephew, Hugh Lonsdale's father. Hugh's father had already inherited Barleythorpe from the Silent Colonel, and he now inherited all the Lowther estates and the great mansion in Carlton House Terrace.

Chapter 2

The young Hugh was to know little of his heritage for the first fifteen years of his life. His father Henry, now the third Earl, had never been a favourite of his bachelor uncle, with the result that the family had seldom gone to Lowther and even more seldom to Carlton House Terrace.

Hugh was born on the 25th January 1857 at 21 Wilton Crescent in London and spent most of his childhood at Asfordby, which his father rented, near Melton Mowbray. He was the second son of a family of four boys and two girls.

His father, up to the time of his inheritance, had lived his life in the approved Lowther tradition. After a career in the Life Guards, he had entered Parliament as the Member for West Cumberland. Once elected he retired to Asfordby and devoted himself almost exclusively to the pleasures of the hunting field and the table, his appearances in the House of Commons being almost as rare as his visits to Lowther.

Although he hunted five days a week it did not provide sufficient exercise to keep pace with his huge appetite. So great was his capacity for food that within a few years of his retiring from the Army there was no horse in the country which could carry him. When he eventually died at the age of fifty-eight he weighed twenty-two stone and it took eight men to hoist his coffin to its last resting place in the family mausoleum.

His ideas on the education of his four sons were on the elementary side. When his wife insisted on a tutor for the boys, who were running wild, he appointed Trooper Hall, his old batman in the Life Guards, to the responsibility. Hall's only qualification seems to have been that he had been the Regimental heavy-weight boxing champion.

Mrs. Lowther was a gentle, retiring woman, known affectionately to everyone, including her children, as Pussy. One afternoon she returned home to Asfordby from tea with friends, to find a scene of indescribable excitement on the front lawn. Maids from the upstairs windows shouted shrill encouragement whilst, around an improvised ring amongst the rose beds, stable boys and gardeners, led by the redoubtable Hall, were enthusiastically egging on two blood-spattered devotees of the 'noble art'.

It consoled her not at all to learn that she had arrived just in time to see her son Hugh knock his much larger opponent to the ground and win a famous victory; nor did she derive any satisfaction from the victim being, in the true David Copperfield tradition, the butcher's boy who was the local bully and had 'had it coming to him for a long time'.

As a result of this incident, Pussy, for once, put her foot down and the following term the ten-year-old Hugh was sent off to join his elder brother St. George at Eton.

The only record of Hugh's scholastic career is his own claim in later years that he had sung in the choir. At all events his formal education was short-lived. He left Eton at the age of twelve, which was the sum total of his schooling.

On the other hand, his father was determined that his physical education should not be neglected. To this end he put him in the charge of no less a personage than Jem Mace, the last barefist champion of England, the Pride of the Fancy, and the generally acknowledged father of boxing in the form in which it is known today. Jem Mace was supposed to share his duties with a tutor, which sounds like an amicable husband-and-wife compromise in the Lowther household.

They reckoned, however, without Hugh, who objected strongly to having his hunting and the other country sports interfered with by the necessity of attending schoolroom lessons. One day he lured his French tutor M. Ciro down to the river on the pretext of introducing him to the old English art of catching fish in a casting net. When Monsieur tried his hand at throwing the weighted net across the stream, instead of holding the other end, Hugh took the precaution of surreptitiously anchoring it to one of the big decorative buttons on the back of his father's coaching coat, considerately lent to M. Ciro because of the extreme cold, with the result that the unfortunate man succeeded also in casting himself into the river.

The joke almost misfired for, entangled in the net and the heavy coat, Monsieur would certainly have drowned if the local miller had not come promptly to his rescue. It was too much for the mild-mannered Frenchman who, the following day, fled back to Paris.

Successive tutors fared no better until finally the good-natured Colonel gave up the uneven struggle, consoling himself no doubt with the thought that his eldest son at least was showing himself to be an apt pupil at Eton.

It was during his only year at Eton that Hugh was taken to his first Derby. It was one of over sixty that he was to attend, so it was appropriate that it should have been one of the most memorable of all time. It was the 'snowstorm' Derby of 1867, which, he always used to assure people afterwards, was not run in a snowstorm at all, but in brilliant sunshine. It was the background to the race, however, which really made it so remarkable.

A neighbouring estate to Asfordby was Blankney, which belonged to a close friend of the Lowthers, Harry Chaplin.* A couple of years earlier, Chaplin, a wealthy and eligible bachelor, had been the victim of an extraordinary scandal which had rocked London Society. He had become engaged to the beautiful Lady Florence Paget. A few days before the fairy-tale wedding was due to take place he had driven his fiancée to the unromantic front door of Marshall and Snelgrove in Oxford Street, where, she said, she had some last-minute shopping to do. Alas, for the course of true love! Whilst Harry waited patiently in his carriage at the front entrance, the beautiful Florrie was making a get-away at the back with his erstwhile friend Lord Hastings, one of the wildest young rake-hells in London. Harry Chaplin took the disaster with dignity. He withdrew to his country estates and dedicated himself to horses and breeding of hounds. In later life Hugh was to describe him as the greatest judge of hounds of all time. Lord Hastings, on the other hand, left no stone unturned to try and blacken the name of the man he had wronged.

It was against this background of Victorian melodrama that the Derby of 1867 was run. Chaplin had entered Hermit, a very likely colt, and it soon became known around the clubs in St. James's Street that Hastings was giving almost any odds anybody wanted against the horse winning. 'He is backing against Hermit,' wrote his already disillusioned young wife, 'as if the colt were already dead.' Ten days before the race it looked as if the great Hastings

* Later President of the Board of Trade and created Viscount Chaplin, he remained a close friend of Hugh Lowther all his life.

gamble would succeed. Hermit, going on a trial gallop, burst a blood-vessel, and it was long odds against him running, let alone winning. Chaplin was determined to keep his entry in, but Hermit came into the paddock with a substitute jockey and looking so out of trim that the betting lengthened to a contemptuous 66–1. The result of the race is now history. In the last few strides the gallant Hermit 'came from nowhere' to get his nose in front, and win. The result broke Hastings, and within a few years he was dead. Harry Chaplin, however, as in all the best story books, became a Lord himself, and lived happily ever after.

It was a Derby to capture the imagination of a much less devoted horseman than the young Hugh Lowther.

Pussy made one more effort to complete Hugh's education. A year after her husband inherited the title, she sent him to an expensive finishing school for young gentlemen in Switzerland. With his in-bred love of hunting, horses, and the English countryside, it was not a gambit that was likely to succeed. Nor did it.

Within a month of his arrival he gave up the unfamiliar scholastic routine and joined a travelling circus. He stayed with them for a blissfully happy year only returning to England on his eighteenth birthday when he learned that his father was prepared to allow him a private allowance of £1,000 a year.

Henry, Earl of Lonsdale, paid as little attention to his family in adolescence as he had in their schooldays. No longer able to hunt because of his great weight, his chief ambition for his boys was that they should ride well to hounds. To him, like most of the Lowthers, hunting was a way of life and a religion. Only in the case of St. George could he see any sense in Pussy's ineffective fussing about education. So far as he was concerned the failure of the Swiss experiment only went to show what a waste of time the whole thing was. Switzerland indeed! And in the middle of the hunting season too!

When, after his return, Hugh announced his intention of spending the summer in London the Earl raised no objection. Henry hated London himself but he knew plenty of hunting men who quite enjoyed it—out of the hunting season of course.

Hugh took a small flat in Jermyn Street and set about exploring a strange new world. It must have been hard going at first. Tall, athletic and not conventionally good-looking with his sandy hair and prominent features, he suffered from a shyness which never left him all his life. Most of the young men of his age had already got an intimate circle of friends formed at school or during the holidays. They belonged to the exclusive clubs of Pall Mall and St. James's as their fathers had before them, and they conversed with confident sophistication in the fashionable slang of the day. Hugh had none of these advantages. His father was definitely not in Society. He had made few friends in the short time he had been at Eton and he had a much more intimate knowledge of stable yards than of Mayfair drawing-rooms.

On the other hand the second Earl William, Hugh's great-uncle, had been one of the leaders in the political world and his glittering *soirées* and powerful influence were freshly remembered. Soon the extravagantly engraved invitation cards from London's ever-alert hostesses were falling thickly through the modest letter-box in Jermyn Street.

In the same way it was not long before he collected around him a circle of bachelor friends with tastes similar to his own. His next-door neighbour in Jermyn Street was 'Chicken' Hartopp of the 10th Hussars, a bluff giant of six feet five with little money but great charm. Chicken's size was matched by his thirst and his capacity for hell-raising wherever he went. In his native Ireland he used to drive to meets in a coach into which were piled unlimited quantities of liquor and a brass band, which was apt to turn the whole affair into a carnival. He was just the sort of colourful character that Hugh loved. He found himself at home with the brash, hard-living set of young men who put hunting above all else and regarded the posturings of their less athletic contemporaries with scorn. Most of the grand invitations went unanswered. The less reputable assembly rooms, like the Argyll Rooms* and 222, Piccadilly,† offered much more amusement.

Amongst Hugh's friends, the essence of living in the eighteen seventies and eighties hinged round one essential—for a man to prove that he had 'bottom'. This expression which was current in the nineteenth century was the near equivalent of having 'guts' today. It also meant rather more. It could mean having 'background and breeding' as well as simply being a 'jolly good chap'. But in either context nobody could have 'bottom' unless they had guts as well. Thus the primary ambition of those who hoped to be well

* This meeting place for the young bloods and the ladies of the town stood on the site now occupied by the Trocadero.
† Even seamier than the Argyll Rooms, it was alternatively known as 'The Pic' or 'The Three Bloody Twos'.

thought of by their contemporaries was to prove that, whatever else they lacked, they did not lack guts. To defeat the bailiffs was a way of showing that one had bottom. So was gambling for more than one could afford (always provided one paid one's debts); so was drinking quantities of port after dinner; so was bedding an actress; and so, above all, was any sort of sporting achievement.

In spite of his many bedroom conquests, the Prince of Wales, whose exploits were beginning to be the talk of London, was not considered to have much bottom, principally on the grounds that his position gave him an unfair advantage. On the other hand, for a man to steal one of the Prince's mistresses was to show bottom of the highest order.

To demonstrate their prowess was a religion, particularly with the young men who were heirs to immense second or third generation industrial fortunes. They devoted their lives to proving that in everything but the novelty of their wealth they were gentlemen of the old school. Their heroes were men of a previous generation like Squire Mytton, whose exploits were legendary, and who eventually died as a result of setting fire to his nightshirt to prove a theory that it would cure his hiccups; or Squire Osbaldeston, hero of innumerable wagers on his own sporting achievements.

Hugh Lowther entered into the game with zest; indeed, he played it with such dedication that he was still proving to the world at large that he had bottom long after the very expression had been forgotten. His favourite story on the subject concerned a group of swaggering young men who entered an inn which was well known as a haunt of Irishmen. 'I smell an Irishman,' remarked the leader, looking round pugnaciously. 'Well, you will never smell another,' remarked a customer drawing a knife and slicing off his nose. This, in Hugh's eyes, showed first-class bottom, even for an Irishman.

One of Hugh's earliest exploits was the result of a five pound bet. It arose out of a discussion one morning in the shop of Mr. Poole the tailor, where young men of fashion were accustomed to meet to discuss the affairs of the day. Poole's in those days was more like a club than a tailoring establishment. Someone remarked on the arrival from America of a Mr. Weston, who was credited with some remarkable performances as a road walker. Hugh at once remarked that anything an American could do an Englishman, and Hugh Lowther in particular, could do very much better. It was a ready made situation to prove himself and, the bets being made, the bewildered Mr. Weston was contacted, and in no time at all he found himself the focus of attention far beyond the confines of St. James's Street.

The match was fixed to take place from Knightsbridge Barracks to the Ram Jam Inn beyond Stamford on the Great North Road, a distance of almost exactly one hundred miles. The referees, mounted on horseback, were the Duke of Beaufort and Sir John Astley.*

The race started on the evening of 17th June 1878, with a third competitor, a Mr. Pulteney who had decided to join in the fun. It was all over before midday the following day. Hugh, stopping only three times for an hour each time,† covered the course in 17 hours 21 minutes, to record a speed of a little under six miles an hour. By any standards this was a remarkable performance, and a tribute to his terrific physical fitness.

When he heard of the fortunes of his opponents, he wrote out a statement for publication in the Press, which, if not notable for its modesty, at least had the virtue of brevity. It read:

Result of walking match 17th June 1878. The Hon'ble Hugh Lowther, representing England, the winner. Mr. Weston, representing America, gave up at Herne Lane on hearing that Mr. Lowther had won. Mr. Pulteney, the independent, stopped at Kate's Cabin, his feet having given out.

The match earned the plaudits of Hugh's new sporting friends. He had set out to impress them and he had succeeded. It also caused quite a public stir. Ever since Crockfords with its unique collection of characters had closed its doors, much of the spice had gone out of London life. The aristocracy, if they indulged their traditional tendency towards eccentricity, now did so discreetly behind closed doors, from beneath which the breath of scandal seldom escaped. It was a disappointing time for the lower classes, whose humdrum existence was much enlivened by the excesses of their betters. It was a gap which Hugh, in his later life, was to do his best to fill.

Hugh's walking exploit, however, did not recommend him to the

* Nicknamed 'The Mate' for some reason now forgotten. Sir John was a bearded giant of a man and one of the best-known sporting characters of the time.

† He, also, by his own account, stopped every five miles to put on new shoes and socks. To this precaution he attributed his freshness when he finished. After the race he strolled on to Asfordby to arrive in plenty of time for dinner with his mother, who by then was living at Cottesmore.

stuffier elements of Society who clustered round the Court. Public display of any sort was, in their eyes, deplorable.

It was perhaps unfortunate for Hugh that his introduction to London life should have come at a time when Society was going through a period of straight-laced Puritanism which was as dull as it was hypocritical. The Prince of Wales had not yet emerged as the leader of the Champagne Set, and Queen Victoria was at the nadir of her popularity with the public. The nation was growing out of sympathy with the little old woman who seemed, year after year, to cast deeper and ever deeper rings of melancholy round the throne. Whilst the Empire in the forcing frame of commercialism rose to new heights of power and splendour, the hand of the Queen Empress at home turned everything she touched to dross. From behind the half-drawn blinds of Buckingham Palace, Osborne and Balmoral, she ruled resentfully. There was no glitter, no pomp, no circumstance. Even the traditional act of opening Parliament was distasteful to her. 'The Queen *must say,*' she wrote angrily, 'that she feels *very bitterly* the want of feeling of those who *ask* the Queen to go to open Parliament. . . . She *will* do it this time—*as* she promised it, but she owns she resents the unfeelingness of those who *clamoured* for it.' It was not an attitude that the ceremonial loving British public could be expected to be in sympathy with indefinitely.

Unpopular or not, however, conventional Society took its lead from the ageing Queen, whose epitaph was to be, 'We are not amused.' The social rules were as rigorously observed as regimental orders at a Guards' Depot. To break them was to risk social ostracism. It was as if the whole of Society were in perpetual mourning. It was the age of black-edged notepaper (the depth of the border mathematically laid down according to the relationship to the mourned), of plumed funeral carriages and widow's weeds. Sex did not officially exist, so that even the bare legs of the grand pianos in the drawing-rooms were covered up lest they excited unseemly passion.

Above all, in the greatest commercial nation in the world, commerce was looked down on by Society. Everybody in Society knew everybody—and not only knew them but knew their pedigrees, their financial standing and their expectations. To enter Society was, for a rich man who had made his money by his own efforts, much harder than ever it was for the Biblical camel to pass through the eye of a needle.

A few, through prodigal expenditure, succeed in achieving tolerance, but nothing else. Occasionally an actress of impeccable reputation might receive qualified acceptance by virtue of her marriage to a leading member of the aristocracy. Mistresses were never recognized, and kept discreetly in the background by their protectors. On the other hand, Society would defend to the death the right of a married gentleman to keep a lady, providing she was suitably housed in Maida Vale or St. John's Wood—a part of London where it was quite impossible for anyone else who had pretensions of being 'in the swim' to live. Indeed, it was almost expected of any respectable married man to have an *alliance de la main gauche*, and perfectly in order for him to leave a dinner party early in order to visit his mistress, provided he did not actually declare his intention. It was one of those things which were understood but never mentioned.

The ladies of the *demi-monde* were not in the least put out by the formidable barrier between them and their respectably married 'sisters under the skin'. Rather they gloried in it, smothering themselves in diamonds and driving through the Park in all their finery to the excited admiration of the public, who were remarkably well informed about their identity. The ribald comments of the spectators were regally accepted by them as their just tribute.

One of the most popular was a pert, pretty little thing called Caroline Walters, who was universally known as 'Skittles'. A few years older than Hugh, she was one of the first of the belles of the era to catch his eye and she featured in many of the stories he used to tell in later life. She arrived to conquer London from the back streets of Liverpool where she earned her nickname from her job of setting up the pins in a skittle alley. Skittles had a sharp wit and a poise which lifted her out of the general run of Bedroom Beauties. She became mistress to Lord Fitzwilliam, who allowed her unusual latitude in the matter of meeting his friends. She was a first-class horsewoman, and hunted regularly with the Quorn. Socially ineligible to be invited to any of the hunting house-parties, she would stay at the Haycock Hotel at Wansford and arrive at the meets impeccably mounted on her lover's superlative hunters. The sensation was all the greater because women in the hunting field in her day were the exception rather than the rule.

Her great enemy was Lady Stamford, herself a woman of great personality and beauty. Of her it was rumoured that, like Jem Mace the boxer, she was of gypsy origin,* and that before her marriage she had been 'in competition' with Skittles. The battle between

---

* She was supposed to have been the daughter of a Norfolk gamekeeper.

the two women added considerable zest to the Quorn meets, and was as avidly discussed as the events of the day's hunting. In the more liberal atmosphere of the Shires, Skittles was widely accepted. Lady Stamford's airs and graces, on the other hand, did nothing to make her liked. Of her a wit once remarked, 'You can never satisfy a woman who is accustomed to nothing.'

The rivalry reached its climax when Lord Stamford took over Mastership of the Quorn. At the opening meet at Kirby Gate, Lady Stamford, taking a leaf out of the book of the famous Duchess of Montrose, turned out in a dazzling habit of blue velvet. Forewarned by George Fitzwilliam, Skittles arrived in an equally striking outfit of bright scarlet—a choice of colour which was not lost on an amused field. Lady Stamford, quivering with rage, and using her authority as wife of the Master, ordered the offending Skittles home in front of the whole field. She reckoned, however, without Lady Grey who was also at the meet, and who immediately arranged for Skittles to change into less conspicuous dress at her house, which was nearby, and rejoin the hunt. Delight knew no bounds when, at the end of the day, Lady Stamford inquired the identity of the young lady who had ridden so well ahead of her, only to discover that it was her hated rival!

Incidents like these were the very stuff of life for Victorian society. Gossip was the most sought after commodity of all, and life revolved around the process of obtaining it and passing it on. When in London all Society repaired to Rotten Row in Hyde Park for this purpose. Here in the mornings it was usual for the ladies to dismount from their carriages and stroll along the rails, the better to see and be seen, and of course the easier to discover the tittle-tattle of the day. The hub of this daily activity was the Achilles Statue at the Hyde Park Corner end of the Row. It can only be assumed that the anatomical accuracy of this splendid nude bronze escaped the notice of the ladies sheltering from the facts of life beneath their wide brimmed hats.

Those who complain about the dubious advantages of the telephone should be grateful that it provides a much less cumbersome medium of communication than this morning ceremonial, where a reputation could be destroyed with everyone who mattered in the time it took for a leaf to blow from one end of the Row to the other.

The afternoons were spent in visiting, a ritual which was hedged round with a complicated set of conventions of its own. No lady could be seen on foot in the afternoon, but only in her carriage.

Calling cards were left on which various corners were turned down in a generally understood code to indicate whether the cards had been left in person, whether it was required that the call should be returned, and so on.

When the time came for Society to depart to Goodwood, or to shoot grouse in Scotland, or to visit Deauville, they took wing of one accord like a flock of starlings, leaving behind them acres of dust-sheeted drawing-rooms and shuttered windows.

Eventually it became that the very term 'week-end' was reserved, together with flat hats and ice-cream sliders, for the working classes. For Society, Friday to Monday was spent at their own or somebody else's country house. If anybody was unfortunate enough not to be able to comply with this convention, they drew their blinds just the same, and, swearing the servants to secrecy, passed the time in Stygian darkness until convention allowed that they should re-advertise their presence.

Altogether it was not an atmosphere in which a high-spirited Hugh Lowther, with his limited personal fortune, was likely to find acceptance—nor did he.

Chapter 3

Hugh Lowther's father died suddenly in 1876 when Hugh was nineteen, and his elder brother St. George had not quite come of age. It was the first time that a young man had held the Earldom, and so St. George's accession was greeted with more than usual enthusiasm by the tenantry at Lowther—that remote, grey family kingdom, which so far had played such a small part in their lives.

Certainly Hugh and his younger brothers Charles and Lancelot regarded Lowther as the Buckingham Palace of their lives—a place they visited reluctantly and where life was hedged in with convention and duty. The fun was to be had in London, at Newmarket, or in the Cottesmore country, where their magnificent hunting-box, Barleythorpe, was surely as much home as anything could be.

From the beginning St. George was determined to take his responsibilities seriously. He was a tall man, over six feet three in height, and with the slight stoop common to very tall men. If not exactly an intellectual, he was a man of wide interests. 'Poor old St. George,' Hugh once said of him, 'he was the only one of us all who ever read a book.'

St. George planned his arrival at Lowther with all the precision of a military operation. Assembled on the platform at Clifton, the Lowthers' private station, were all the local dignitaries, and the heads of all the departments on the estate. Special police were drafted to keep back the crowds. Outside the station a procession of immaculately turned out carriages waited to carry the new Earl and his party to the Castle along a route lined by the local Yeomanry.

The whole effect was somewhat spoiled by the new Earl himself. Of a naturally nervous disposition, he had dined rather too well on the train to fortify himself against the coming ordeal. The result was that, far from being able to rise to the dignity of the occasion, the first view the assembled company had of the Earl was a fleeting one as he was hurried on an improvised stretcher from the train to his carriage.

It was an unfortunate beginning, and all the more so because his inability to control his drinking was the symptom of an illness from which he was to die six years later. Inevitably it made him irritable and unpredictable, so that his good intentions more often than not remained unfulfilled.

It also showed him in a pale, unattractive light by comparison with the great good nature of his three extrovert younger brothers—and particularly with Hugh whose exploits as a young man about town and in the hunting-field were already providing food and drink for the gossip-hungry Society matrons. With St. George in control of the family fortunes, Hugh set about the business of 'living it up' with even greater determination.

There is no doubt that there had been little love lost between the two brothers since they left the nursery. It would hardly have been surprising even in brothers of more similar temperaments; they were in fact in no way alike. Second only in his devotion to animals, Hugh worshipped physical fitness and virility in men. For him life was a matter of the survival of the fittest. He set his standards by the only standards he had been brought up to understand—the standards of the hunting field. 'I can tell everything I want to know about a man by the way he sits on a horse,' he once said, and it was indeed almost his only criterion.

By contrast, St. George was much colder and a less colourful personality. Aware from his early teens of his destiny, he took his responsibilities seriously and without humour. Although a fine horseman and a good shot, his real passion was the sea, and after his inheritance he spent much of his time aboard one of his two steam yachts, making protracted voyages to distant parts of the world. His meticulous studies of the behaviour of the Gulf Stream were of sufficient importance to be published in book form by the American Hydrological Department.

Differences in character apart, however, it was the disparity in their fortunes which Hugh found hardest of all to accept. Following the custom of most of the great families of the day, St. George inherited not only all the lands, but a fortune which provided an income greater in one week than Hugh and his younger brothers had for a whole year.

One of St. George's first acts was to buy a string of thirty-five racehorses in training from Captain Machell, one of the best-known racing men of the day. It was the sort of act that Hugh could not forgive. Although not particularly enamoured of horse-racing himself, he felt keenly the almost casual way in which St. George could overnight buy himself into being one of the leading bloodstock owners in the country; even worse almost was that he should have put himself at one blow in terms of familiarity with men like Machell, who had been one of Hugh's boyhood heroes, and now became merely St. George's racing adviser.

The only weapon Hugh could find to fight the swamping of his own personality by his brother was in exhibiting his own prowess. If St. George had the reputation of being a cold fish with women, Hugh would demonstrate that he was a great lover. As his brother's horses, such as Petrach, won classic after classic, Hugh would show that he was a better and more courageous horseman.

St. George had inherited the Cottesmore hounds as well as Barleythorpe while Hugh had to be content with hunting with the far less fashionable Woodland Pytchley. He was already recognized as one of the best horsemen of the day, so that his appearance at any meet in the country caused a stir of interest. Unable to buy expensive hunters, he would scour the country for well-bred hunters which had a reputation for being difficult or dangerous, and buy them for a song. After a few days of almost living with a new horse it would become as tractable in his hands as a riding-school hack. 'There is no such animal as an unrideable horse,' he would claim, and for him it certainly seemed to be true.

One of his greatest triumphs was with a horse called Quirk, which was bought by Lord Calthorpe who expected to win the Grand National with it. Quirk was an Irish horse and a wonderful looker. Unfortunately when he was brought over to this country nothing could be done with him. Even Joe Cannon, the leading steeplechase jockey, confessed himself beaten. Eventually Calthorpe gave Quirk to Hugh, remarking that if he wanted to break his bloody neck on him he was welcome.

Hugh took him to his stables, and a week later, against all expectations, came under starter's orders with him in a Liverpool trial 'chase. Riding him on a rope bit of his own devising, he won comfortably. Although to the end of his days Quirk would never go for anyone else, Hugh hunted him for years and claimed he was the best hunter he ever had. When Machell organized the last six-mile steeplechase ever to be run in England, Hugh entered Quirk, although the general opinion was that the horse was too old for such a strenuous race. He won in the most leisurely fashion against odds of twenty to one. It was a victory which gave him particular satisfaction.

Hugh was never prepared to let St. George have his way. When he heard that he had had a substantial win at the Casino at Nice, Hugh immediately set out with Chicken Hartopp, Moreton Frewen and J. B. Roche, Lord Fermoy's younger brother, with the express intention of wiping his brother's eye. On this occasion fortune favoured the brave. He quickly lost the modest capital with which he had started out at the roulette tables. Then, with a borrowed ten pounds and an extraordinary run of luck, he finished up by winning a small fortune—£1,800.

The following night with his newly won capital he ventured his luck at the big table playing baccarat. Punting against the wealth of the Russian grandees, whose extravagant gambling was the talk of Europe, he increased his fortune to £8,000 before news that the frost had broken in England sent the whole party hurrying back to resume their hunting.

Few gambling stories have a happy ending and Hugh's was no exception. In London a man could gamble just as heavily as in the South of France but it was altogether a much more dangerous business. In the Casinos a man's credit was the amount of ready money he had to play with. In England a gentleman's credit was never in doubt. Cully, the great racecourse bookmaker of the day, would take a bet of £10,000 from a young man of good family, simply at the nod of a head. He knew that to default meant social ruin. In private gambling parties where the fashionable Regency game of *écarté* was being superseded by the even more hazardous game of baccarat, a loser was expected to redeem his chits the following morning even if it meant selling up his estate to do so—a fate which was far from uncommon.

Hugh met his Waterloo one night during the summer after his big win at Nice. After a day's racing at Newmarket he settled down to play in the Duke of Devonshire's house in a rich company of hardened gamblers like Jubilee Juggins Benson and Sir Beaumont Dixie (whose devotion to the bottle earned for himself and his wife the nicknames of Sir Always and Lady Sometimes Tipsy). Also playing was Captain Machell, about whom Hugh had a sizeable chip on his shoulder which may have caused him to show off rather more than usual. He finished up losing £18,000 which, for him, was a very serious matter indeed. His £8,000 had long since been dissipated and the sum he had lost was far beyond his means.

He would have had to go to St. George for help if the old family friend, Lord Calthorpe, had not come to his rescue. He paid Hugh's debts in full but extracted a promise from him that he would never gamble again. To his immense credit Hugh never laid a bet on a horse or touched a card for the rest of his life.

In after years, explaining his aversion to any form of gambling he would tell the story of the fateful night at the Duke of Devonshire's with a slightly different ending. According to Hugh it was he who had been the big winner. The following morning Lord Calthorpe had called upon him and lectured him on the folly of gambling with people who could not afford to lose on the same scale as himself. 'Do you realize,' Calthorpe is reported by Hugh as saying, 'that it would break all those good fellows who lost to you last night if they had to meet their commitments.' Thereupon he handed Hugh a cheque for all he had won on the condition that he would never play again.

It was just one of the many myths he was to create about himself in later life when there was no one left to dispute them. At the time his misfortune was another thing to be held against St. George whose own high scale of betting was well known.

The climax in Hugh's war of attrition against his brother came when St. George announced his engagement to Lady Gwladys Herbert, who was the sister of the Earl of Pembroke.

Gwladys was quite one of the most beautiful women of her day. Her close friend Lady Augusta Fane describes her in her reminiscences: 'Nearly six feet in height, she had the most superb figure and, with her lovely dark eyes and brilliant colouring, she made any woman near her look pale.'

Hugh had never made any disguise of his contempt for St. George as a ladies' man. In consequence he found the good-natured legpulling which he had to put up with when his brother made a match that any man might envy, hard to take in good part. It was definitely one up to St. George.

There was only one thing to do about it, and that was to make a match himself which would eclipse St. George's in the eyes of Society.

The chances of Hugh making a good match in London were remote indeed. Mothers with eligible daughters protected them from impecunious young men with unimaginable ferocity. Better by far that they should remain on the shelf to comfort their mothers in their old age than that they should fall victim to a fortune hunter who would squander their dowries and involve them in goodness knows what scandals besides.

The number of families who could be counted as being in the top flight of Society was only about three hundred. They clung together with impregnable aloofness. Not only did everybody know everybody else but they knew the state of each other's finances down to the last penny piece. They knew who would inherit from whom and how much. They knew what family estates were mortgaged and who would benefit from the entail of others. A man might be as dull as ditchwater, and as unprepossessing as a gargoyle, but if he was wealthy and of good family he was a good marriage prospect. No one else, however dashing and gay, had very much of a chance. By contrast with the free-for-all entertainments given today when anxious mothers vie with each other to drag in no matter what young men to partner their daughters, the *entreé* to the grand Society balls was as zealously guarded as the vaults of the Bank of England.

Hugh Lowther, with his modest private income and his reputation for fast living, could on no account be considered a good catch. Within a year of his *début* in London he had been crossed off the lists of eligible young men assiduously kept by ambitious mothers.

It was not a situation which caused Hugh any loss of sleep until St. George exploded his unexpected bombshell. Then his thoughts turned with greater determination to Lady Grace Gordon with whom he had been having an on-and-off romance since he was sixteen.

Grace was a sister of the Marquis of Huntly and one of a big family of six sons and six daughters which was ruled over with an iron rod by their widowed mother.*

The Gordons had a family house at Orton Longueville in the middle of the hunting country between Stamford and Peterborough which was Hugh's spiritual home. They were unusual amongst aristocratic Scottish families in espousing the English sport of

---

* When the 10th Marquess of Huntly died he left the following family: Charles, his heir; Lewis, lost at sea 1870 on H.M.S. *Captain*; Bertrand, died at Sydney 1869; Douglas, died unmarried 1888; Esme, died 1900; and Granville Armyne, died 1907—and daughters Mary, *m.* 1st Earl of Ancaster, *d.* 1921; Grace Cecilie; Margaret Ethel (Maggie), *m.* 3rd Baron Harlech; Elena Mary, *m.* Major J. L. Wickham and her twin sister Edith Blanche who died 1862; another daughter Ethelreda Caroline was born posthumously in 1864, *m.* Lt.-Col. Hy. Wickham and died in 1962.

hunting, and the family spent much of the year in the South.

At one time in Scottish history the Gordon family had wielded almost more than Royal power from their fortress, Aboyne Castle in Aberdeenshire. The head of the family was the premier Marquis of Scotland and held the proud title of Cock o' the North. As a result of political miscalculation much of the family fortunes had been lost. The uncompromising grey turrets of Aboyne still stood, but the lean years showed in the crumbling masonry and under-furnished rooms. The family put in an appearance every year at Aboyne for Christmas but that was about all. Only their proud titles remained to them in Scotland. For the rest they just about managed to keep up appearances in their country estate at Orton Longueville. There were never quite enough hunters to go round the sons, let alone the daughters, who were only able to hunt if a friend was kind enough to give them a mount; and there was never quite enough money to present the girls in proper style in the London Summer Season.

Lady Grace Gordon was the third eldest of the girls and quite the plainest of them all. Yet it was Grace who first caught the youthful Hugh's eye. Straight as a hop pole, and angular in her movements, she was in every way a tom-boy. She was a superb horsewoman— one of the best of her day—an excellent tennis player and even played billiards and cricket well enough to hold her own with her brothers.

From the very first Grace was attracted to Hugh by his skill as a horseman. With little entertaining being possible at Orton Longueville they met for the most part in the hunting field or at country house-parties. When Hugh came back from his year on the Continent they took up a childhood friendship again, and soon, for the only time in her life, she was desperately in love. While Hugh sowed his wild oats in London she stayed at home playing tennis with her brothers and sisters, looking after her bantams, of which she was immensely proud, and waiting for Hugh to come tearing down for a few days' hunting. For the most part it was a dull monotonous time for Grace. Here is a typical entry in her meticulously kept diary:

Cold today. Mr. Tyrwhitt came. We began to dance about half past ten and danced till one. Mama played one or two things and Mademoiselle everything else, and we had a variety of dances. The only contretemps was that there were no men to dance with so the maids had to twist round together. Monty and Mr. Hall exerted themselves very much.

Beautiful bright day. Fed my fowls and ducks. Walked to Woodstone in the afternoon. I took 'Gladys' and coming home let her out in the field and she had a rare gallop. After dinner we played cribbage with Mama. We each won a game.

And so it went on, day after day, until Hugh's reappearance brought momentary colour and excitement to her life.

Surprisingly, with all London to discover, and the world opening out for him, Hugh's schoolboy affection survived the first flush of adolescence. One night after a dance at nearby Burley Park he proposed to her. He was eighteen and she almost twenty-one.

When she blurted out the news at the family breakfast table the following morning, there was a moment of stunned incredulity. 'I will see you in the morning-room directly,' announced Mama coldly, and left the table.

By lunch-time it was all settled. A tearful Grace had given her word not to see Hugh for two years and Mama had dictated a letter for her to send to him giving her decision in the coldest possible terms.

It was of course unthinkable that the Gordons should allow one of their daughters, from whom they expected so much, to marry Hugh Lowther; poor they might be but the family was one of the proudest in the land. Lord Huntly, on his return from London, thoroughly endorsed Mama's decision. 'Huntly returned from London today with more stories of Hugh's doings. You would really think he was the worst man in the world. I cried myself to sleep,' Grace recorded sadly.

It was the beginning of two unhappy years for Grace. Every day she patiently entered a record of the weather, the number of games of tennis she had played, the people she had met and the dances she had attended. Sometimes even she tried to interest herself in other men. 'Pratt came out and he and Lord Burghersh bowled to me for a long time. Lord B. bowled me four times and Pratt once. Lord B. is so nice!'

But it was no use. Hugh was never very far from her thoughts, although the very mention of his name was enough to cause a furious row with Mama. 'At dinner My Lady and I had a few words and she was very angry with me. Oh goodness what it all is!' Mama's social aspirations for her she found intolerable. 'Dressed after dinner and went with My Lady to Mrs. White of Ardanrock's Concert, whoever she may be. Such a collection of people! The rummiest I have ever met. He a real Scotsman, she a painted lady of the highest order. Her Ladyship storming because I did not stay amongst the swells and pay attention to the young men.'

Unavoidably she and Hugh met from time to time at parties and it was only then that her painstaking diary showed any animation.

. . . Granville went to shoot at Walcot. I went to dinner with Everard Digby. We did not begin to dance till near eleven o'clock, everyone came so late. The room looked very pretty and the music capitally led by Mr. T. Wills and Finney's band. The room got very hot and at one time was overfull. I think I danced every dance and chiefly with the men of the house who were very energetic. The Bushy party arrived latish and I was at the top of the stairs when they came and saw H. long before he saw me. It was dreadful not being able to dance or talk to him, but as I had been asked not to so do, I did not, and only had one polka with him. He danced several times with Maggie and in the cotillion I had several turns with him. He led the cotillion capitally and it was great fun only there ought to have been presents. Charles Lowther came with Dick Fryons and was terribly drunk. I had a square with him early in the evening. Kept it up till five and I enjoyed it very much but might have enjoyed it fifty million times more and my feelings were rather worked up.

'Oh, how I long for Feb. 20 '78,' she recorded time after time, like a schoolgirl ticking off dates until the end of term, but as the months passed the possibility of an engagement seemed further and further away. Mama's resolution was hardened rather than appeased with the passage of time and the continued bad reports of Hugh himself did nothing to help. Hugh's younger brother Charles, although still in his 'teens, was drinking with a dedication he kept up until his death at the age of twenty-six. Even St. George, with his heavy gambling and drinking, and sudden disappearances to outlandish parts of the world, was regarded with suspicion by a carefully regulated Society. It all confirmed Lady Huntly's views that the Lowther brothers were far from being suitable companions for her daughters.

Towards the end of the summer of 1877 the position must have seemed increasingly hopeless even to Grace. 'Walked with Ethel [her sister] and talked about Hugh. I found out that there is a regular storm brewing. No rest for the weary. Not one of my relations sticks by me either.' And a few days afterwards, 'Dinner at home. Mama and Maggie went out in the evening. I did not, but before Huntly and My Lady came to give me a long jaw, Huntly having received a letter from Hugh which he showed me, and they talked and talked, most of it nonsense—it was settled that I had best write to Hugh and tell him no pledge or engagement. Bed sorrowful.'

Nobody knows what brought about the dramatic change in the situation some time after the 28th January 1878. At this point the carefully kept diary, which recorded even the pennies she spent from her tiny allowance on 'sweeties', comes to an abrupt end. It is not resumed until she had been married for a year. Did St. George's engagement to the glamorous Gwladys Herbert spur Hugh on to redoubled efforts? Or did Grace's steadfast determination in the end win the day? There is no record. It is only known that they were married from Orton Longueville on the 27th June 1878, after an engagement that could only have lasted a few short months. It took place a fortnight before St. George's own wedding, and neither brother attended the celebrations of the other.

St. George's marriage almost straight away ran into serious trouble. Within a year he was writing strict instructions to his head agent at Lowther, Mr. Little, on the subject of how the glamorous Gwladys was to be treated during his absence on yet another of his voyages on his yacht *Northumbria*. He wrote:

I am off tomorrow, but before starting I write one line to say that I have written some more orders in the order book.

You will see that I have allowed people to stay at Lowther because, when I came to think matters over, I believe it is better not to give my Lady the excuse that she had to go and stay at *all sorts of fast houses* because I would not allow her friends to come and stay at Lowther. . . .

The heavy underlined instructions continued for eight closely written pages, ending with the injunction that the orders must be 'carried out to the letter, come what may'.

Whether Lady Lonsdale had her guests at the Castle during St. George's six months' absence is not known. All that is certain is that, if she did, they must have had a fairly miserable time. Nobody was to ride any of his horses, carry any gun or rifle anywhere on his 100,000 acres, use any of the reception rooms, which were to be kept locked up or attend any of the local functions.

As for her Ladyship, she was not even allowed to stable her horses at the Castle without authority from Mr. Little. In the event of her attempting to do so, 'they will, without fail, be sent down to the Crown Hotel at Penrith, there to be kept at Her Ladyship's expense, due notice having been given to Siddle that we refuse to pay one farthing for their upkeep, and that he must look to My Lady for payment'.

My Lady was to have her wings clipped with a vengeance. A

scribbled postscript to this extraordinary document goes part of the way to explaining the cause of the trouble which had blown up so seriously in the marriage which caused such a social stir. It reads: 'We cannot afford to suffer from her wilfulness in not taking advice and in going contrary to her statement to me, that is the whole secret—if we pay she does not care, if she pays she will take care.'

There is no doubt that Gwladys led St. George a considerable dance. She much preferred Carlton House Terrace to Lowther for there she had far more scope to entertain her friends. She gave wonderful parties to which everyone came—even old Lord Beaconsfield, dandified to the last, his fingers glittering with rings, his heavy-lidded eyes still keenly observant.

Lady Augusta Fane could find only one fault with her great friend. In her book *Chit-Chat*, she remarks 'Gwladys had a fine character, and a broad outlook on life. She had however . . . an overwhelming curiosity to know everything and experience every sensation, and this inquisitiveness led her into dark places and amongst undesirable people, but, fortunately it neither altered nor debased her mind. . . .'

Hugh Lowther, who disliked his sister-in-law and Lady Augusta Fane with almost equal intensity, used to claim that after St. George's death Gwladys indulged in all manner of excesses. It can safely be taken that most of these were mere colourful flights of his imagination. Her second marriage to Lord Ripon was a great success, and in later years her closest friend was Queen Alexandra.

So within a year St. George and Hugh had both found wives in the marriage market. The reserved, introverted St. George, dogged with ill-health and imbued only with a desire to travel to further and more remote corners of the world, matched with the flighty, gay Lady Gwladys to whom the bright lights and parties were food and drink. The lusty, red-blooded extrovert, Hugh, married to the strictly proper, careful Grace with her rigid sense of duty and aversion to the life of a social butterfly. St. George's first act after marriage was to sell his string of racehorses and plan a trip to the Arctic; Hugh's was to throw himself with renewed vigour into the increasingly hectic merry-go-round of a London which was taking its lead from the party-loving Prince of Wales.

The present-day psychiatrists would no doubt find the whole thing perfectly logical, but Victorian society literally gaped with amazement.

Chapter 4

Lady Huntly's objections to her daughter's marriage were well founded. Hugh was head-over-heels in debt and there seemed little prospect of his ever being anything else. It was a gloomy outlook indeed for the young couple until, from out of the blue, a solution of at least a temporary nature presented itself.

Amongst the more formidable of Hugh's hunting companions was Moreton Frewen, a very fine horseman and one of the outstanding characters of the hunting field. Frewen's interests, however, ranged further afield than Melton and the surrounding countryside. His father was a solid country squire of comfortable means, but young Moreton and his brother were of the stuff of which pioneers are made.

It was the time of the great cattle boom in the American Middle West. In the clubs and coffee houses of St. James's Street and Prince's Street, Edinburgh, the talk was all of the great fortunes being made almost overnight in the Texas Panhandle and the virgin lands of Wyoming. A five-dollar bull calf, it was reliably reported, could be fed on the limitless free grazing available, and be sold at the end of it for ten times what it cost. Everywhere there were stories of people who knew people who had laid out a modest capital sum in the spring to find it turned into a fortune by the end of the summer.

One of the local Wyoming papers, the *Laramie Boomerang*, wrote a leading article which was intended as a satire on the cattle fever which was sweeping the country. A Texas cowhand, it was reported, tongue-in-cheek, had ridden up to Wyoming bringing with him one lone steer, and found himself in no time, due to the miraculous fertility of the area, to be the owner of six thousand head of cattle. Whilst the ranchers up in Johnstone County rocked with laughter, the report was passed from mouth to mouth in London as proof that everything that had been rumoured was true, and more.

The real truth was that Victorian England was bulging at the seams with money to invest. In a safe, comfortable society a spirit of adventurous commercialism combined with greed stalked the land. Keeping up with the Joneses meant keeping on making fatter and fatter profits. Even Queen Victoria herself, it was freely claimed, was investing her personal fortune in Texas cattle under an assumed name. It was the same dangerous, heady atmosphere which, a hundred and fifty years earlier, had created the South Sea Bubble.

To the two Frewen brothers the challenge was irresistible. In 1877 they plunged, with all the capital they could lay their hands on, into the great cattle rush.

The Frewens set up their headquarters just north of Cheyenne, where Moreton indulged his love of the theatrical by building a vast wooden edifice to serve as his home, and which became known as Englishman's Castle.

From the beginning his extravagance made him an unending source of astonishment to the hard-bitten ranchers whose pioneering herds were sweeping into the area from the south. They goggled at the indoor sanitation he insisted on installing, at the silver knives and forks which adorned his hospitable table, and the fresh flowers he had delivered regularly by the railroad—and they rolled in their saddles with glee when a trader managed to sell him the same herd of cattle twice in one afternoon.

Hugh Lowther, however, fretting in idleness through the summer of 1879 with only the parlous condition of his bank account to occupy his mind, had no doubts about Moreton Frewen. To him the rumours of his friend's exploits were like 'the brave music of a distant drum'. When he received an invitation for himself and Grace to go out for a few months' big game-shooting he accepted for both of them with the utmost alacrity. Grace, too, was delighted to leave London. It was to be a belated honeymoon for them both.

They arrived at Cheyenne on 12th August to join a number of other well-known young aristocrats invited by Frewen. Amongst them were Lord Rodney, the Hon. Charles Fitzwilliam and the Hon. James Roche.

The Frewen brothers had established their newly formed 76 Ranch far up in Johnstone County along the banks of the North Powder River and the Crazy Woman. It was practically on the site of General

Custer's famous last stand, which had taken place only three years previously, and was over three hundred miles from the nearest railroad at Little Rock. Once out in the wilds the party split up into small groups. Then the fun really started.

The only woman in the original party besides Grace Lowther was a Mrs. Brockhurst. She proved an early casualty. Finding that the ground was unsuitable for carriages, she and her husband returned to England. The other groups, however, pushed on to the main hunting grounds on the fork of the Powder River. This area was one of the last refuges of the buffaloes. They were, in fact, only to survive persecution and the influx of the Texas Longhorns for another few years, but at the end of the 'seventies they still grazed over the Great Divide in considerable numbers.

Reports of the expected buffalo herds proved the undoing of the excitable Sir Maurice de Bunsen, another of Frewen's distinguished guests. Out commendably early one morning, he spotted what he took to be a rather thin buffalo grazing by itself some distance from the camp. Determined to steal a march on his slumbering companions, he set off on a long and painstaking stalk. His shot was unerring, but alas, his victim turned out to be the dairy cow on which the party depended for its supplies of fresh milk.

James Roche was the most experienced member of the party. It was his second trip to the Middle West, and he was a particularly keen buffalo shot. His method of killing them was unique, and founded on a strange lack of the instinct of self preservation which he had observed in the animals so far as white hunters were concerned.

The slaughter of the buffalo in earnest only started with the white invasion of the Indian territory. At its peak it reached a fantastic thousand head a day. Yet the buffaloes never learned to fear the white man in the same way as they did the Indians.

James Roche had a technique of riding his horse right in amongst a herd, picking his animal and shooting it dead at point-blank range, between the shoulder-blades—the surest way of hitting the beast's heart which is placed very low down in its massive chest, between the forelegs. Being a sportsman in the best English traditions, however, he would always stampede the herd first and shoot the animal he had selected on the move, and the weapon he used was a ·41 revolver!

Roche teamed up with the Lowthers when the big party split up, which would appear to have been a rather unfair distribution of talents. Roche was easily the most experienced hunter and what

Hugh lacked in experience he made up for in enthusiasm and hardiness. Grace, too, proved to be a great asset to the party. She could ride with the best of them, undaunted by long hours in the saddle. She cooked excellently and kept the camp supplied with trout which she caught herself—a skill she had learned as a child on the Scottish Don and at which no one in the party could match her.

Lord Rodney's party by contrast suffered not only from lack of experience but, apparently, also from a lack of a sense of direction. James Roche and Hugh Lowther came upon him hopelessly lost and out of touch with the rest of his party, who were supposed to be hunting an area seventy miles away. They set him off again in the correct direction, only to find him at their camp again the following morning, the unfortunate man having ridden enthusiastically all night, to discover when dawn came that he had described a complete circle.

The Lowther party had some misfortunes of their own. Grace, delighted with her role as camp cook, set fire to the prairie by mistake on their second day out. They lost practically all their equipment and had to send back to Cheyenne for further supplies. The fire itself continued to burn for two weeks, which stands near to a record for the Middle West.

In the midst of all this high comedy and confusion, the Arapahoe and Ute tribes were spoiling for trouble. The Lowthers' party watched the comings and goings between the tribes with apprehension. Fortunately the Indians were too involved in their own politics and in trying to get Chief Sitting Bull to come out of retirement on his reservation in Canada to bother about the sudden influx of Leicestershire hunting folk to Sioux territory! They did, however, get quite a scare from another quarter.

Roche and Hugh Lowther had been out with a half-breed trapper since early morning in search of grizzly bear. On their way back to camp in the late afternoon they came across the trail of a lone rider heading in the direction of their base, where they had left Grace alone to prepare the evening meal.

The trapper examined the tracks closely for some minutes, shaking his head with foreboding.

Then he announced that they had undoubtedly been made by 'Little Henry'.

Everybody in the Big Horn knew of Little Henry. He was a notorious horse thief who would not hestitate to murder to steal. The Lowther camp, with its pack ponies, mules and hundreds of pounds worth of valuable equipment guarded only by Grace was temptation indeed.

Thoroughly alarmed, the party set off at breakneck speed to the rescue. As they neared the camp they unslung their rifles and edged round the corner of the track, fearful of what they would discover. Little Henry was there sure enough, squatting by the fire with his horse grazing nearby. The guide was all for shooting him out of hand. After all, was there not a five-thousand-dollar bounty on his head? Roche and Lowther would have no part in such an unsporting suggestion. Nonetheless they rode into camp with their fingers on the trigger.

There followed a reunion at least as classic as when Stanley met Livingstone, for Hugh Lowther and the notorious horse thief fell to pumping each other's hands and slapping each other's backs. Little Henry, it turned out, had been at Eton with Hugh.

Eton or not, however, he thoroughly deserved his reputation as a dangerous horse-thief, and eventually met his fate at the gun of Bat Masterson, Sheriff of Dodge City. It is interesting to speculate how his death would have been reported had the College authorities got to hear of it. This was one of Hugh's favourite stories. Unfortunately nobody ever managed to discover Little Henry's real name.

The Lowthers stayed on in the Big Horn until well into November. Then they returned to New York with James Roche, to be met by a battery of Press-men. Even if the Wyoming cow-pokes thought little of the Frewen brothers and their aristocratic guests, socially conscious New York was delighted with them.

In an extravagant eulogy to Lady Grace Lowther the *New York World* wagged an admonitory finger at American womanhood. 'Are the daughters of Albion to be allowed to carry off all the sporting honours of the Great Divide?' it asked. 'If not it is time for the American votaresses of Diana to be up and doing.'

In terms of sporting achievement the trip was certainly a great success, particularly if the number of trophies is anything to judge by.

The same paper, reporting a personal interview with Hugh Lowther recorded the scene in his suite at Brevoort House as follows:

The large sitting-room looked like a hunter's camp, carpeted. Over the backs of the large lounges were thrown great robes of fur. One of skunk fur, another of wild cat skin. Beaver skin mats lay on the floor, and out of a large packing case brought in for inspection were taken skin after skin of all the wild creatures that walk the western forest two by two, Noah's Ark fashion.

On the sideboard were spread out Indian trophies by the dozen. Among them were tomahawks which had seen service before bullets from the United States carbines laid their owners low. To one of these was still hanging the scalp which ornamented it when it stuck in the belt of the Ute who once carried it. There were moccasins and sandals enough for a small tribe. . . .

and so on for a whole closely printed column which chronicled everything from papoose cases to witch-doctors' bead necklaces. The final item was thirty-one grizzly bear skins, the largest of which had weighed 1,200 pounds.

Hugh Lowther sailed back to England the following week but he took back with him more than the dozens of packing-cases of trophies to prove his hunting prowess. He had also caught cattle fever from Moreton Frewen.

*

Back in London before Christmas Hugh did not return immediately to the Woodland Pytchley country as might have been expected. Instead he sought out Sam Lewis, the doyen of moneylenders, and asked his advice. The problem was not the usual one that he was fed up with trying to make ends meet on the allowance he had from St. George. What he needed was capital. Money he could put into buying cattle which Frewen would graze for him on the 76 Ranch and from which a golden flow of dollars might be expected—enough even for his extravagant ideas of what a young man with sporting instincts required.

It was not an easy matter to arrange, but in the end it was done. He managed to sell his contingent reversionary interest in the vast Lowther estate for a parsimonious £40,000.

Hugh Lowther was not by any means the only contributor to the Frewen formula for quick fortune. Lord Rosslyn weighed in heavily; so did several others. But it was Hugh Lowther who was the real fairy godmother of the scheme. Fired with enthusiasm by his recent trip he plunged in with every penny he could raise.

In fact he was right in his estimate of the future possibilities, as was proved by the vast fortunes that were later to be made in Wyoming. They were not to be made, however, by the British financed companies—or at least by very few of them. Many millions of dollars were invested by English and Scottish fortune seekers, and, at the height of the boom, British capital controlled well over twenty million acres of American territory.

Frewen's company, the 76 Ranch, at the peak of its prosperity, owned 80,000 head of cattle grazing on the Powder River.

Already the big dividends being paid and the upward spiralling price of beef were causing head shaking in more cautious quarters. The slump was to come, but, before it did, a far worse disaster overtook the fortunes of the 76 Ranch. Early on in the autumn, the snow came. Soon the lush prairie was blotted out and the hunger maddened cattle were ranging far and wide for anything they could find to eat. The early snowstorm caught Frewen napping. He had no store of winter feed, and with the railhead over two hundred miles away, little chance of getting any. His only hope was that the phenomenally early storm would let up. It didn't.

In the severe winter of 1878 when drifting snow had buried many thousands of cattle, the cattlemen thought they had learned their lesson. To combat the danger they constructed miles of drift fences behind which their cattle could shelter. Now their foresight was to prove disastrous. Vast hordes of cattle on the wrong side of the drift fences, driven crazy by hunger and the snow sleeting in their faces, turned their backs on the storm and stampeded for what they hoped would be safety. The drift fences checked them long enough for the first cattle to be brought to their knees. Those behind, forced irresistibly forward, piled up on top of them. When the thaw came, a hundred yards' wide swathe of decomposing cattle stretched along mile upon mile of fencing.

Frewen made a brave effort to salvage the emaciated remnants of his herd. With hundreds dying every night he headed for the shores of Lake Superior. Here he housed them in hurriedly constructed sheds and fed them with refuse from the nearby grain elevators. Finally he prevailed on Lord Lansdowne, then Viceroy of Canada, to lobby for permission for the cattle to enter England in spite of the quarantine barriers against pleuro-pneumonia.

To help his cause, Moreton Frewen dashed back to England. The arrival of the 'Wyoming Cattle King', as the Press called him, caused quite a stir. Controversy raged. 'One thing is certain,' claimed one paper, 'Mr. Frewen knows how to perform with figures. He tickles with microscopic fractions and anon he thunderbolts with crashing thousands.'

Even his persuasive voice, however, could not win the day. He returned to Wyoming and sold up. The land on which West Superior

City now stands he let go for a song, thus missing one of several opportunities he had in his lifetime of amassing a fortune.

Frewen's enterprise was by no means unique in the magnitude of its failure. Whilst freight charges and fodder bills remained high, the price of beef plummeted down from nine dollars a hundred to a rock bottom of one dollar eighty. The English and Anglo-American companies, which had started out with such *élan*, shrivelled and died on the frozen prairies of the winter of 1880, and with them went Hugh Lowther's chance of a fortune. Further south in Texas, the story was the same, even without the appalling weather.

The Earl of Aylesford, for example, was so hard hit on his 40,000-acre ranch that, after paying for thirty-odd horses, thirteen dogs and five servants, he had no money left for buying more cattle. Known by his neighbours as 'the Jedge', his performance with the whisky bottle was remarkable. He would always open a new bottle for any cowboy who cared to drop in, and as one of them reported, 'He doesn't stop at one neither. I've been to the ranch many a time to stay all night and woke in the mornin' to find the bottles lyin' around thick as fleas, the boys two deep on the floor snorin' like mad buffaloes and the Jedge with a bottle in each hand over in the corner.'* Aylesford went the way of all the rest of them, but he certainly enjoyed himself on the way out!

The reactions of the London backers to the Frewen failure varied. Lord Rosslyn wrote to Frewen, 'I fearlessly challenge anybody to prove that you have not always been right in your actions, your prophecies, your suggestions for escape from a most difficult crisis. Your only fault latterly has been that you could not raise money fast enough.'

Others were not so charitable.

Hugh Lowther had no doubts whatever about Moreton Frewen. With all his money sunk without a trace he simply drew a line through Frewen's name. He never mentioned him nor the ill-fated venture again. In the after years he would delight in re-telling stories of his days in Johnstone County and of his friendship with Buffalo Bill, but Longhorns and the 76 Ranch might never have existed. Hugh Lowther would never recognize any part of his life which was not a success.

Moreton Frewen emerges from the whole affair as a rather enigmatic figure. He gained world fame afterwards as the great champion

* *Cattle v. Men* by C. W. Towne and E. N. Wentworth (*University of Oklahoma Press*).

of bi-metallism. He preached his theories in almost every capital in the world and many of the world's statesmen became his friends. He found time to set right the corruption in the Nizam of Hyderabad's Treasury, made a fortune with a method of separating tin from zinc and lost it all again in a scheme for extracting gold from mine heaps.

Scheme after scheme sprang from his fertile brain, each one breathtaking in its conception and each in turn failing through some unforeseen quirk of fate. In the end he began to run short of both funds and friends. When he died in 1924 he was struggling to prove his title to a thousand acres on the Pacific Coast, worth many millions of dollars today.

A man of brilliance and charm, history has never decided whether Moreton Frewen was a genius *manqué* or a rogue with a silver tongue. Some of the most powerful men of the day, such as Lord Desborough and Earl Grey, remained his staunch supporters to the end. Others nicknamed him 'Mortal Ruin' and gave his schemes a wide berth.

Of all the participants in the Wyoming fiasco perhaps the strangest future of all lay in store for Lord Rodney.

Rodney was not well off by comparison with most of his friends but he excelled them, if anything, in a taste for rich living. Returning from his club one night, in the small hours of the morning, he decided to walk home to clear his head and reflect on the money he had just lost at cards.

In this way he fell in with a stranger and, on an impulse, poured out his troubles to him. Failing to persuade Lord Rodney to change his way of life, the stranger prophesied that one day he would want to do something useful. 'I shall wait at this hour and at this place on each anniversary of this meeting,' he said. 'One day you will keep the appointment and I will help you.'

Six years later, Lord Rodney was at the end of his tether when he remembered the arrangement. As a last resort and wondering at his own credulity, he kept the appointment. The stranger was waiting.

He persuaded the young peer that his only hope of happiness lay in helping others worse off than himself.

Next day Lord Rodney moved lock, stock and barrel down to the East End of London where he kept open house for any of the youth of the East End wanting to make use of what he had. The youth organization which he formed, called 'The Rods', set a pattern for movements like the Dockland Settlement which still do so much good.

As for the stranger, he disappeared into the night and was never heard of again.

Chapter 5

With the collapse of the Wyoming venture, Hugh was faced with an outlook of unrelieved gloom. His capital had disappeared and his hopes of financial independence had been dashed for ever.

He had rented Catmose Cottage in Oakham as his and Grace's first family home. It was as small as its name indicates and he had only intended it to serve until he would be able to afford something more suitable. Now, with nothing more than his allowance from St. George to live on, it looked like becoming their permanent home.

There was only one bright spot on the horizon. Grace was going to have a baby. Even their financial troubles could not spoil their delight. Pussy suggested that they move into Cottesmore until the baby arrived so that Grace could have every care and attention, with Pussy keeping an experienced eye on things. They accepted gratefully.

Hugh managed to add a little to his income by travelling all over the country buying and selling horses. For the rest he occupied himself in hunting with the Woodland Pytchley or with one of the neighbouring packs. Even with keeping expenses down to the 'minimum', however, they could not manage to make ends meet.

Grace, with her careful Scottish instincts, shuddered to see how profligately Hugh spent what little money they did have. Since he had heard about the baby he had not, it was true, gone up to London so frequently on mysterious business, but there were still plenty of outlets for his extravagance around Cottesmore.

Grace was continuing to hunt, although both Pussy and Hugh tried to persuade her to give it up after Christmas. The baby was not due until June, which seemed a long way off to Grace with the best of the hunting season still to come.

Nobody knows today quite how the accident happened. It is

probable that her horse put its foot in a rabbit hole and, after falling, rolled on top of her. Whatever the reason the result was the same. The baby was lost. Grace herself was so gravely ill that it was some days before the doctors would give their final verdict. When they did it was worse even than anyone had feared. She would never be able to have another child. The specialist, down from London, took Hugh aside and told him that a normal husband and wife relationship would not be possible for at least three years. Perhaps never.

It was a shattering blow and each of them reacted differently.

For Grace it was not only an end to her hopes of children of her own, it was the beginning of a long history of chronic ill-health. She withdrew more and more into herself. Unable to hunt regularly or to play tennis or to take part in all the tom-boy activities of which she was so fond, she took to spending hours in her own room, remote from the activities and interests in which Hugh became increasingly absorbed.

It may be that in time her 'illness' became largely psychological, giving her an excuse to withdraw from a life which had lost much of its savour. She was to live until she was eighty-seven, but there were few days when she did not see a doctor. There were trips to all the fashionable spas of Europe in search of relief from the pains which kept her awake at night. When she travelled abroad her first concern was to find yet another doctor who would treat her.

In particular her attitude to children changed. Having been brought up in the rough and tumble of a large closely-knit family, it was not unnatural that she should have regarded having a family of her own as the highest ambition. Unable to do so she felt uneasy with other people's children, and the children, sensing it, shied away from her strange remoteness. In after years, nephews and nieces visiting Lowther found her a forbidding and rather frightening person.

From the time of her accident her personality grew further and further away from the fun-loving Grace Gordon of Orton Longueville. She was to make few close friends outside her family circle. Everybody else she treated with an immaculate courtesy which never thawed to greater intimacy.

Even with Hugh she could never recapture the gaiety which had characterized their trip in Wyoming. The memory of those carefree months was perpetuated in a habit which they had both fallen into on the trip. Wyoming in the early days had been known as Johnstone County, after the pioneer Tom Johnstone. Playing a game of make-

believe they had christened each other Mr. and Mrs. Tom Johnstone—and Mr. Tommy and Mrs. Tommy they remained to each
other for the rest of their lives.

Hugh's reaction to the disaster was completely the opposite to
Grace's. He fought his own sadness in the only way he knew—by
pitching the pace of his living higher and higher. The knowledge
that he could never have a son to succeed him was a terrible blow
and it is doubtful whether he ever altogether recovered from it.

When Hugh and Grace returned to London in the summer, the
pattern was already set. From then on Hugh was to grow larger than
life, seizing every opportunity to project himself in bigger and more
colourful disguise, while Grace flitted more and more in the shadow
of his personality so far as the public were concerned.

If she had not been such a strong character, the disaster might
have overwhelmed her. Her childhood dreams of her marriage lay
in ruins, but she emerged from the tragedy as the one strong influence
in Hugh's life. As he skipped on his colourful, extrovert way,
tumbling in and out of trouble, there was always Grace in the background ready to advise him when he needed advice most. That she
should become more of a mother to him than a wife was perhaps
inevitable.

Chapter 6

London in the early eighteen eighties was beginning to be a much gayer place than it had been during the earlier years when the Queen was ruling the Court with her rod of iron swathed in black crêpe. True, the socially ambitious middle class and the dyed-in-the-wool courtiers continued to strive to preserve a rigorous régime where every day was a Victorian Sunday, but the Prince of Wales was already making his presence felt as leader of the Champagne Set. Whilst half of Society stood on the touch-line and frowned, the other half played a riotous game of follow-my-leader hanging on to the coat-tails of the inexhaustible Prince. It was the beginning of the end of a régime.

The Prince of Wales's taste for enjoyment was as catholic as his taste in friends. Any beautiful woman, whatever her background, who managed to sparkle for a moment in his firmament was likely to find favour with him. His men friends, some of whom had actually made their money out of trade, caused if anything even greater eyebrow-raising. Where the Prince of Wales led there were many who tried to follow. The eye of the needle had grown bigger, and all kinds of strange camels were squeezing their way through, into a Society half-light. Suddenly, solid respectability was less admirable. The pendulum was swinging the other way so that life was becoming more colourful and extravagant.

It was altogether an atmosphere much more to Hugh's liking. It was this more liberal climate that allowed men like the notorious George Baird to attract a certain following, particularly with the sporting public.

Because Hugh was later to be one of the instruments in effecting Baird's eclipse, and because he was an extreme example of the Regency revival which was in the air, Baird's brief, tempestuous passage across the scene is interesting. There were many young men of Baird's background and suddenly acquired wealth who would have followed in his footsteps if the revolution in moral standards had gone a very little further than it actually did.

Baird's income at Cambridge, derived from the family coal-mines, was over a quarter of a million pounds a year. He set about using it to prove that he was a 'sportsman' of the old school. Not caring to be known as plain Mr. Baird, he took a leaf out of the Osbaldeston or Mytton book and insisted on being known as Squire Abingdon, a name he took from one of his Scottish properties. Sent down from the University, he went about the business of being the 'Squire' with fantastic energy.

On his estates at Lickfield he kept a stable of over a hundred horses in training. At Moulton Paddocks at Newmarket he had another hundred and fifty. Even horse-mad England had never seen his like before. Living on practically nothing but brandy and soda, his short life was one long struggle to keep his weight down, yet there was hardly a meeting when he did not ride one or two winners against the toughest opposition.

Even those who admired eccentricity on a grand scale could not quite take the 'Squire'. Sometimes, however, his exploits amused them. He had the reputation of being the dirtiest rider on the turf. On one occasion, taking advantage of a mêlée on a tight bend at Wolverhampton, he tried to put the favourite out of the race by doing his best to shove Lord Hartington through the rails. He was disqualified and afterwards offered one of the few apologies in his life. 'Beg pardon, my Lord,' he remarked genially, 'I thought you were a bloody farmer!'

He scoured the streets of London looking for fist-fights and betted huge sums on his gamecocks. He saved the Marquis of Ailesbury's financial troubles by eloping with the Marquis's actress wife Dolly Tester. He paid fifteen thousand pounds compensation. The romance was over in a month.

Surprisingly Lily Langtry fell in love with him, and their romance survived the outrageous scenes he created whenever he turned up to watch her performances in the theatre. The end nearly came one wet Sunday afternoon when the 'Jersey Lily' was resting at home after a strenuous week at the Haymarket theatre which she had leased for a season. An agitated messenger burst in upon her to tell her that there was what appeared to be a riot at the theatre. She hurried round there to find that the Squire and his friends, the day proving boring, had transformed the foyer into a rat pit. Wildly excited men crushed round the improvised ring yelling extravagant wagers to one another as their terriers were let loose amongst two and a half dozen great black sewer rats, whilst around the walls bloodthirsty-looking assistants held heaving sacks, promising further fun to come. In the centre of it all was the Squire joyfully wagering fistfulls of fivers and yelling encouragement to his dogs. The terrified Lily took one look and fled from the blood-spattered scene. It was all she could do to bring herself ever to enter the Haymarket Theatre again.

There was a sort of madness in the air which permitted scenes like this to become short-lived wonders until the next excitement drove them from people's minds.

Hugh Lowther's own exploits caused widespread eyebrow-raising but they fell far short of the Squire's excesses.

Baird was too much for anyone to take and perhaps most of all too much for Hugh. It was an odd contradiction of Hugh's character that, although he flouted convention, he was himself at heart a conventionalist. The men he admired most of his own generation were the great figures of the hunting-field like Lord Henry Bentinck, Harry Chaplin, and the Duke of Beaufort. They were all rich men, who not only lived for hunting but were acknowledged by their contemporaries as the most knowledgeable men of their day. Hugh longed with all his heart to be recognized in the same company. He had the knowledge and love of the sport in ample measure. It was only his lack of money that let him down and he felt it very bitterly.

Fifty years earlier, Creevy, the diarist, had nicknamed Lord Durham 'King Jog' because of his lordship's expressed opinion that 'one can jog along on £40,000 a year'. In the company to which Hugh aspired this was little more than the truth. With his tastes, Hugh's £1,000 a year was little better than a pittance. To cover up this deficiency and, perhaps to some extent to cover up his own shyness, he became involved in more and more colourful incidents.

During the summer of 1881, after Grace had lost her baby, the pace of Hugh's life in London became more furious than ever. Pussy had lent them her house in Wilton Crescent so that they had a roof over their heads. For a young man with aristocratic connections, credit was easy enough to come by, so that while Grace stayed at home, there were few nights when Hugh was not to be seen in one or other of the haunts popular with the young bachelors of the day, and few occasions when he missed a race meeting near London.

Hugh's companions were men like the 'Mate' (Sir John Astley) and 'Chicken' Hartopp. They were men who lived cheerfully on the brink of bankruptcy and yet managed by one device or another to have an extraordinarily good time.

There were plenty of people on the fringe of Society and in the sporting world who were ready to assist in preserving the illusion of spacious living. If Hugh's friends were not the most fashionable and if he attended more race meetings on the 'wrong' side of the rails than in the Members' Enclosure it did nothing to lessen his enjoyment.

In later years he used to delight in telling stories of what must have been one of the blackest years of his life, in spite of the fun there was to be had.

Largely as a result of his own powers of invention, legend and truth have become so intermingled that it is difficult to distinguish one from the other. One story, however, is certainly true. It happened at the July Meeting at Newmarket in 1881, when another of his friends, Sir George Chetwynd, had occasion to be grateful for Hugh's democratic connections.

Immediately after the third race Chetwynd discovered that he had lost his tie-pin. It was not only a valuable one but had great senti-mental value. The obvious person to turn to for help was Hugh, who not only knew but was on Christian-name terms with many of the more dubious racecourse personalities.

There was one thoroughly disreputable villain called Probyn who ran a racecourse gang. When Hugh sought him out he admitted that he had seen the pin which he agreed looked a valuable one.

'It is,' said Hugh, 'but it is also known to every jeweller in London. All that anybody is going to get who tries to sell it is a stretch in gaol.'

In the end, Probyn agreed to have it returned for twenty-five pounds.

'Tell your pal to go to the left-hand gate of the enclosure,' were Probyn's instructions. 'When he sees a gentleman in Holy Orders he must hold up the money so that the "reverend" can see it, and say "cuckoo" in a loud voice. If the reverend says "cuckoo" back, every-thing will be in order.'

Rather self-consciously the immaculately dressed Sir George set about carrying out the instructions. Sure enough, there was a rather seedy-looking parson and sure enough when he waved the money and managed to squeak 'cuckoo', the parson replied 'cuckoo' in the measured tone of a man born to the Cloth. After that the transaction was neatly completed.

Later, when Sir George was hurrying to catch the racing special back to Town, he was accosted by a ragamuffin about ten years old, who demanded to know how much he had paid the parson to get his pin back.

'Blimey!' exclaimed the boy, when Sir George told him. 'Twenty-five nicker! 'E only gave me ten bob, and I stole the bloody thing.'

Sir George was the most charming of men, if rather naïve. 'D'ye know what?' he used to remark when telling the story afterwards, 'I think there was something damned fishy about that vicar fellow!'

*

Perhaps the most famous story of all which Hugh used to tell of his young days was of the time he beat John L. Sullivan, the heavyweight champion of the world.

At the beginning of the eighteen eighties, the formidable figure of the American, John L. Sullivan, dominated the boxing scene. There may since have been more skilful holders of the proud title of heavyweight champion of the world, but for sheer power and ferocity John L. still stands head and shoulders above his successors.

As some men are born with a greater than average mental capacity amounting to genius, so some inherit a physique so much above the average as to set them above and apart from their fellow men. Sullivan was one of these. In his home town his feats of extraordinary strength had earned him the title of the 'Boston Strong Boy' by the time he had reached his 'teens. Add to this a naturally ferocious and anti-social temperament and there were all the ingredients of a champion in the days when the kings of the fight game were the men who were the least destructible.

Sullivan's rise to pre-eminence from a poverty-stricken childhood was meteoric. He would fight anyone and everyone. As world champion he toured the United States offering £200 to anyone who could knock him down. He never had to pay out. 'I'll fight anyone except pigs, dogs and niggers!' he would roar, sweeping all the glasses off the counter of the saloon, and happily taking on anyone who objected to his conduct. He was a braggart and bully of the worst description, particularly when he had drunk too much, which was very often.*

* It is only fair to add that after his retirement he 'got religion' and ended his days as an evangelist for teetotalism.

In spite of his heavy drinking his massive frame stood up to all the punishment his opponents could hand out, until he was finally stopped by Gentleman Jim Corbett after more than ten impregnable years.

The champion of England at the time was Jem Smith, and there was much talk of a match between Smith and Sullivan to take place in the presence of the Prince of Wales. Furious at the suggestion that Smith might have the beating of him, Sullivan offered to fight him for nothing, and pay him £200 into the bargain in the, to him, impossible event of Smith getting the better of him. One way and another, the fight never took place, but the general opinion was that Sullivan at the height of his career would have been too much for the gallant Jem.

Hugh Lowther, typically, took the opposite view. He even went so far as to boast one evening to a group of admiring friends that he himself would be quite prepared to put the gloves on with the great Sullivan.

One of the group was Haydn Coffin, the actor, who was leaving the following day to tour the U.S. with a play. Meeting Sullivan some weeks later, he remarked that there was a young aristocrat in London who was game to have a bout with him.

The effect of this challenge on Sullivan was electric. 'If he wants a fight he can have one,' he is supposed to have bellowed, 'and that goes for any other Dooks or Oils he cares to bring with him.'

Haydn Coffin carefully stirred the pot, working on the vanity of the two men. Eventually a match was arranged under the terms of the greatest secrecy, and Hugh Lowther sailed for New York.

His party must have been one of the strangest ever to leave these shores to meet the heavyweight boxing champion of America. It included a stage comedian, Arthur Roberts, Lionel Brough, one of the matinée idols of the day, and Lydia Kyasht, the dancer whose name was being freely linked with Hugh's by the gossips.

The only member of the party with any practical knowledge of boxing was the redoubtable Charlie Mitchell who was later himself to meet John L. Sullivan in an epic battle which took place in France and ended in a draw. Mitchell was a brilliant boxer and an ideal sparring partner for Hugh Lowther. He might have had an even more successful career if he had not become involved with Squire Abingdon. He managed the Squire's stable of fighters and became his boon drinking companion and general nursemaid. When he travelled to America with Hugh he had to book his passage under an assumed name as he was wanted by the police on a charge of 'breach of the peace'. It had arisen out of one of the Squire's brawls for which Mitchell, for a consideration, had agreed to take the blame.

The match had been arranged at the Central Park Academy, a riding-school in which Sullivan had a financial interest, and was to be with the still illegal six-ounce gloves. Hugh Lowther used to say afterwards that he would have met John L. with bare fists, but elected to use gloves to prove that as much damage could be inflicted with them as without.

One of Hugh's friends in New York was the wealthy American sportsman Richard K. Fox, the proprietor of the *Police Gazette*—a distinct misnomer for a paper which was concerned almost exclusively with sport and in particular with boxing. Richard Fox helped Charlie Mitchell to get his protégé ready for the contest, providing, amongst other things, special gloves stuffed with human hair as opposed to the more generally used horse hair. Human hair, it was claimed, was finer and more resilient than horse hair, the difference between the two being as silk to wool. Horse or human hair, however, the contest was still illegal, and would in all probability have been stopped by the police were the facts known—in spite of the support of the *Police Gazette*.

As to the fight itself, Hugh Lowther himself wrote an account of it all in later years for *The People*, which is worth quoting verbatim:

Just as in the old-time jockeys, men like Archer and their like, used to scare the life out of timorous rivals by their murderous shouts as they thundered along the course, so the boxers often used to try to frighten their opponents by snarling and shouting before ever the battle began.

Naturally, the people who came along to witness our contest were more than inclined to bet odds on Sullivan.

That was only to be expected. But all the time in my secret heart I felt I could show them something different. . . .

For the first round we just sparred and padded around taking each other's measures. I could see that Sullivan was a bit puzzled—just a little bit. I don't think he expected to find daring Mr. Lowther quite such a game proposition.

I saw him run his eyes over me when I entered the ring, and he seemed—perhaps I imagined it—to be rather surprised.

In the second round I felt once or twice that I had taken on something that was beyond me altogether. Sullivan got in one or two mighty blows that shook me, and I wasn't able to land any of mine. But I held on grimly and managed to sidestep the worst punches, and in the last few seconds I got in a beauty on the champion's nose.

Sullivan's face changed when that blow made contact. He began to wear that bear-cat expression which terrified his opponents. But I wasn't easily terrified in those days, and I kept on telling myself that even if I did take the count in the end, I had at least drawn the claret. . . .

It was in the third round that Sullivan crashed home that sledge-hammer right of his straight into my ribs, and I thought I was done for.

The blow was a capital one. It took all the wind out of me, and sent me staggering up against the ropes.

But it really served to put me on my mettle. I felt a fierce shooting pain in my ribs, but I didn't know that Sullivan's fist had done much damage.

I fought back after that for all I was worth, and got home several stingers on the big fellow's head and face. There was feinting and clinching, and then I put over a rattler of a smack to John L.'s chin.

All this time, too, I was taking punishment. One of my eyes was closed up, and I had an ugly cut on my shoulder. But though I was certainly hard pressed, I knew quite well that Sullivan was in a much worse plight. I had shaken him up time after time, and he was breath-ing hard, and finding it difficult to time his punches.

As he came at me in the opening of the sixth, I decided it was now or never.

I let fly with my right and caught him solid in the solar plexus, and he went down without a sound, apart from a faint grunt.

He lay there for several minutes after the final count, and when I went over and put out my hand to shake his, his face wore a dazed sort of smile as he accepted my grip.

As it half-clasped mine, I could feel its old, instinctive strength, while a shrinking pain ran up the back of my hand between fingers and wrist. This sudden stab made me realize that a bone had been broken!

But I HAD BEATEN JOHN L. SULLIVAN!

So, you see, though Jim Corbett got the credit for defeating the Boston Strong Boy as heavyweight champion years later in New Orleans, actually he was vanquished by—me.

And considering that Sullivan when I met him was quicker, lighter, younger, and in every way a finer boxer than when time, fame and drink had combined to lull him on to a state of complacency, then perhaps you will admit that I may be forgiven for thinking that my victory was no mean one.

Yes, now after all these years, I can look at my strong right hand and say with truth 'This hand put to sleep John L. Sullivan!'

Certainly false modesty was never one of Hugh Lowther's weaknesses!

Because of the secrecy with which the whole affair was conducted, it was often afterwards doubted whether the fight took place at all, or whether, if it did, it ended in the way claimed by Hugh. John L. Sullivan, who in after years was questioned about the fight would not deny that it had taken place, but was always extremely reticent about the result. Richard Fox and Charlie Mitchell on the other hand openly supported Hugh's version, and both claimed that Hugh Lowther had both the skill and the physique to have become a heavyweight champion of the world.

Whatever the real truth of the matter, the effect of the reports on the fight on Hugh's reputation with the sporting public was immense.

Back in London his attendance at a boxing match or his appearance at a racecourse was the occasion for knowing nudges amongst the fraternity. His jaunty open-handed manner coupled with his impressive physical appearance lent credibility to the many stories which were in circulation about both his sporting prowess and, it was beginning to be whispered, his bedroom conquests.

Inevitably Hugh's way of life could not last. As the pace in London got faster and faster there was less and less money to keep Catmose Cottage going, economical though Grace might be. Something had to crack very soon.

Unexpectedly in 1881 St. George's wife had given birth to a baby daughter.* With the birth of a son to St. George Hugh's remote hope of inheriting the Lowther estates would have disappeared altogether.

When Hugh had gone to moneylenders with his reversion, he had pledged the whole of his expectation of inheriting. That this money had all gone was bad enough. Even worse in Hugh's eyes was that St. George, discovering what his brother had done, had bought the loan off the moneylenders. To St. George it had only meant a few weeks' income.

St. George returned from a cruise to the Balearic Islands after the Christmas of 1881, and summoned Hugh to Lowther for a few days' shooting. It was a summons that Hugh dreaded. St. George at a distance was bad enough. To have to put up with his condescension under the same roof was intolerable. However, Gwladys had gone to the South of France for a holiday, and for once St. George

* Now Lady Juliet Duff.

seemed more cheerful. The voyage had done him good. He went out with the Lowther Harriers, of which he was the Master, and the brothers had several days together shooting pheasants.

The whole visit might almost have been enjoyable if it had not been for St. George's knack of reminding Hugh of his inferior position, simply by virtue of his own existence. Even the new portrait which St. George had had done of himself, and which now hung in pride of place above the fire in the great hall, irritated him. It was a relief when the party broke up and they went their own ways, St. George to London and Hugh to Catmose.

Just before they left St. George had complained of a cold, but then St. George was always suffering from colds and other minor complaints.

Grace met Hugh at the door of the cottage looking pale and worried.

It only took one glance for Hugh to know that the worst had happened. Two large men, still in their raincoats, with their bowler hats laid neatly on the circular dining-room table in front of them, were seated staring uncomfortably into space. The bailiffs were in. It took Hugh only a second or two to get over the shock. Then he shrugged his shoulders and, arming himself with a couple of bottles of champagne, went in to join his unwelcome guests.

It was well on in the evening when there was another knock at the door. This time it was a telegram. St. George's illness had taken a turn for the worse and the doctors were worried. They wanted Hugh to go to London at once.

The summons was not to Carlton House Terrace, but to 30 Bryanston Street, a small house which St. George had recently taken for his own use. (Rumour had it that he used it as a house of assignation.)

He was met at the door by a grave-faced man in a frock-coat whom he recognized at once as Sir William Jenner, the distinguished doctor.

'Your brother is dying,' he told him bluntly, 'he cannot last many more hours.'

St. George, in fact, lingered on until the middle of the following morning.

Lord Rosebery describes the scene in his diary:

I drove with Tyrwhitt to 30 Bryanston St., where Lonsdale is dying. He is dying in the house he took to give actresses supper in. His wife does not leave Monte Carlo till tomorrow night. His brother is here in the next room cheerfully smoking cigarettes till the end comes, passing away incognito as it were from a world which appeared to reserve every blessing to continue for him, and where he never spent a happy hour.

Unhappy St. George, who had tried so hard to live up to his heritage, but whose well-intentioned endeavours seemed always to finish up as tragi-comedy. He was not even able to leave his life with the dignity which he so ardently desired. His body had to be smuggled back to Carlton House Terrace in a hansom cab before the announcement of his death could be made. There followed the long journey back to Lowther; the slow lines of mourners filed past his coffin as it lay in state in the great hall at Lowther, heavy with the scent of exotic flowers from the Lowther greenhouses. Then there were the sonorous tributes from the pulpit meticulously reported in the long, closely printed columns of the Press, and the words of sympathy for his widow, distinctive and elegant even in her weeds.

One curious story about St. George's death concerns an ancient oak tree in the park at Lowther, which is supposed to have been planted in the reign of King John. Tradition had it that whenever a reigning Earl died, a branch would fall from 'Jack's Yak', as the tree was called in the Cumbrian dialect. Before the news of St. George's death had reached Lowther, a branch was seen to have fallen from the tree.

It was the last time the tree was able to prove the tradition. Subsequent Earls have seen to it that dangerous looking branches were firmly propped up!

Chapter 7

Hugh was twenty-five years old when he so suddenly succeeded as 5th Earl of Lonsdale, Viscount Lowther and Baron Lowther of Whitehaven, Lord Warden of the West Marches. At once he set out to play his part with all the lusty virility of his ancestors.

Within three weeks of St. George's death he had bought a team of chestnuts from Colonel Ewart for £1,000. They were acknowledged to be the finest in the country but it was still a price which brought gasps of surprise from the horse-dealing fraternity.

It was only a beginning. From then on he started collecting horses like a schoolboy collects postage stamps. His standard was exacting. The chestnuts had to be not a fraction more than 15 hands 2 inches in height and not a pound more than 9 cwt. If the measurements were right, price was no object. His hunters had to submit to equally rigorous standards; not less than 16 hands, 6 feet round the girth and 8¾ inches of bone. Grace too had to have her own stable of ponies, of which a commentator in *The Country Gentleman* remarked, 'We do not happen to know the essential qualifications of her ponies, but if the standard is fixed by the pair the Countess was seen driving in the Park there will never be anything in this stable but symmetery, action and good manners.'

Soon the lavish stabling behind Carlton House Terrace was filled to overflowing and additional accommodation had to be rented in the vast Police stables at Scotland Yard. Barleythorpe, the luxurious twenty-bedroomed hunting-box which Hugh had inherited in Rutland, vied with Squire Abingdon's stables both in the numbers and the quality of the horses he kept there.

It was not long, however, before he discovered new and even more extravagant ways of impressing himself on a startled Society. In the days when the fashion for liveried servants and dandified dressing had largely fallen out of vogue, Hugh Lonsdale set a standard of colourful perfection with his turn-outs, which, almost overnight, became one of the sights of London. All the Lonsdale servants were dressed in canary-yellow jackets with dark-blue facings, white beaver hats and white buckskin breeches. Hugh himself, if immune from the extravagance of the Regency bucks, was always dressed in the height of conventional fashion. In London he would quite frequently change his clothes four times a day.

When he stubbed out the final cigarette in the ante-room of his brother's death chamber, it is likely that he never lit another. His six-inch cigars were specially made to his order, and christened by a gratified tobacconist 'Lonsdales'. The cigar became almost as much his trade-mark as the perfect white gardenias which he wore in his buttonhole, and which were sent to him daily regardless of cost wherever he might be.

The empire which Hugh inherited had been designed, ever since the days of Wicked Jimmy, exclusively for the enjoyment of the incumbent. Each successive Earl had added some new brilliance to the diadem. William the Good had purchased Barleythorpe and the surrounding lands for his second son, the silent Colonel. They had become joined again to the estate through Hugh's father. William the Bad had brought in Carlton House Terrace. St. George had contributed two yachts the *Verena* and the *Northumbria* which now rode at anchor at Cowes and which Hugh had never even been aboard.

There was an army of officials and servants to protect Hugh from the administrative headaches of his great inheritance. The offices at Whitehaven and Lowther were staffed by highly qualified professional men and each headed by an agent with powers as great as those of the managing director of a million pound business today. In an office in Pall Mall a secretariat was devoted exclusively to the handling of his personal finance and Grace had her own secretary to help her with the housekeeping accounts.

Hugh set about adding to his entourage until his household was little if anything less in grandeur than the Court of a minor European Royalty. He appointed his own Master of Horse, his own Chamberlain and his own Groom of the Bedchamber. A private orchestra of twenty-five musicians under his Master of Music travelled with him whenever he moved from one of his great houses to another.

For him the 'business of living' was in truth a business and he entered into it with zest. For Grace, with her carefully kept records of how every penny of her hundred-a-year private income was spent, it was an overwhelming experience; yet it was to Grace that Hugh was to turn scarcely two years after his inheritance, to help him out of the biggest financial crisis of his career.

In embarking on his Homeric spending spree, Hugh had overlooked one thing. When he had sold his reversion to finance Frewen's cattle in Wyoming, it had been bought, at St. George's instigation, by the estate. Now it was the estate which owned Hugh and not vice-versa, and the estate was represented by a body of Trustees whose job it was to see that the estate was protected. Hugh was only entitled to enjoy it as life tenant. The Trustees were bound to keep up Lowther and administer the lands as a first charge on the income. Only after this was done was Hugh allowed to draw his pocket money. Even so his income was somewhere between eighty and a hundred thousand pounds a year. The Trustees could afford to be generous with him but there was a limit to their generosity.

The limit was reached just before Christmas 1884.

For months Hugh Lonsdale's cousin and senior Trustee, James Lowther, had been urging moderation on Hugh. The admonition had fallen on deaf ears. Carlton House Terrace became more like Tattersalls every day, as dealers and gentlemen with horses to dispose of sought to by-pass the sale ring by seeking to see Hugh personally. He seldom refused anyone. Grace, who had managed quite happily during the first few years of their marriage with the few pieces of jewellery which she had brought with her from Aboyne, now found herself embarrassed by the gifts Hugh showered upon her. After the slightest argument Hugh would rush round to his jewellers and order yet another expensive trinket.

As Christmas approached, and the spending rose in a new crescendo, the blow fell. James Lowther, having failed to make any impression on Hugh, decided that there was no alternative but to apply sanctions. There was to be no money, absolutely no money at all, for anything but the bare essentials, until the backlog of bills had been worked off. To add weight to the decision, James Lowther deputed Mr. Birch, the Trustees' solicitor, with the task of delivering the ultimatum.

Hugh was shaken. As he often did in such circumstances, he took his troubles to Grace. It was a situation which she understood, and she knew what must be done. On Christmas Eve she sat down and wrote a letter to the senior Trustee:

My dear Mr. Lowther,

Hugh says he did not in the least realize the serious position of affairs, and did not think the debts had so increased until he saw Mr. Birch on Sunday last.

He had the day before ordered some things of Henry Lewis* (much to my annoyance), and says he would not have done so, had he understood how matters stood.

I am writing in a very great hurry as I am just off to catch the train to go to Orton for two nights. You may depend on me to do all I can to help you to make Hugh try to see the position.

Yours sincerely,
Grace Lonsdale

It must have been a gloomy party at Orton Longueville that Christmas, with Hugh and Grace worried about their finances. All his life, Hugh was never to understand the value of money. When the lack of it was brought home to him it affected him like a physical illness.

On Boxing Day Grace wrote again to James Lowther. She had had forty-eight hours to preach her own brand of Scottish thrift, and it looked at last as if Hugh was going to listen.

Dear Mr. Lowther,

Hugh is going to make a list of horses for sale at once, and let you know. I suppose Tattersalls will be the best place to send them to. I forgot to tell you in my hurried letter of Wednesday that Hugh telegraphed after seeing Mr. Birch last Sunday to Lewis the jeweller, to stop sending the things he had ordered last week, but I am sorry to say they had already been sent off.

You will not mind my asking you not to say to the 'family' anything about our affairs. I do not know that you ever do, but I am always hearing that the relations know the ins and outs of our money affairs, and it is not very pleasant. For other reasons too I think it is so important that the state of finances should be kept as quiet as possible, so as to avoid a 'panic' amongst the creditors. I hope you will not mind my saying this.

Hugh begged me to tell you that he is quite willing to do everything you wish.

Yours very sincerely,
Grace Lonsdale

It was an overwhelming victory for James Lowther and, for that matter, for Grace, but it was by no means the end of the war. That was to continue for the whole of Hugh Lonsdale's life.

* The jeweller.

It was said of 'Jim' Lowther that he was the only man who ever had any control over Hugh, and it was true. He had a very great influence until his death just after the turn of the century. He represented the Isle of Thanet in Parliament, which had been a Lowther seat for two hundred and ten years, since the days of Wicked Jimmy and his 'nine-pins'. He had been Under-Secretary for the Colonies in the Disraeli Government of 1864, and later Secretary of State for Ireland, where he won the remarkable distinction of being popular with the Irish.

Like all Lowthers, he loved horses, and kept a large racing stable at his country seat, Wilton Castle. It was his proud boast that he never made a bet nor smoked a cigar, although he tolerated such luxuries in others.

Perhaps his greatest claim to fame was his Parliamentary ability to talk round any subject, and if the result looked like going against him to resort to obstructive tactics.* It was an ability which was to stand him in good stead in carrying out his duties as Trustee for the Lowther Estates.

For almost a month Hugh kept the need for economy in mind, and even resigned his Mastership of the Woodland Pytchley. It was a serious blow to the Pytchley, who had been one of the chief beneficiaries of Hugh's boundless generosity. As an act of contrition Hugh wrote to Jim Lowther himself to tell him of his decision.

My dear Jim,

I have written to Langham† today to tell him that owing to my head I do not see my way to continuing hunting the country after this season. I have had a talk to one or two people, and think it was thoroughly understood that I was giving up the country . . . but I think it would be better to make my retirement due to my fall‡—and being true—rather than to the shortness of funds. As my credit is now good and the sharks might get nervous if they knew the real reason. The fact of ill health is a true one, and the doctors say often that I should not hunt hounds myself for two years. . . .

As Hugh concerned himself in the literal sense of the phrase with

---

* In his obituary in *The Times* it was remarked: 'With the late Mr. Cavendish-Bentinck he was an expert in contributing to Parliamentary debate such sounds as are produced by the crowing of cocks, the braying of donkeys, or the inarticulate crying of cats.'
† Huntsman to the Woodland Pytchley.
‡ Two months earlier he had one of his rare falls, cracking two ribs. It only kept him out of the saddle for a few days. Now it appears as a convenient excuse.

putting his stable in order, Grace struggled with other equally knotty problems brought about for the most part by Hugh's own generosity.

Dear Mr. Lowther,

I hope you will forgive my bothering you with the enclosed, which Captain Saunders* gave me today, but I do not see how to settle it without asking you. Sir George Grove seems to be in a very great hurry for the money, and as Hugh has none in the bank he cannot send it, and I am not able to send it myself. The story is this: The boy Smith is an orphan and was for some time in the Cumberland Militia band, and afterwards in our band was such a promising musician that Hugh sent him to the Royal College of Music and paid for him for a year. Then when he was leaving Sir G. wrote and said he was one of the best of his pupils and getting on so very well that he begged he might have another year's tuition, to which Hugh consented. They expect this year's payment in advance. It seems rather nonsense bothering like this, but I suppose it is the rules of the College. If you would very kindly give orders to pay it for me and settle about it as you think right, I should be so very much obliged.

Yours very sincerely,
Grace Lonsdale

The fees were paid.

Deprived of his favourite sport of hunting by his own excuse of ill-health, Hugh moved up to Carlton House Terrace at the beginning of the London Season, and immediately set about providing the Trustees with a new set of problems.

Second only to his passion for hunting foxes was his love of the pursuit of beautiful women. He was now able to devote much more of his attention to it.

Carlton House Terrace suited Hugh Lonsdale admirably. It had all the advantages of living in London with many of the facilities of being in the country. The Terrace, overlooking St. James's Park, provided an exercise ground for his dogs, whilst the Park itself he regarded to all intents and purposes as his own personal property. He had his own key to all the London Parks, which were then fenced in with high railings and closed to the public after six o'clock at night. He took a personal interest in the bedding out of the flower-beds and the welfare of the ducks, and did not hesitate to give instructions as to what was to be done. On Sunday afternoons he would take his dogs on a tour of inspection through St. James's Park, Hyde

* Grace's Personal Secretary.

Park and Kensington Gardens, puffing vigorously at his cigar and noting every detail. Later, a chit would be sent to the Head Gardener suggesting alterations or variations in the colours of the flowers, or other attractions. No one seems ever to have questioned his authority.

Carlton House Terrace itself was a very large house. The first floor was entirely taken up with a ballroom which ran the whole length of the two original houses. All the rooms were papered in dark colours which had survived since the days of Great-uncle William, and furnished with the ornate gilt furniture which he had collected on his European travels. Nothing had been moved or changed since his day. Nor could it be, for behind the pictures and the furniture where it stood against the walls, the paper, protected from the soot of London, was several shades lighter. To move a piece of furniture was to have to redecorate the whole room. Nobody thought it worth while.

On the ground floor was the library, Hugh's own sitting-room with steps leading out on to the Terrace, and the great dining-room, which was served from the kitchen quarters below. Inside the front door footmen were always on duty ready on an instant to fling open the doors at the first touch of the bell—a practice which could prove unnerving to the unwary guest.

Nothing had been touched in the house since the turn of the century, save for a bathroom or two installed by St. George, and an extremely dangerous lift to the upper floors. The lift was open at the sides and was little more than a caged platform affording no protection to the passengers from the walls on either side.

On one occasion, Grace, who always travelled with her personal footman, was waiting to catch the train to Newmarket. Her footman, bringing down her trunk, got wedged between the trunk and the walls; when the lift arrived at the ground floor the footman was dead.

It was all very awkward, for Grace not only lost her personal footman but very nearly missed her train. It was a rule in those days that no tragedy, however great, should be allowed to alter the ordered routine once the wheels had been set in motion.

During the whole of the spring of 1885, Grace was far from well, and particularly at nights suffered almost continuous pain. In conformity with tradition she was able most days to ride out in the Park, and even to go calling in the afternoons, but late-night balls and dinner parties were too much for her. The invitations which showered like a snowstorm on Carlton House Terrace during the summer season were for the most part refused. Only on exceptional occasions, like a State Ball, was she able to make the supreme effort, and then she usually had to pay for her sacrifice with two or three days in bed afterwards.

Hugh was not expected to accept any invitations without her so, rather than spend a gloomy evening by himself after she had retired with a cup of bread and milk, he went out, not to the parties which his wife's indisposition had forced him to refuse, but to the music halls, the Gaiety Theatre, with supper parties afterwards in St. John's Wood, and other bachelor entertainments. Occasionally, long after the footman had sleepily gone to bed, some of his friends would creep in to keep him company in his sitting-room.

If only Grace had been well, what 'lovely fun' it would have been to take the dust sheets off the gilt chairs in the ballroom, uncover the crystal chandeliers, turn on all the lights and fill the house with people.

If only, he must have thought, as often in the small hours he stole upstairs to bed past the ballroom, dark and silent under its dust sheets. On the second floor, in her great gilt bed, with its hanging draperies which had once belonged to Marie Antoinette, Grace lay sleepless, listening to the clock ticking the hours away. It was a room he never entered except to bid her good morning. On the top floor overlooking the Park, Hugh Lonsdale slept soundly surrounded by his dogs.

*

Financially embarrassed or not, Hugh was quite determined, whatever happened, that not a whisper of his predicament should gain currency in London Society.

Soon his doings were the talk of the town, so that almost every morning in the Park there was some new extravagance to report associated with his name. Where his contemporaries conducted their affairs with the greatest discretion, Hugh was incapable of doing anything by stealth. It was one of the most endearing characteristics in his make-up, but one that was to cause him endless trouble.

If he wanted to take an actress riding in the Park, he would do so without the slightest regard to what might be whispered in all the Mayfair drawing-rooms that afternoon. Whilst Mr. Taylor, his private secretary in the Pall Mall office, was wringing his hands in despair over the mountains of bills for champagne, flowers, cigars

and costly presents, his Lordship's turn-out was never more glittering, nor his appearances more eagerly awaited by the man-in-the-
street and Society alike.

Lily Langtry was the reigning beauty of the day, and, it was well
known, the Prince of Wales's favourite mistress. This fact did not
in the least deter Hugh from a determined attempt to win her favours.
His old friend, Sir George Chetwynd, whose tie-pin he had so
dramatically recovered, also considered himself to be in the running,
and both men strove to outdo the other in proving in what direction
the 'Jersey Lily's' real affections lay. Soon everybody, with the
possible exception of the Prince himself, became aware of the competition.

As always, Hugh was determined not to be outdone, and what
started as a harmless and amusing rivalry began to take on all the
overtones of a serious feud.

Perhaps the most concerned person was Mrs. Langtry herself,
who had every reason for not letting it be thought she favoured
either of them. The whole situation was further complicated by the
fact that Grace, who did not give her friendship easily, had taken
a great liking to Lily, and had paid her the signal honour for a woman
in her position of asking her round for tea at Carlton House Terrace.

The climax came when Lily Langtry found that she had arranged
to ride in the Row with both Hugh and Sir George on the same
morning. It was an impossible *impasse*. To put off either of them
would have been an unforgivable insult. As she was appearing at
the time at the Prince of Wales Theatre, it was equally impossible
for her to plead a sudden illness. The only thing to do was to forget
that she had invited either of them, and hope for the best.

The best did not happen.

As both men waited impatiently under the Achilles statue, peering
anxiously at their watches, each became aware of the other's predicament, and it was not long before they established that they were
both waiting for Lily.

From then on events are graphically described in a current newspaper report.

'Don't meddle with my Lily!' shouted Sir George, as he struck Lord
Lonsdale with his whip across the shoulders.

Lord Lonsdale returned the blow with his whip. The horses of both
combatants became frightened, began to plunge and kick in a lively
manner, and the riders were forced to dismount. Dropping their whips,
they continued to fight with their fists. Sir George soon got his

opponent's head 'in chancery',* and pummelled him repeatedly. Lord Lonsdale struggled to free himself, and both men rolled in the dust. They regained their feet, blood flowing from their noses and mouths, their clothing torn, and renewed the fight. . . .

Eventually the Duke of Portland and Sir William Cummings managed to separate them and drive them home, still swearing vengeance.

London fairly buzzed with excitement. The Queen, it was rumoured, had sent for Lord Lonsdale to remonstrate with him about his conduct. The Prince of Wales pretended to have heard nothing of the affair, but there is little doubt that Lily was given a sharp private talking-to for her part in the matter. So far as the public were concerned, however, both of the contestants came out of the business several inches taller in popular estimation. One of the justifications for the aristocracy in the public mind has always been that they can behave outrageously and get away with it.

* Perhaps Sir George may be excused for the gross breach of boxing etiquette of tucking Lonsdale's head under his arm when the known prowess of his opponent is considered, as well as the fact that the Queensberry Rules had still to be written.

Chapter 8

Not all the activities which kept Hugh in the public eye were romantic ones. He was already a familiar figure at almost every sort of sporting event, and particularly at boxing matches.

Boxing was still illegal, and although it had amongst its devotees some of the greatest names in the land, including the Prince of Wales, both the contestants in a fight were liable to prosecution as disturbers of the peace, and the spectators for aiding and abetting the offence.

In the eighteen seventies prize fighting in England had reached one of its periodical low ebbs. Although there was a pretence of running championship fights, the real purpose in staging contests was for the opportunity it provided for betting. Where twenty years before it had been a popular sport with the aristocracy, it had by degrees fallen into the hands of the worst types of bookmakers and gamblers. To the danger of arrest was added the much more real danger for the spectators of having their pockets picked at best, or, at worst, receiving a beating-up at the hands of the roughs who attended matches for that very purpose. The police would seldom take action on the grounds that it was not their job to protect a citizen who was himself breaking the law.

Socially, it was completely beyond the pale. Everybody connected with the 'noble art' was regarded, not without justice, as belonging to the lowest and most degraded sections of the community. A few, a very few, of the aristocracy continued to support prize fighting. For the most part their interest sprang from the fact that they were proficient performers themselves, and ready at any time to put on the gloves with leading professional fighters of the day. Lord Drumlanrig* and Lord Verulam were two of the leading exponents,

* Later the Marquis of Queensberry.

so was Sir George Chetwynd and, of course, Hugh Lonsdale himself.

The popular idol of the day who did more for the sport than any of his contemporaries, was Hugh's mentor Jem Mace.

Mace is remembered as the last of the bare fist champions, but he fought well on into 'the glove era', and genuinely earned the title of a world champion by going to America to beat the best they had. He had the interests of the game very much at heart, and blamed the promoters and the gamblers for the depths to which it had sunk. He wrote in a book published after his retirement:

Either carelessly or by design, the roughs were allowed free access to the places of the meeting, with the result that the more respectable patrons of the ring were driven away. It is true that some attempt was made to keep order and protect the peaceably inclined spectators from the depredations of these human vermin. But such were not always successful. Indeed, it not infrequently happened that the special ring keepers, who were appointed at a wage of a guinea a day by the Pugilists' Benevolent Association, were themselves overpowered and in some cases badly beaten by the ruffianly mob. As these ring keepers were invariably trained boxers, specially selected for their strength and skill, it may be imagined what sort of chance the ordinary spectator would stand, did he venture to resent the loss of his property, or the ill-usage to which he was too often subjected.

Boxing was, however, on the brink of a golden era.

The revival came about in an almost casual way. It owed much to an unworthy individual called 'The Shifter' who earned a precarious living as a tipster on the *Sporting Times*—otherwise and better known as 'The Pink 'Un'.

The Shifter, whose real name was William Goldberg, spent much of his time hanging around the resorts of rich Bohemia, where sporting gentlemen mixed on equal terms with lesser mortals, and where racing tips were to be picked up without the uncomfortable necessity of lying behind bushes at first light on Newmarket Heath or on Epsom Downs with a powerful pair of field-glasses. To glean these rich crumbs, a ready supply of money was required to purchase such necessities as bottles of champagne, and this was a commodity that The Shifter found in uncomfortably short supply. Daniel Nichols, the owner of the Café Royal, had refused him further credit, and Alfonso Romano of Romano's was in much the same state of mind. 'Looka here, Missa Shif,' he expostulated vigorously one evening, 'I give credit to gentlemen up to the hilt. But you—you hit below the hilt!'

The Shifter's answer to this predicament was to start a club on his own. He hooked a prosperous Lewisham grocer, with sporting ambitions, and opened a club in Denman Street, behind Piccadilly Circus.

The club premises were roomy but sleazy, the area unsavoury and the name—the Star Club—unlikely. Yet out of this improbable alchemy one of the most successful sporting clubs—the forerunner of the National Sporting Club—was compounded.

Quite why the club was such an immediate success it is impossible to say, but much of the credit must go to a gregarious character, Ernest Wells, universally known as 'Swears', a nick-name derived from his colourful mode of expression.

Swears and Shifter got together and new finance was found for better and bigger premises. The club, rechristened 'The Pelican' in honour of a large stuffed pelican which shared a mammoth glass case with a flamingo above the mantelshelf in the smoking-room, was reopened in Gerrard Street, thanks to the efforts of the tireless Swears, who soon became a partner in the enterprise.

Almost at once it became a meeting place for the most extraordinary characters it would seem possible to gather together under one roof. The bearded, colourful Sir John Astley was elected chairman. He presided over as aristocratic a committee as would be found in any of the exclusive clubs of St. James's. The Marquis of Queensberry was a most active member, so were the Dukes of Hamilton and Manchester, Lord Marcus Beresford and 'Derry' Rossmore. Hugh Lonsdale, perhaps on the strength of the story of his fight with John L. Sullivan, was elected chairman of the boxing committee, helped by Grace's brother Lord Esme Gordon and 'Bay' Middleton.

Exclusiveness was not, however, one of the attractions claimed for the establishment. The notorious Squire Abingdon, who was banned from most of the pot-houses in London, let alone the more choosey clubs, was a member; so was Billy Harris the sausage king, and so was Sam Lewis the moneylender, whose services were in constant demand. Actors and managers, finding it to be one of the few social clubs whose doors were not locked against them, flocked to join. The great impresario, George Edwardes, was a member; so was Fred Terry, Lionel Brough, who had travelled with Hugh to America, Haydn Coffin, and a host more besides. Even journalists and Jews were not excluded.

Somehow this *pot-pourri* managed to achieve an exclusiveness of its own, and, certainly so far as sporting matters were concerned, became a very real influence.

Hugh was fascinated by the Pelican Club. He enjoyed the raffish company, the lack of ceremony and the conversation, which was never far removed from his two favourite subjects of horses and boxing. There were few nights when he did not take the leisurely stroll from the cloistered quiet of his house in Carlton House Terrace, past the garish attractions of Haymarket and Panton Street to the cigar-laden atmosphere of the Club, where the scene was more reminiscent of a rag in a public school common room than anything else.

Another story well worth repeating in describing the atmosphere which prevailed at the Pelican Club concerns Sam Lewis the money-lender, to whom Hugh had gone a few years earlier for advice about his reversion.

One day Lewis received in the mail a very fine diamond ring. With it was a note from a young subaltern, stationed in Dublin, who was in urgent need of five hundred pounds. He wrote: 'I realize you would not *lend* me five hundred on the ring, but I need the money very badly and am willing to sell the ring, although it is a valuable family heirloom. Only it is five hundred or nothing. Please don't waste time in haggling.'

The ring was well worth the money, and would stand Sam in at a nice profit, but to pay what was first asked went against the grain. He wrote, therefore, a long letter explaining why he could not offer more than four hundred. Back came the reply by telegram: 'Five hundred or return the ring.'

But Sam was not to be beaten so easily. 'Dear Friend,' he wrote. 'Your troubles have caused me a great deal of worry. I hate to disappoint a client in need, but what am I to do if the ring will not fetch more than I am offering? I know that I am running a terrible risk but for old time's sake I will give you four hundred and fifty for it. If you accept, don't even bother to open the box but send it back by return of post.'

The box arrived neatly tied up the following day. The officer was sorely tempted, but in the end decided to stick to his original price, and he opened the jewel box. Inside there was no ring. Only a tiny piece of paper on which was written: 'All right. Five hundred!'*

* Sam Lewis, one of the most loved of an unloved fraternity, left five million when he died. Over three millions was bequeathed to various charities.

It was the sort of story which the Pelicans loved.

Up to the time of the opening of the Pelican Club, fights had had to be held either in noisome, unventilated booths where they got away with it on the grounds that the entertainment offered came under the description of sparring matches, or in remote parts of the countryside, when spectators wishing to be present had to get up at the most uncomfortable hours in order to reach the secret rendezvous in time.

The match for the championship of England held in 1885, the year before the Pelican opened, is a typical example of what enthusiasts had to put up with. Those in the know were invited to assemble in the small hours of the morning at an obscure café behind Leicester Square. They were to equip themselves with fishing rods and shotguns in the hope that the police noticing such a tweedy gathering at such an unusual hour would be misled as to their real intentions. Of those who turned up, any who had not been forearmed with the password 'London Bridge' were not allowed to proceed further. Only a handful of spectators had the privilege of driving at breakneck speed through an icy December dawn to the scene of the contest outside East Grinstead.

In the event, Jem Smith the champion dealt with Davis, his challenger, in double quick time, but only just in time to beat the arrival of the Law. As Smith was being proclaimed Champion of All England the cry of 'Police' was raised and the spectators, the pickpockets, the bookies, the officials and the contestants of one accord took to their heels and scattered to the four winds. A rather striking contrast to the manner in which the Heavyweight Championship of England is decided today.

At the Pelican Club for the first time patrons were able to enjoy boxing contests in comparative comfort, and in the reasonable certainty that the high percentage of nobility in the audience was sufficient protection against police interference.

In spite of the light-headedness which characterized the general conduct of the affairs of the Club, Hugh Lonsdale, in his role of Chairman of the Boxing Committee, took his duties extremely seriously. From the very beginning he set out to eliminate some of the more glaring evils of the game.

Contests were decided on a timed round basis over a specified number of rounds. Previously a 'round' was deemed to have been completed when one of the contestants was knocked to the ground, and the fight over when one of the contestants, after a thirty-eight-second rest, was unable to 'come up to the scratch'.

Hugh, with his committee, set about laying down the standard pattern for a fight as we know it today. He was not only concerned with the contestants. He regarded the behaviour of audiences as very much within his province. Although he did not at first attempt to interfere with the heavy wagering which took place between members, he did discourage in the most forcible way the indiscriminate shouting of bets around the ringside whilst the fight was in progress. Even loudly voiced comment was apt to earn his displeasure, which he did not hesitate to demonstrate with a sharp poke of his stick if the offender was within reach. Those were unheard-of innovations in a day when the contestants could count themselves lucky if the spectators stopped at verbal protest. Active participation was by no means unusual, and a fighter who looked like winning against the odds could expect to be tripped or even hit on the back of the head with a loaded stick if the money looked like going the wrong way. Now the balance of the whole fight game was to be altered. It was the fighter who was to be all important, and the backers who were to be the also-rans.

And leading the reformers, with a new-found missionary zeal, was Hugh Lonsdale.

Chapter 9

Hugh had come to boxing with a much narrower knowledge than perhaps he would have had people believe. He had never been to a bare-fist fight, nor seen the inside of a boxing booth, nor got to know the real underside of the game. To begin with, the colour and the novelty of it all gripped him, but it could not contain his adventurous spirit for very long.

Almost equally fascinating to him amongst the mixed collection of members who gathered every night at the Pelican Club was the theatrical element. Before long Hugh was finding the stage-door just as distracting as a ringside seat at a boxing match and his yellow carriages and his big cigars soon became as familiar to first-nighters as they already were to the sporting public. The crowds were all the bigger when the Yellow Earl, as he was coming to be known, was in the house, straining to see which actress was to be swept off with a flourish to dine with him at the Café Royal, at Verrey's or in one of the private supper rooms at Kettner's.

There was a headiness in the air which Hugh found altogether delightful. The country as a whole, and particularly London, was enjoying an unprecedented wave of prosperity. The new underground railway was nightly bringing in from the outskirts their quota of pleasure-seekers determined to have a good time. The great British middle-class were in the making and the gaiety of the Naughty Nineties was already casting its shadow before.

On the great Lowther estates and in the town of Whitehaven, however, Hugh's image did not shine so brightly. One newly started local paper, *The Northern Counties Gazette*, attacked what they called 'Lowtherism' with a virulence which would be unthinkable in modern journalism. Hugh's absenteeism and his much publicized life in London made him an easy candidate for the pillory.

Even St. George was not allowed to rest untroubled in his grave. A story was started to the effect that he had married bigamously. 'If it should turn out that the late Earl had a wife living, and knew of it at the time he married Lady Gwladys, I, for one, won't be surprised,' the Editor, Mr. George Windross, stated baldly.

About Hugh and Grace he was equally blunt.

'Why does not the Colliery Office tell us something about the Earl and Countess of Lonsdale,' Windross wrote a week later. 'Their movements, especially after his Lordship's fight with Sir George Chetwynd, ought to be peculiarly interesting. ... As the present Earl is only a sort of pensioner on the estates and not the proprietor, he has not the power the late Earl had. He is consequently not thought as much about; and perhaps this is why the Colliery Office men don't care to bring him too prominently before the public; and perhaps at the present time his domestic affairs should be kept dark.'

Here was rather more than a hint that Hugh's private life was not what it should be. Events were to prove that Windross knew what he was talking about. In London Hugh continued to espouse the role of the open-handed sporting peer with all his vigorous enthusiasm. If the older generation in Society peered disapprovingly at him through their lorgnettes or from behind their whiskers, it did nothing to usurp his good content. He was in step with the times and just to be alive was such 'lovely fun'.

It was in this dangerous climate that Lionel Brough introduced him to Violet Cameron, one of the great stage beauties of the day. Hugh was soon completely captivated. Within a few weeks of their meeting Violet Cameron was to be seen everywhere on Hugh Lonsdale's arm.

In Whitehaven, Windross continued his attacks unchecked, but when Mr. Edmund Yates in *Truth* took an indiscreet tilt at Hugh's romance, Hugh hit back quickly and hard. Yates was prosecuted and was sent to prison.

Perhaps as a sop to local feeling, and no doubt encouraged by Jim Lowther, Hugh and Grace travelled to Lowther in August of 1885 and gave an immense garden party for the Whitehaven miners. By all accounts it was a badly managed affair. The food ran out and many of the 1,700 miners and their wives who attended went hungry.

Another highlight of the visit was when Hugh travelled to Whitehaven to make a speech in support of the 'Lowther candidate' Mr. (later Sir) George Cavendish-Bentinck.

'If the Conservative colours are yellow, and the Liberal colours are blue, what are the colours of the Earl of Lonsdale?' asked one earnest seeker after knowledge from the body of the hall.

'Why, Violet!' chorused the delighted miners who were well abreast of the current gossip.

After Hugh had returned to London even the loyal *Whitehaven News* showed signs of disaffection.

'I wonder what the fêtes at Lowther, tea-drinking, muffin-eating and junketting generally all mean?' the leader writer asked. 'One thing is certainly not intended, namely that the Earl shall do Whitehaven the justice of residing and spending his money there for a short time. His Lordship may be proud to learn that there is an analogy between himself and Royalty, though the instance is not so creditable as it might be. The depression in London would be mitigated if the Queen would once more hold Court at Buckingham Palace. The depression in Whitehaven might disappear if the Lonsdales held Court at the Castle and circulated the money they take from the town amongst the townspeople.'

It is doubtful if Hugh ever read the attack. Certainly all criticism of him was carefully edited out of the Press-cutting book kept by his secretary. In any case, he was already deeply involved in affairs of his own; far more deeply than the newspapers could even have guessed.

The full story did not break until August of the following year. Violet Cameron, it appeared, had been married only two years before to a M. de Bensaude and had had a baby daughter by him. Shortly after being introduced to Hugh by Lionel Brough she had started the Violet Cameron Operatic Company and with Brough as her leading man, set off on a provincial tour. De Bensaude had first of all been included in the arrangements but very soon had been pushed out altogether.

The real manager of the Company and the financial backer was Hugh Lonsdale. He took his managerial duties seriously, travelling everywhere with the Company and booking adjacent suites in the best hotels for himself and Violet whilst the penniless de Bensaude had to manage as best he could in cheap boarding-houses. Matters came to a head when the Company reached Newcastle. After the show Hugh returned with Violet Cameron to her sitting-room in the Turks Head Hotel to find de Bensaude waiting for them. Without more ado Hugh threw him out.

De Bensaude had had enough. He sued Hugh for assault and the case was heard two days later before the Newcastle magistrates.

Hugh was fined forty shillings and received a stern lecture about his conduct from the Bench and the affair was blazoned in spicy detail in all the papers in the country.

It also sparked off a series of petitions and cross-petitions between de Bensaude and his wife, with Hugh in the middle, which were to entertain and scandalize the country for many months to come. Violet Cameron sued for protection against her husband and de Bensaude petitioned for divorce, citing Hugh. Hugh gave his version of the affair freely to the Press saying exactly what he thought of de Bensaude and de Bensaude sued Hugh for libel.

At the height of the scandal, Hugh abandoned the tour of the Violet Cameron Operatic Company and, putting the whole cast on a boat, set out to conquer New York. Somehow de Bensaude managed to raise enough money to follow them there, and all the rows and dirty-linen-washing started afresh.

Now de Bensaude was frankly after getting as much money as he could out of the situation. Offers and counter-offers were made which Hugh happily made public, with an aside thrown in that anyway de Bensaude had made off with the capital he had put up for the Operatic Company.

One American paper reported: 'The interviewers stalked the hotels where the parties lodged, in the expectation that blood was about to be shed, and it is hard to say whether they were relieved or not when they found that Lord Lonsdale and M. de Bensaude breakfasted at Delmonico's in the friendliest and most sympathetic manner.'

The truce did not last long. Shortly afterwards Hugh invited a reporter of the *New York Herald* to witness a meeting between de Bensaude and himself, 'When the whole truth will be made clear'. The report read:

The Earl was seated upon a table by the window, while Miss Violet's husband was calmly smoking a cigarette of the Earl's giving. Lord Lonsdale arose, closed the door, and then calmly drew from his portmanteau a small mahogany box with the gold 'L' surmounted by a coronet on the lid. This box he unlocked and placed close by his hand on the table.

'Now,' said his Lordship to M. de Bensaude; 'Did you or did you not take those three hundred pound notes and place them in another theatrical venture than the one for which they were intended? Just answer yes or no.'

'I did not exactly; they were in my wife's name at any rate.'

'State publicly that in any difficulty which you had with your wife I was entirely uninterested.'

'No. I can't do that.'

'Then,' said his Lordship in the same calm tone, 'if you want to obtain satisfaction, if you came here to look for any row, here is your chance. Pistols for one!' Saying this, Lord Lonsdale opened the box at his hand and pushed across a handsome pearl-handled revolver with the ever-present 'L' and crest on the handle. 'Now is your chance, my boy; if you want to take the first three shots, here you are. Load up and I will stand down here.'

The terrified de Bensaude pushed the pistol away begging Hugh 'not to fool around'.

On the whole the Americans were even more censorious than the English. 'We have no patience,' wrote the *New York Star*, 'with a theatrical combination of a noble patron, a wayward wife, and a complaisant husband that has recently landed on our shores. Their nasty rows and grievances, which they discuss so volubly, are nothing to us. They should have left them at home if they come to us for an artistic judgement.'

In the end de Bensaude finished up in jail for threatening his wife, and the Company sailed home again.

Only once in all the publicity was Grace's name mentioned. A reporter in New York asked Hugh where she was. 'I have no idea,' replied Hugh blandly. 'As she is one of Miss Cameron's closest friends I think that it is likely she is on her way out here.' Grace, however, did not arrive.

Nor does it appear that Hugh was in any hurry to see her again. Back in London he calmly moved into a house in Hampstead with Violet Cameron where they lived under the name of Mr. and Mrs. Thompson. Soon it became known that Violet was to have his child.

There is no knowing where the affair might have ended if, improbably, Queen Victoria had not taken a hand in the matter. She let it be known that she expected Lord Lonsdale to leave the country until the scandal was neatly tidied away.

The edict suited Jim Lowther admirably. Hugh let loose in London had definitely not been a success. Apart from the scandal, the Violet Cameron Operatic Company had been disastrously expensive. If he could get Hugh away from the flesh-pots of London for a year, it would give him time to mend the broken financial fences. The only question was where he could persuade Hugh to go. To send him to France, the usual refuge of the out-of-favour, would be to invite goodness knows what new extravagances. Already it was rumoured that the Prince of Wales was setting a pace in Paris and Biarritz that even the Russian grandees with their fabulous wealth and love of ostentation were finding it hard to match. The thought of Hugh in that setting made the Trustees break out in a rash of apprehension.

The only place where Hugh would really be out of harm's way was somewhere where there were no beautiful women, no champagne, and no horse-flesh—and where on earth was that?

A solution hit the worried Trustees like a thunder-clap.

The Scottish Naturalist Society wanted somebody to go to the wastelands of Canada to collect specimens of the fauna in that still relatively unexplored part of the world. If only Hugh could be persuaded to undertake the journey!

As usual the diplomatic Jim Lowther was given the task of selling the idea. In the event it did not prove a difficult task.

Hugh could never resist a challenge to his manhood, nor an opportunity to prove that it was Hugh first, and the rest nowhere. Jim had prepared his bait carefully, and Hugh rose to it like a hungry trout. Within a month it was all arranged—a month filled with obtaining maps, charts, letters of introduction, and going through a mass of detail of what should be taken and what should not, on the long trek.

Grace watched the preparations with mixed feelings. She knew from Jim Lowther all the reasons for the journey, and could not but approve of them. During the whole Violet Cameron affair she had preserved a dignified aloofness. There is no doubt, too, that her loyalty never wavered. The agony she must have been suffering went unrecorded in her diaries. Perhaps even to herself she would not admit that it was happening or perhaps she knew that Hugh would soon need her more than ever. On the other hand she could not conceal her apprehension as her Hugh blithely made arrangements to plunge alone into one of the great uncharted areas left in the world. The North-West Passage was still only a dream in the minds of a few pioneers, and the North Pole the very epitome of hopeless endeavour.

Hugh sailed on the steamer *Republic* from Liverpool one cold wet day in February 1888, in a storm of publicity. It was freely rumoured that his real intention was to reach the North Pole. So great was the legend already growing up around his name that few really doubted that this was so.

Hugh himself can have had little idea of the rigours of the journey he had undertaken. His idea for companionship on his 3,000-mile trek across the frozen wastes was four springer spaniels and a far from enthusiastic valet!

It was fortunate for Hugh that one of the introductions arranged for him in London was to Donald Smith of the Hudson Bay Company, who met him in Montreal. Smith was one of the most remarkable men ever to work for that most remarkable company. He was fourteen when he left Scotland to join his uncle who was a company employee. He spent sixteen years in the Northern woods during which time he never saw a white man. The Indians called him Silver Cloud because of the silver coins with which he paid for their skins. One night in the middle of a fierce storm an Indian girl, on her way south to join her husband, sought refuge in his log cabin. She stayed with him for the rest of her life. When the law rescinding the ban on marriages between white men and Indians was passed Donald Smith, by then Sir Donald Smith, married her. Every year he gave a great reunion party for all her relations who would come to her house in Montreal and sit on the floor of her drawing-room to smoke the traditional pipe of peace. When Donald Smith retired he took her back with him to his native Scotland. The last years of their lives were spent on their estates in Glencoe as Lord and Lady Strathcona.

On Donald Smith's advice Hugh sent his dogs home in charge of his much relieved valet, and a team of Indians, who were prepared to make the journey, were assembled with their dog teams at a point three hundred miles up the Saskatchewan River. When all the preparations were completed, Hugh set off on horseback to join them. The journey was scheduled to take a week. With typical flourish he covered the distance in three days, taking only two hours off to sleep.

From then on the journey was grim and earnest. It had been an exceptionally hard winter, and in the next two hundred miles he counted no less than three hundred Indians who had died from starvation. Crossing Buffalo Lake, three of his party had their faces so badly frozen that they had to go back. By the time they had reached Chippewayo at the other end of Lake Athabaska, the original party of Indians was down to two, and many of the sixty-seven huskies had died from the cold.

Hugh Lonsdale was in his element. As his friends in London languidly discussed the prospects for the Derby, he was engrossed in battling his way through the most appalling conditions known for twenty years. 'Worked for thirty hours non-stop in freezing water to get the canoes through,' he records happily in his diary, adding modestly, 'Even the Indians worked for twenty hours.'

As they pressed on into the Arctic Circle they came across nomadic tribes of Eskimos. These were the 'Huskey' Eskimos, whose hostile attitude towards strangers was well known. Hugh was more than equal to the occasion. To quote from his diary again:

> There was one particularly surly fellow who, I learned afterwards, had killed two or three men, and terrorized his fellows. On my way back to the camp (from a meeting with the head of the village) I saw him skulking behind me. As I passed an upturned boat he jumped out at me with his knife raised. I straightened my right arm and he went down. When the other natives rushed up and found their bad man lying down quite stupid, they could not understand it. They took his knife from him and gave it to me as a token of submission. I gave it back to him, and after that we were friends.

At another stage of the journey the Indians rebelled. Hugh recorded:

> It was one of the worst parts of the journey, the temperature being sixty-four degrees below zero. There were some mountains to cross which everyone said were impassable, twelve men having died in the attempt. It was worst after walking and running all day to have to lie in the snow to sleep. The Indians refused, so I took one by the neck and made him go before, and I walked after him. At the foot of the mountains I got up at three in the morning and, collecting all their rifles and snowshoes, put them on my sled, and sat on them. When they got up at six, planning to creep away in the dark and desert me, they were surprised to find me there before them.
>
> I started at six that morning, and crossed over the highest point, which was 5,200 feet. The cold was intense, and terrible storms would blow up from time to time.
>
> When I got across I had only seven dogs left out of sixty-nine, and there were seven Indians and five sleds missing. I set off back to find the missing men. Eventually I brought them down safe and sound, they being frozen only about the hands and feet. All the dogs however were dead.

Years afterwards, talking about his adventures in the Arctic, he would chortle delightedly and say, 'Ah! It was such lovely fun!'

One year and two months after setting out he arrived at Kodiak in Alaska, and promptly went down with a chest cold which lasted a week.

Back in England, rumour had bred on rumour. Hugh Lonsdale had died in a last desperate effort to reach the North Pole. He had fallen down a crevass and been killed. He had broken a leg, and was being nursed back to health by a tribe of Eskimos. Each time a new extravagance was produced by the Press, Grace would hurry down to the offices of the Hudson Bay Company to see if she could get either confirmation or denial of the reports. Usually the Company, with their network of trading posts and unique contact with the most remote corners of the territory, were able to set her mind at rest.

Anxious though she was it was not altogether an unhappy time for Grace. Ever since she had been married, Hugh's personality had completely overshadowed her. His strange taste in friends, his irresponsible attitude towards money and the scandals which constantly surrounded him had kept her in a constant state of tension. She had never had a chance of living her own life and every day with Hugh was fraught with financial or emotional anxiety.

The Catmose Cottage way of living had been banished for ever, but it had been replaced by far more difficult problems.

With Hugh out of the country she began to regain some of her old feeling of independence. For the first time she was mistress of her own household, able to give orders to her servants and direct her own daily life as she wanted it. She could entertain her own friends at Carlton House Terrace and generally enjoy a normal social life.

Within a few weeks of Hugh's sailing she records in her diary that she is sleeping better. The pains and headaches did not afflict her again until the fourteen-month respite was over.

Hugh's year of exile created a set of different problems for Violet Cameron. Anticipating that letters back from the trapping stations would have to pass through many hands before being committed to the anonymity of Her Majesty's mails, Hugh had arranged that his letters to Violet should be sent in an outer cover addressed to his personal secretary, Taylor, at the Pall Mall office. It was Taylor, too, who was charged with making the regular payments to Violet which Hugh had undertaken before leaving England.

Time hung heavily on her hands. Her daughter was born in the summer but there were few visitors to the house at 37 Acacia Road in St. John's Wood which Hugh, in accordance with the traditions of the day, had provided for her. 'Many, many thanks for sending me the letters so promptly. His Lordship seems to be in much better spirits this time,' she wrote to Mr. Taylor at the beginning of

October. 'He says I may get some letters next *January*, so the return seems so very far distant. I am glad to be able to tell you that he has received several of my letters, which is a great comfort to me.'

A month later she was thinking of going back to work.

Dear Mr. Taylor,

Many thanks for the money. I missed Mr. Edwardes last Thursday when I called, but went to the Gaiety on Thursday night. He came to see me in the box, and I arranged to play on Xmas Eve. He seemed very nice and I think I shall be all right. I am pleased to say that I am gaining strength every day, and hope by Xmas to be quite myself again.
                                        Yours sincerely,
                                        Violet Cameron

On the 23rd December, the night before she opened again at the Gaiety, she found time to drop Mr. Taylor a note.

Thank you very much for the posie, which you kindly sent, and also for the doll you bought. Baby is quite delighted with it.

But it must have been a sad and lonely Christmas for Violet.

The suspense ended on 16th March with a telegram from Katmoi to say that Hugh was safe and well, and was making his way by boat to San Francisco.

*

A month later, past scandal forgotten, the first reports of his adventures burst into print across two hemispheres. The San Francisco *Daily Reporter* was first in the field. 'A FEAT—ONE OF THE GREATEST ON RECORD,' screamed the headlines. 'THE EXPLORER RETURNS TODAY.' 'The Earl,' they explained, 'is a large man, above six feet in height, and muscular to admiration. He is as a matter of course a member of the House of Lords, and has won from forty to fifty cups by his muscular performances. . . .' There followed a five thousand word description of his experiences which make any G. A. Henty tale seem tame by comparison.

The rest of the world Press took up the theme with enthusiasm. Some were adulatory, some incredulous, some frankly disbelieving.

In the midst of all the excitement, Grace slipped quietly out of England to join him in New York.

All the way across the Atlantic she was in excellent health. It was a rough crossing but Grace loved the sea and was never seasick in her life. Shortly before the ship arrived in New York the weather improved. Grace records in her diary, 'All the poor sick passengers appeared on deck seeming well again. I sat in my deck-chair all day basking in the sun and the air delicious.'

She arrived in New York before Hugh and immediately became ill.

Sunday May 12th: In the middle of the night I had such a horrid pain that I sent Goddard [her maid] for a doctor who came at once and gave me an injection of morphia.

Monday May 13th: Saw Dr. Partridge. Sir Bache [Cunard] looked in.

Tuesday May 14th: Dr. Partridge came before 11 a.m. I could not report myself much better after restless night. Bed all day. Telegram from Hugh from Montreal saying he would be here in the morning.

Wednesday May 15th: At a little past 7 a.m. my Hugh arrived and all day long he was showing me some of his furs, curiosities, photographs, etc., and between times talking to newspaper reporters who were hanging about all day and took up a lot of his time. I only got up for dinner in the next room.

Thursday May 16th: Read account in various newspapers of Hugh's travels. Saw Dr. Partridge who thought me much better. Hugh had representative of *Harper's Magazine* here some time later, and Mr. Gilder and Mr. Sartoris with whom he lunched downstairs and brought them up after. Hugh went for a walk.

Friday May 17th: I sat up at dinner but very tired later. Mr. Cunningham of *The World*, a vulgar reporter, appeared and talked a lot.

Saturday May 8th: Saw Dr. Partridge who reported well of me. I got up a little after luncheon. Hugh went out for a bit. Then Sir Bache Cunard came for him, they dined at the Delmonico and went to see a play, *Clovis*, which H said afterwards was very stupid.

And so the pattern went on, with Grace never quite well enough to join in the fun. They stayed for another few days in New York before sailing for England. They sailed on May 22nd. A final extract from Grace's diary reads:

Ready about 11 a.m. and went down to the *Celtic* in a tram-car. Found H there with Billy and the four Eskimo dogs and a sea-otter which I saw for the first time. Sir Bache Cunard, Mr. David Millikin and Mr. Cunningham of *The World* came to see us off and the waiter turned up with a mocking-bird. I laid down in the afternoon feeling very tired.

Back in England they were met by Jim Lowther, Pussy, Lancelot, and his wife Gwen.

It was June before they could find time to travel to Lowther where all the livestock had been sent on ahead of them. Long before their train was due in Penrith, the station square was packed to suffocation. All the town dignitaries lined the platform and, as the train drew in, the town band, dressed in gay Hussar uniforms specially ordered for the occasion, struck up with 'Home, Sweet Home'. There were long speeches, while the townsfolk strained at the crash-barriers and the local police sweated to keep them from bursting on to the platform. They were then towed through the streets, preceded by the band playing 'See the Conquering Hero Comes', while Hugh waved his acknowledgements to the crowds which packed the road all the way to the castle gates.

'The Earl looked in exuberant health,' recorded the *Penrith Observer*, 'but the Countess by his side looked pale and fagged by her long journey.' One cannot help hoping that some of the cheers at least were for her.

By the time the last word had been written and the last cheer had died away, Violet Cameron was as forgotten by the public as if she had never existed.

There was no doubt that her love for Hugh was sincere and lasting. Hugh himself never forgot her although he never allowed her to appear again in his life. The cure had been altogether too drastic to risk repetition. Ten years later there is a letter from Hugh to Mr. Taylor asking him to start paying Violet an allowance again. 'I see from the papers that her show has closed. She has not asked me but you know what she is like about asking for money.'

Of all the *personae dramatis* Grace in her off-stage role proved herself to be the strongest character of all. At the height of the clamour she continued to live her impeccable life as if Violet Cameron, the Operatic Company and de Bensaude did not exist. When it became necessary to 'show the flag' at Lowther, she went without question and not by the blink of an eyelid let it be known that she knew anything of the drama boiling just below the surface; at Carlton House Terrace she continued to entertain to tea whilst Hugh careered around the country in a blaze of adverse publicity.

During Hugh's year of exile, she found new strength. It is quite certain that thoughts of divorce were never considered, although she must have known that there would certainly be other women besides Violet Cameron in Hugh's life in the future. By the time he had settled down again they must have come to an understanding about their future way of life.

From now on Grace was to be mistress in her own house, free of Hugh's whims and caprices. Only people she personally approved of were allowed to stay at Lowther or Carlton House Terrace or Barleythorpe. The actresses, the Pelican Club and all Hugh's rakish entourage were put firmly on the other side of the fence. Grace established a strictly conventional background for Hugh and he accepted it gratefully. That it had continued to exist during the Violet Cameron crisis was the only thing which had, in the end, enabled him to extricate himself, and it was to continue to be important to him all his life.

It was Grace who had really won the day and, from now on, so far as the public were concerned, Hugh's married life was beyond reproach. That Grace was to grow more and more spinsterish and Hugh was to live his life, to all intents and purposes, as a bachelor was inevitable. On the other hand, their affection and regard for each other grew stronger rather than faded with the passing of the years.

What happened to de Bensaude never became known. Probably he got what he wanted in the end—money.

One sad echo of the affair was sounded a year later in Whitehaven. George Windross and his *Northern Counties Gazette* slung one stone too many at the Goliath of 'Lowtherism'. The Lowther interests sued him for libel and got small damages, but the cost of defending the case made Windross personally bankrupt. He recovered and returned to the attack more vigorously than ever. His enemies hit out again, this time by getting their friends to withdraw advertising support from the paper. Within a few months Windross retired, broken in health, and the paper folded up quietly a few weeks later.

It was the last ripple in the pool. From then on Hugh's popularity in the North was to increase year by year.

223248

Chapter 10

Hugh more than anyone else benefited from the rigorous months he spent in Canada and the Arctic. All his life his personal disasters had a way of turning to his advantage. In London he found his reputation much enhanced. Scientifically the trip had been reasonably successful, but much more important from his own point of view was the new stature he enjoyed in the eyes of the public generally and of his fellow-members at the Pelican Club in particular.

In his absence great changes had taken place in the Club. It was now housed in a new and grander building in Gerrard Street, and to the new premises had been transferred all the precious paraphernalia of the old. The waxed moustaches which Lord Esmé Gordon had skilfully shaved off Major Hope-Johnstone were proudly mounted on purple velvet and silver, boxing mementoes were reverently enclosed in glass cases, and the famous stuffed pelican gazed from a point of vantage over a large modern smoking-room which even boasted a cocktail bar. The building now contained the largest boxing hall in London, gymnasiums and changing-room, bedroom suites and a billiards-room, with enough dining accommodation for all the members to sit down at one time.

Unfortunately before it really opened, the death knell for the new venture was to be sounded by the disgraceful affair of the Jem Smith–Frank Slavin fight, which was engineered from its inception to its disastrous end by the Pelicans, and in particular by their match-making manager, John Fleming.

It was a fight that was managed in a way that Hugh Lonsdale would never have countenanced, but the agreement was entered into without consulting him. Besides, he had come back from his travels with boxing interests of his own.

Hugh's boat had hardly passed the Golden Gates of San Francisco on his way back from Alaska before he was hearing rumours of 'The Black Diamond', a coloured fighter who had made his way from Australia, where he had been coached by Hugh's own tutor, Jem Mace, and was now employed as a boxing instructor at San Francisco's fashionable Californian Athletic Club.

His first night ashore he took the opportunity of seeing the wonder boy in action. Writing of their meeting afterwards, Hugh recorded: 'The moment I laid eyes on that dark skin, sleek and shining with health, and the exquisite harmony of those easy, powerful limbs, I knew that here was something uncommonly good....'

He lost no time in arranging for his protégé to travel to England at his expense, with the result that when his boat docked at Southampton he had more to show for his trip than cases and cases of specimens, a complete Arctic sled with twenty stuffed huskies and four live ones, several tons of geological samples, and a complete skeleton of a musk ox. He also brought with him Peter Jackson, one of the greatest boxers, white or coloured, the world has ever known.

While Hugh travelled north to Lowther, Jackson was spirited quietly off to Hugh's mother's house, Cottesmore, where he was put into strict training. It must have made quite a surprise for the gentle retiring Pussy.

Jem Smith was then the idol of England, and the generally acknowledged heavyweight champion. The previous year he had fought the greatest match of his career in a bare-fist contest with Jake Kilrain. It had lasted for one hundred and six rounds before the two men had agreed to a draw. Now Smith looked England's brightest hope to win the heavyweight championship of the world under the new rules with gloves. He was the particular protégé of the Pelicans, so that when Hugh claimed that he had an 'unknown' to beat their favourite, he was met with cries which were both incredulous and indignant. Even 'The Mate', Sir John Astley, Hugh's close friend and the president of the Pelicans, took leave to doubt whether it was even safe to let an unknown fighter into the same ring as the great Jem. If Hugh had been a betting man he could have taken any price against Jackson surviving a few rounds against the champion.

Hugh stayed up at Lowther into the autumn. Grace seemed very much worse in health, complaining of constant pain, so that if she went out at all it was in an invalid carriage. Towards the end of October they travelled down to Cottesmore; Hugh bubbling with enthusiastic plans for his protégé, Grace relieved at the prospect of a rest from the public life they were expected to lead at Lowther.

The match between Jackson and Smith had been fixed for 11th November, and was to be the first contest to be held in the new premises of the Pelican Club.

At Cottesmore Hugh found Peter Jackson in tip-top condition. He was a quiet boy with natural good manners, and a calm temperament which it was almost impossible to upset. It was said that the only thing which would make him rise was an insult to the coloured race. He had a lot to put up with, not only in America, but in England, where coloured boxers were by no means popular—especially with other fighters—ever since 'Molyneux the Black' had come so near the Championship of England. 'I hear you niggers can't take a punch in the belly,' a loud-mouthed pug once remarked to Jackson. 'Are you claiming to be one of the white men who can?' he replied with enough menace to close the incident.

At Cottesmore, Hugh, whose admiration for Peter Jackson was boundless, would spar with him every morning. 'He could have floored me at any time,' he admitted, his boasting of how he had beaten John L. Sullivan forgotten. 'If I managed to land him a good one he would just shake his head and remark, "That's better, my Lord. That's better."'

In the evenings, after dinner, Jackson would amuse Hugh's guests by throwing right-hand punches at the tall candles on the dining-room table. So accurate were his punches that he could extinguish the flame without touching the candle.

On the appointed night of the battle a fashionable crowd stumbled over the planks and still-wet cement of the new Club to pack the ringside to suffocation. The audience was one of the most title-studded ever to patronize the still illegal sport of boxing. Even the officials were in large part drawn from the aristocracy. Sir John Astley had appointed himself as ring master, Lord de Clifford was the timekeeper, and Hugh himself was in Jackson's corner, splendidly immaculate with his cigar and gardenia.

The proceedings did not take long. By the end of the second round the pride of the Pelicans had been beaten to a pulp by the 'Black Diamond'. Technically, Jackson won on a disqualification, as the maddened Smith tried with one last desperate manoeuvre to man-handle his opponent out of the ring, but even Smith's most ardent supporters admitted that if he had not been disqualified he would have been unfit to go on.

It was only a short six weeks after this that a group of Pelicans who had lost heavily over Jackson's unexpected win planned to recoup their losses by matching Smith with Frank Paddy Slavin, the 'Sydney Cornstalk'.

For reasons of their own, which were to become all too apparent, they decided not to hold the match at the Pelican Club, but to seek a secret rendezvous on the Continent.

It eventually took place, improbably, on the tennis lawn of a retired British army officer living outside Bruges. It was to be a bare-fist fight, at which Smith excelled, and enormous sums were wagered on the result. On form the Pelican backers were on to a good thing, particularly as they had backed their man 'not to lose' as distinct from 'to win', so that in the event of a draw they still stood to collect.

Even before the contest was due to start, however, it appeared that the big gamblers had taken steps still further to narrow the chances of their losing. In spite of the customary security precautions, which were even more necessary to prevent police interference on the Continent than in England, Bruges on the eve of battle presented a spectacle calculated to strike fear into the heart of a lesser man than Frank Slavin. Every rough in the game appeared to be there, and none of them made any disguise of the fact that they were under orders to see that whoever won it would not be Slavin.

At the start of the contest Slavin's corner looked one of the loneliest places on this earth. The highly partisan crowd, who roared encouragement to their champion Jem, made little pretence of hiding the coshes, truncheons and even revolvers with which they were liberally equipped. In spite of this show of force, however, Slavin pitched into his opponent with such effect that by the fifteenth round nobody could have been in any doubt of the result. This was the signal for the appearance of Squire Abingdon, inarticulate with drink and rage, shouting encouragement to his supporters to 'do in the Australian bastard'.

Lord Mandeville, fearing for Slavin's life, drew a bowie knife with which he had had the foresight to equip himself and faced the mob. A few of the braver spirits like Jim Carney joined him; at this show of resolution the Squire and the battered Smith staged a precipitate withdrawal, whereupon much to the delight of the heavy gamblers who included both the Squire and Fleming, the match was declared a draw.

Back in London, there was all hell to pay. At one blow all the glamour of the Pelicans was stripped from them. Worse, the reputation which Hugh, 'Mate' Astley, Lord Queensberry and a few others had worked hard to build up for boxing as a clean sport, was all but destroyed.

At a hastily called meeting, presided over by the 'Mate', Squire Abingdon was blackballed from the Club, and Fleming dismissed from his position as boxing manager. It could not, however, save the Pelicans. With the paint scarcely dry on their splendid new headquarters, their popularity went into a decline from which it never recovered. Within a few years the Club had to close its doors.

Squire Abingdon caused a minor sensation the following year by trying to get the Chancery Court to rule his expulsion illegal. He failed. Undeterred, he determined to make his mark in the history of boxing by backing his own fighters to beat the world. In 1893 he fitted out an expedition to America ostensibly to match Charlie Mitchell with the world champion Jim Corbett. It was doomed to failure. Corbett was too busy making money appearing in the play *Gentleman Jack* to bother about the Squire's challenge.

To fill in time at intervals of getting drunk and generally hell raising, the Squire appeared in Jem Hall's corner in his fight against Bob Fitzsimmons in New Orleans. Hall was beaten, but it still called for a celebration. Still dressed in an open-necked silk shirt soaked in perspiration and whisky, the Squire set out to beat up the town. Next morning he went down with a bout of pneumonia. Within three days he was dead. His retinue of prize-fighters, gamblers, drunks and hangers-on dressed him in full evening dress, put him in his coffin, and carried him back to England.

His death at the age of thirty-six marked the end of one of the worst eras in the history of British boxing. The new broom, as represented by Hugh Lonsdale and his friends, had already started on the job of making boxing respectable. They were now to go from strength to strength.

*

For a long time membership of the Pelican Club with its own way of selection of members had been the ambition of sporting-minded City businessmen. It represented for them a rakish glamour. That eminent respectability was almost a complete bar to acceptance by that strange company, made it perhaps even more desirable.

The man to recognize this anomaly and decide to take advantage of it was a city businessman, A. F. (Peggy) Bettinson. A chance meeting on a suburban train with the out-of-favour John Fleming, late of the Pelican Club, resulted in a new club being formed.

With the Pelican in its death throes, there were many boxers looking for a new Club where they could display their talents as a means of gaining recognition.

Bettinson wisely realized that to attract the right sort of member he must somehow manage to invest his new club with some of the glamour of the Pelicans, whilst at the same time set a standard of respectable behaviour for members, and fair play for boxers. The solid middle class which he hoped to attract might envy the high jinks of the Pelican from afar, but they would not long remain members of a club where they were quite likely to lose their trousers or find their moustaches being forcibly shaved off. Nor would they enjoy the regular appearances of the bailiffs, whose efforts to collect their just dues were such a constant source of merriment to Pelican members.

As Bettinson was pondering these matters, Hugh Lonsdale was becoming involved in one of the great *causes célèbres* of boxing.

Billy Madden, the American promoter, had brought over to England Jack McAuliffe, one of the best fighters of America, to fight the now immensely popular Frank Slavin for a purse of £1,000. With the memory of the Slavin–Smith fight still very much in the public mind, the announcement caused the greatest excitement. It also presented a challenge to the anti-prize-fighting campaigners, who had had much strength given to their cause by the affair at Bruges.

The fight was scheduled to take place at the Ormonde Club on 22nd September 1890. Richard K. Fox, the American sportsman, gave the proceedings an international flavour by offering a valuable belt, in addition to the prize money, for the winner.

Altogether it was a situation which the police could not ignore. By no stretch of imagination could the conditions of the fight answer to the description of a sparring match, which was the usual way of evading the strict interpretation of the law. Three days before the fight was due to take place both contestants were arrested, and bound over in the sum of £1,000 to keep the peace. It was the chips down with a vengeance.

Fox, representing the American contingent, stood bail for McAuliffe. 'Rats' Piesse, however, who stood in much the same position *vis-à-vis* Slavin, was notable only for his absence. Public interest reached fever-pitch when it was known that Hugh Lonsdale had stepped into the breach and bailed Slavin.

The personal intervention of Lord Lonsdale caused yet another shudder to ripple through polite Society circles where boxing was regarded as one of those things that it was almost a breach of good taste to mention. But there was worse to follow.

Hugh was quite incapable of doing anything by halves. Having once entered the lists in support of Slavin and McAuliffe, he was determined to see the matter through to the end. Not only did he stand bail for Slavin, but he undertook the whole financial responsibility for the defence.

Overnight, Carlton House Terrace became the headquarters for the defence of British boxing. Hugh was in his element. Step by step, he prepared every detail of the defence with his lawyer Wightman Wood. The hearing was before the Lambeth magistrates and lasted three days. Hugh himself was called to give evidence as to the fairness of the new rules under which contests were held. When the case was committed to the Surrey Sessions, he hired Sir Charles Russell* for the defence.

His hard work and financial generosity were amply justified when Russell's fluent pleading resulted in the Treasury being given leave to withdraw, and Slavin and McAuliffe were released.

It was by no means the end of the battle, but it was certainly the first step towards the recognition by the authorities of the legality of boxing contests carried out under properly constituted rules. It also solved a problem for Peggy Bettinson. The name of Lonsdale was now firmly associated in the minds of the sporting public with fair play and a square deal. Who better to be the President of the new Club, whose aim was to stage contests for the enjoyment of a thoroughly respectable audience, under conditions very far removed from the not-so-long-gone days as represented by the 'Affair at Bruges'?

Hugh was invited and accepted. He thus became the first President of the National Sporting Club—an institution which was to play such a decisive part in the development of boxing, not only in this country but all over the world. He held the office for thirty-eight years.

For Hugh the Presidency of the N.S.C. was to prove one of the most important happenings of his life.

From such small beginnings it was to grow immensely, and with it Hugh's own stature was to increase in a way which would not have been possible in any other sport.

* Later Lord Russell of Killowen, and Lord Chief Justice of England.

Chapter 11

Before the cheers of the sporting public and the agitation of his social equals over the Slavin–McAuliffe fight had died away, Hugh got himself involved in yet another affair which was still further to increase the affection in which he was held by a sensation-hungry public. Only this time he was to be one of the chief participants in the drama, and not the *deus ex machina*.

If Hugh had any Gods in his life, certainly one of them was the eccentric Squire Osbaldeston who had lived during the first half of the nineteenth century. Osbaldeston was a leading supporter of prize-fighting, a noted horseman, and a great character. Anecdotes about him are legion, and some of his sporting achievements were extraordinary.

On one occasion Osbaldeston wagered that he could ride a distance of two hundred miles in ten hours, even taking a bet at ten to one that he would complete the distance in under nine. By dint of using fifty changes of horses, he accomplished the feat in eight hours, forty-two minutes, including time for changing mounts. His actual riding time was seven hours, thirty-four minutes.

Tales like these thrilled Hugh Lonsdale. He had more than a streak of the Walter Mitty in him, which, coupled with his determination to impress his prowess on his contemporaries, led him to regard himself as well nigh invincible.

It was this attitude of mind which got him involved in a contest with Lord Shrewsbury which was to make both their names headline news for many months.

It started at a shooting party at Ingestre Hall, Lord Shrewsbury's country estate. In the smoking-room after dinner, Shrewsbury claimed that a horse's speed at a good gallop was twenty-four to twenty-five miles an hour. The irrepressible Hugh said he had a trotter which could beat that. It led to an animated debate whilst the brandy continued to circulate.

The rest of the company included such redoubtable figures as Admiral Stevenson, Mark Bouverie and 'Bay' Middleton, the idol of the hunting-field who piloted the Empress of Austria when she hunted with the Quorn. Sensing a bit of fun after their own hearts, his companions egged Hugh on, knowing that he would never give anyone best when it came to discussing feats of horsemanship.

At first a straight trotters-versus-gallopers race was suggested, with the two Earls riding their own choices. Not satisfied with this, Hugh capped the proposal by suggesting that postillion riding be included in the match. There were few other than professionals who had any knowledge of riding postillion. Hugh had learned the art in the stable-yard at Asfordby, and was extremely proud of his skill. In Lord Shrewsbury, however, he had a man who could match him. Like Hugh he had, to use his own words, 'been to all intents and purposes born in a manger'. He accepted the proposal with alacrity.

The atmosphere was soon thick with cigar smoke and furious argument. The original point was forgotten and, with Hugh in full cry to prove himself in this fine company, a most elaborate match was arranged. The contest, for a hundred pounds a side, was to start with the famous Lonsdale trotter in a buggy against Shrewsbury's best galloper, for a five-mile race; the next five miles was to be with a two-horse trap, the next with a four-in-hand, and the final five riding postillion to a pair of horses in an open phaeton.

Among Hugh's friends, news of his wager was greeted with enthusiasm. Amongst the members of the dying Pelican Club there were some of the finest exponents with 'the ribbons' in the country—men like Walter Dickson (Dicky the Driver), 'Swish' Broadwood and Jim Selby. Hugh could count on enough well-meant advice to win the race several times over, whilst the bookmakers and the heavy gamblers chalked up some elaborate wagers for large sums of money on every conceivable aspect of the contest.

In no time at all the news of the match spread, and overnight it became the talk of St. James's Street, and the delight of the journalists. The whole thing had about it a Regency flavour which appealed enormously to everyone on the touch-line. Mr. Arthur Coventry was appointed as referee, with both parties agreeing to abide by his decision in all matters, including the choice of the course.

The two competitors made themselves busy inspecting lengths of highway all over the country. This proved the first bone of contention. Hugh selected a length of the Great North Road by Norman's Cross. Shrewsbury favoured a quieter stretch on the Dorking–Reigate Road. Arthur Coventry gave a casting vote in favour of Shrewsbury.

The matter of the road having been settled, Lord Shrewsbury started to run into troubles of his own. One appeared in the shape of his wife, who regarded the whole thing as a rather dangerous prank in which two schoolboys had got involved, and should definitely be discouraged. A deflating attitude, to say the least of it!

She even went to the length of writing to Hugh Lonsdale on the subject:

Dear Lord Lonsdale,

Boisie [her pet name for her husband] is away today—left before the post arrived. He will not be back in time for this evening's post, doubtless he will answer tomorrow by letter or telegram.

I am afraid I am the person who does not relish the road business. I am *awfully* afraid of an *accident*. You cannot blame me! You know I hate the whole thing, and want Boisie to forego the match! Women are a bore, aren't they!!!

Do *you* feel inclined to back yourself for £100?*

Yours very truly,

Nellie Shrewsbury and Talbot

Lady Shrewsbury was, incidentally, universally known as the 'Shrew', and her influence on her husband was formidable. On this occasion, however, honour insisted that the match take place in spite of her opposition.

In the meantime the national Press were having the time of their lives. The aristocracy were behaving as they expected them to behave, and there was no end of fun to be had out of it. *The Referee* announced that they had exclusive information that Lord Salisbury had challenged his political rival, Lord Hartington, for £100 a side to hop five miles, then go on all fours, roll over and finally walk five miles on stilts.

The 'Pink 'Un' declared the whole excitement, the rumour and counter-rumour, enough to drive two sub-editors crazy, four paper makers to suicide, and ride a master printer to death. As for the competitors, they were both keyed-up to concert pitch, Lord Shrewsbury's condition being no doubt aggravated by the attitude of her Ladyship.

* A shrewd blow at Hugh's known aversion to gambling.

Hugh Lonsdale reacted in a typical way. He reached for his cheque-book. Now that his skill was to be tested in the full glare of publicity, it was unthinkable to him that he should lose. On the other hand, Lord Shrewsbury was regarded by many as the best whip in England. There is little doubt that Hugh regretted heartily that his tongue had lured him into such a difficult position. Hugh started to buy the fastest carriage horses he could find, and searched Europe for the lightest carriages to which he could harness them. Before the startled Trustees could gather their wits about them he had ordered a special lightweight buggy from his American friend Richard Fox, and the bills for everything from horse flesh to special harness were flooding into the office at Pall Mall. This was, of course rather against the spirit of the match, which had originally been to prove who had the fastest horses in his stables. Hugh got round this by claiming that they were horses he had intended to buy anyhow. Shrewsbury retorted by indulging in a spending spree of his own, buying and discarding horses like confetti.

As the time for the match approached, the telegrams started to fly between the two principals like the arrows at Crecy. Spies from each camp reported faster and faster times at the trials which each was holding in secret. The psychological warfare reached its peak three days before the off, when a sharp fall of snow sent supporters of each side scurrying down to Reigate to report on conditions.

Hugh Lonsdale moved his whole entourage by special train from Oakham to the White Hart Hotel at Reigate forty-eight hours before the start. Surrounded by his Pelican Club supporters—and, much to the anguish of the landlord, quantities of their own Pelican Club champagne—he settled down to await the arrival of his adversary.

Public interest was insatiable. On a false claim that the match was to be held at Derby, crowds flocked there from all parts of the country. Furious Chief Constables complained that their police forces were continually occupied dispersing spectators determined that they knew where the match was to take place. Other news was banished from the headlines as speculation followed speculation, and any other subject of conversation was unthinkable.

The anti-climax, when it came, was complete. Shrewsbury telegraphed to say that he was snowed up at Caterham. Whether the excuse was genuine, or whether the 'Shrew' had won the day, as was freely suggested by the Lonsdale supporters, will now never be known. It is likely, however, that the reason was genuine enough, for the telegram was followed by one from Mr. Coventry ruling that the match be postponed for one day.

What drove the Lonsdale camp to frenzied indignation was that Coventry made his decision without ever leaving London, although there was a special train at his disposal. Hugh Lonsdale was having none of it. So far as he was concerned he was at the right place at the right time, and if Shrewsbury was not there he would have his gallop anyhow.

One can almost sense the jubilation in the exchange of telegrams which followed on receipt of Shrewsbury's message.

Lonsdale to Shrewsbury:

Telegram received. Sir John Astley and many others here think road bad but nothing bad enough to stop us. As fair for one as for the other. All agree no need for postponement. Shall expect match to take place, or walk-over, but shall await your reply.

Coventry to Lonsdale:

As referee on all points—according to conditions—advised and confirmed postponement till tomorrow. Coventry.

Lonsdale to Shrewsbury:

Lovely day here. Unless you are at the starting point before three o'clock shall walk over and claim forfeit. Lonsdale.

To this Shrewsbury replied firmly:

Received your two telegrams. Referee has wired his decision. Shrewsbury.

By the time this was received, the victory corks of the Pelican Club were already popping. Indignantly Hugh wired his opponent:

Am much surprised at this unfair behaviour. Thought I had made a sporting match with a sportsman. Instead of which I get unfair treatment and downright discourtesy. Lonsdale.

Having delivered himself of this Olympian bolt, he repaired to the course, where he raced the twenty miles against the clock in fine style to the enthusiastic plaudits of the large crowd who had braved the elements to witness the event. The time recorded was a remarkable fifty-four minutes, fifteen and a half seconds. The actual times for each stage were: 1st stage, 13 min. 40 sec.; 2nd stage, 12 min. 52

sec.; 3rd stage, 15 min. 10 sec.; 4th stage, 13 min. 56 sec. The overall running speed was 22½ m.p.h.

It was reported next day, by the *Daily Telegraph* in particular, in a way which made Lord Lonsdale appear more than a paragon of sporting virtue, and Lord Shrewsbury in a very poor light indeed. After an eulogistic description of the race the *Telegraph* concluded: 'It was a sight which might well evoke the cheers which arose as he shot by the mark having accomplished his feat in less than fifty-five minutes. The cheers went on again and again. The only regret was that Lord Shrewsbury was not present to have shared the applause.'

After a glass of champagne thoughtfully provided on the finishing line, Lord Lonsdale returned to Reigate amidst great enthusiasm. At a splendid luncheon his health was drunk again and, in a speech, he pointed out that he 'had done everything to ensure the fulfilment of the match'. 'I have tried,' he said, 'to act in a straightforward way throughout'—a statement which, echoed the Press, 'needs no confirmation'. At six o'clock he left by special train for Oakham. 'Lord Shrewsbury was not on the platform to bid him good-bye,' the *Daily Telegraph* added acidly.

Lord Shrewsbury claimed that Hugh had not only evaded the issue of the race, but had insulted him and impugned his character as a sportsman. Lonsdale persisted in his claim that he had been unfairly treated. The controversy went on for weeks in the Press, with both sides being urged to revive the match. The various telegrams were quoted and requoted, accurately and inaccurately as suited the supporters of either side. Threats of writ for libel flew to and fro, and to add a final touch to the comedy, a writ was issued against the Earl of Lonsdale for furious driving on the highway. The summons was dismissed with the mild remark from the Bench: 'The Magistrates desire to say that they do not think the public highway is a proper place for a racecourse.' This in turn sparked off a row of gigantic proportions with the increasing number of cycling clubs all over the country. 'Why should an Earl,' they complained in their journal *The Wheel*, 'get away with such a flagrant breach of the law, when cyclists are prosecuted at every turn. Unless they too are noble lords the result in their case will probably be exactly the reverse.'

By the time the row had died down, Hugh Lonsdale and Shrewsbury had met and made up their quarrel, but the match was never revived.

For Hugh the outcome of the whole affair had been highly satisfactory, for there was no doubt that in the eyes of the sporting public it was he who had carried off the honours. To commemorate the event he commissioned a set of sporting prints to be engraved.

'Nothing like enough mud on the faces, hats, rugs, etc.,' he wrote to the artist after viewing the unfinished drawings. 'In fact everything was smothered in mud, and this effect should be conveyed.'

Posterity, at least, was to get its money's worth!

If Hugh Lonsdale had been a gambler, there is no doubt that he would have finished up well on the right side after his 'race' with Lord Shrewsbury, and the successful debut of his protégé Peter Jackson. As it was, he had not had a penny on either event and, indeed, the Jackson fight had only been arranged as a result of his putting up a purse of £800 for the winner and £200 for the loser, with no bets to recoup his outlay.

Chapter 12

Jim Lowther's victory in stopping one drain on the vast income which poured through Hugh's hands like water had only caused the pipeline to spring a series of leaks in other even more dangerous directions. Forlornly he and Grace discussed ways and means of controlling Hugh's incredible capacity for spending. To appeal to Hugh's own sense of discipline was a nightmarish game of shadow-boxing.

By the end of 1891, as Hugh contentedly puffed at his cigar at the ringside of the National Sporting Club, Jim Lowther stared gloomily at the shattered estimates of expenditure which he had imposed earlier in the year. Pinned to them was a typical Hugh note, deeply contrite but exuberantly optimistic about the six months to come.

I may tell you that I am determined to keep within the amount, and if I cannot do it one way, I will do it another, and you may rely on this year's estimates and the years to come being under rather than over the amount allotted to each department. Such being the case, I do not hesitate in saying that I have not the slightest fear, and can give my absolute word, that the estimates shall in no way be exceeded. Everything is in the best possible working order, and I am not aware of a strap or peg that is necessary. I think it is only natural that you should be anxious on this point, and I hope to set your mind at rest by the assurances I am giving you.

Nothing can exceed your kindness to me in every way, and if you have any wishes to express on any point do not hesitate to tell me. The estimates *shall* be adhered to; there is no need for further outlay on any department—with the exception of drains. . . .

Drains, indeed! With something over £6,000 spent over a wager of £100 with Lord Shrewsbury, Jim Lowther might be excused for heaving a rather exasperated sigh.

'I think,' he wrote to Grace, 'that Hugh had better take up hunting again. I really do not think we can afford him in London.'

The difficulties which confronted the Trustees in dealing with Hugh was that their duty was to ensure the proper upkeep of the estates at Lowther and Whitehaven.

The estates were entailed for Hugh's successor, and it was the Trustees' responsibility to see that they were handed over on Hugh's death in the same state of prosperity, so far as was humanly possible, as at the time of his inheritance.

Hugh paid for the upkeep of Carlton House Terrace, which was rented from the Crown, for the Barleythorpe estates which were his own property absolutely, for his permanently staffed but seldom used yacht, the *Verena* (the *Northumbria* had been sold on St. George's death), as well as for his personal office in Pall Mall and goodness knows what other private benefactions besides. His personal entourage concerned in one way or another with his comfort numbered over a hundred. Whenever he moved from one house to another, a special train was reserved for his household. If he travelled overnight, one first-class sleeper was reserved for himself and another for his dogs. Along the route station masters paraded on the platforms on their stations, at whatever the hour, to see the Lonsdale train safely through their station, and to be rewarded with a five-pound note, handed out by Hugh's valet, who was required to stay up all night for the purpose.

By this standard of living his £80,000 a year pocket-money melted like the snows of yesteryear.

The Trustees tried doggedly to preserve and improve the Lowther and Whitehaven estates, whilst Hugh with equal determination strove to extract every penny from the estate to meet his own commitments. Lowther was the no-man's-land over which most of the battles were fought. Where the Trustees advocated a policy of long-term benefit, like planned afforestation or farm improvements, Hugh considered the only proper expenditure to be on something from which he could benefit in his own lifetime.

'I am the last of the Lowthers,' he would say repeatedly, ignoring the fact that, through his younger brother Lancelot, there could still be a close line of succession—and failing Lancelot a collateral branch much closer in relationship than the Swillington Lowthers, his own great grandparents, through whom he himself had inherited.*

His attitude might have been better if he and Grace had been able

---

* Lancelot did in fact marry and have a son Anthony (b. 24th Sept. 1896) who was the present Earl's father.

to have children, but they both knew now that it could never be.

Hugh, adoring children and always at ease with them, took the view that if he could have none of his own he would not recognize the claims that others might have. Perhaps it was his way of revenging himself on Fate. Whatever the cause, without children of his own to inherit, he lived his life as if there were no tomorrow.

*

By the time he was in his early 'thirties, Hugh Lonsdale had earned immense popularity with the man-in-the-street, and the sporting public in particular, but the same could not be said of his standing with his social equals.

Of the great English families of ancient lineage, the only ones which counted in an opulent Victorian Society were those who, through some happy accident of fortune, had managed, like the Lowthers, to emerge from the Industrial Revolution with greatly enhanced wealth and power—families like the Northumberlands, the Londonderrys and the Portlands who had found coal on their estates, or like the Westminsters, the Bedfords and the Norfolks, whose former farmlands had become jungles of brick and mortar with rent rolls which outstripped in magnitude even the formidable royalties from the mines.

For most of them the acquisition of great wealth had made them remote from the affairs of ordinary mortals.

Just as the new industrial magnates closed their eyes as far as they were able to the origins of their wealth, so the former feudal landlords hedged themselves into a tight little circle where even the mention of money was bad taste. It was a world where they were not so much concerned with keeping up with each other as with not letting each other down.

In this company Hugh Lonsdale was not at ease. To them, in spite of his wealth, he was something of a renegade who not only got his name into the papers, and in particular into the more reprehensible gossip columns, but was suspected of quite liking it. Apart from brawling in the Park, which might be put down to the exuberance of youth, and the affair of Violet Cameron which might, with the passing of time, come to be overlooked, there was his deliberate public involvement in the courts with the riff-raff of the boxing booths. Even Queensberry, eccentric, irascible and generally impossible though he was, had the good taste to disappear into the background when it came to a matter of giving public support to a cause he espoused in private. Then, too, there was the ostentatious way that Hugh Lonsdale went about everything he did. Where it was the fashion to live modestly, dress with decorum and plead poverty, the yellow carriages, the liveried outriders, the big cigars and the showmanship were to them intolerable. There was no doubt about it in their view: Hugh Lonsdale was letting the side down.

On the other hand Hugh did not go as far as some of his contemporaries in trampling down the carefully maintained defences of Society. There were some who were completely beyond the pale like the Lord Hastings who had run off with Harry Chaplin's fiancée. Hastings was accustomed to start the day with a breakfast of mackerel bones cooked in gin—a spectacular 'eye-opener' which he did his best to live up to for the rest of the day. Of the Marquis of Hertford Charles Greville remarks in his *Memoirs*, 'there was no such example of undisguised debauchery exhibited to the world. He was in the habit of travelling about with a company of prostitutes who formed his principal society. . . .' Compared with men like these Hugh was a hide-bound conventionalist.

Perhaps the nearest in his way of life to Lord Lonsdale was the Prince of Wales himself, who was held in almost equal distrust by the Establishment. With his thick German accent, his saturnine appearance and his deplorable taste in friends, he was the complete opposite of everything it was felt the heir to the Throne ought to be. Superficially he had much in common with Hugh Lonsdale yet, although they were much in each other's company, they never became great friends. Perhaps their interests too often coincided.

The inherent snobbery which has always existed even amongst those closest to the Throne protected the Prince from much of the censure which was Hugh's portion. That the Prince should compete with Squire Abingdon for the favours of the 'Jersey Lily' could be overlooked. Even his bizarre friendships with social climbers, like the rich American widow Kate Moore, could be regarded with pained tolerance.* But for Hugh there was no excuse. He must either stick by the rules or risk social ostracism.

The great stabilizing influence was Grace. Unable to restrain their curiosity, Society went to Carlton House Terrace to take tea and try to discover some new tittle of scandal to retail in their own drawing-rooms. They went away empty handed. Grace listened with courteous attention to the daily gossip and the confidences given in the

---

* On hearing of Kate's death a wit remarked 'Ah! This will be a great night for Kate, no doubt she will be dining with God!'

hope of receiving confidences in return. She never gave them.

When the 'Jersey Lily', whose name had been so often linked with Hugh's in the gossip sheets, fell out of Royal favour, Grace was one of the very few in Society who did not conveniently forget that they had been friends. Burdened with debt, Lily's house and all its contents were put up for sale to appease the sharks. Grace took the trouble of attending the sale and of writing to the exiled Lily with a report of proceedings. 'Everything went for very good prices, even your little handkerchiefs with your initials on them, so I hope your beastly creditors will be satisfied.'

Grace was fully aware of the attractions of the extrovert way of life, and that places such as the Argyll Rooms and the Holborn Casino were altogether too dangerous as hunting grounds.* From now on Grace insisted that, if Hugh was to have flirtations, it must be within his own circle of friends.

A tacit agreement of this sort was by no means untypical of the age. The growing fashion for giving elaborate house parties gave plenty of scope for amorous affairs among a certain set. Indeed amongst the faster elements who followed the lead of the Prince of Wales it was almost universally accepted. It only became scandalous if it became known outside their own circle of friends.

Illegitimacy carried with it little stigma. Illegitimate branches of noble families were often openly acknowledged. There is a well-known story of a Duke of Norfolk when he was visiting his Northern property of Greystoke Castle. As he was driving through the little village outside the castle gates, half a dozen barefoot children ran across in front of his carriage. Turning to his coachman, he asked to whom the children belonged. 'So far as I could notice,' the coachman replied deferentially, 'those that didn't belong to me, belonged to your Grace.'

---

* It was the heyday of the *demi-monde*, many of whom proved expensive investments. Harry Vane Millbank's father paid Mabel Grey, the leading beauty at the Casino, £10,000 to give up the idea of marrying his son. Emma Crouch, better known as Cora Pearl, squandered something in the region of £15,000,000 in her fantastic reign and was the leading *cocotte* in Europe. Kate Cooke, Rose Wilson and Valerie Reece, all at one time 'girls' at the Holborn Casino, became respectively the Countess of Euston, Lady Verner and Lady Meux. Valerie Meux, who had been second string to Mabel Grey at the Casino, outlived her husband by many years. She was left as a major shareholder in Meux's Brewery and ruled the board of directors with a rod of iron. When she died she left most of her money to her own poor relations. It was her revenge on the Meux family who had refused to recognize her.

The house parties which were given for shooting or to attend the races, were a happy hunting-ground for the amorously inclined.

The popularity of the almost exclusively male pastime of gambling at cards was on the decline. In its place party games were becoming fashionable. At the gayer house parties games like hide-and-seek were much in vogue. As the houses were vast and the number of hiding-places almost inexhaustible the games seldom reached an early conclusion. Somehow, too, it was always the more elderly or the more virtuous of the party who found themselves cast in the role of seekers.

One of the few occasions when Grace accompanied Hugh to a shooting party she records in her diary: 'Jolly fun after dinner when we played games. Finished with a game of hide-and-seek with Lord B. and I as the searchers. We couldn't find many people so after a time we gave up and I went to bed.'

On another occasion, both the Prince and Hugh had been invited without their wives to the same house party at Goodwood. Lily Langtry, her husband being on a fishing holiday in Scotland, was also asked. Long after the last light had been put out and all the guests could be safely judged to be asleep, Hugh decided to try his luck, and, slipping out of his room, set off down the corridor in what he believed to be the way to Lily's bedroom. Feeling his way in the impenetrable darkness, he was manoeuvring round a corner of a passage when his outstretched hand grasped what was unmistakably the royal beard proceeding with equal caution in the opposite direction. Or so the story goes!

It was during Doncaster race week in 1890 that the Tranby Croft affair occurred. Tranby Croft was the home of a wealthy shipowner, Mr. Wilson, who was the host of the Prince of Wales who was to attend the races. The other guests had been carefully selected to ensure that the Prince would be able to enjoy his favourite after dinner relaxation of a game of baccarat.

One of the guests was a wealthy and respected Scottish land-owner, Colonel Sir William Gordon-Cumming. It has never been established for certain whether Sir William was in fact cheating or not. On the face of it it would seem unlikely but the fact remains that he was accused of it and did, on the insistence of his host, sign an undertaking that he would never play cards again.

That would normally have been the end of the matter, but on this occasion it did not remain safely swept under the carpet. Other members of the house party talked, and soon the details of the affair were so widely known that Sir William decided that he must sue for slander in an attempt to clear his name.

When it became known that the Prince of Wales was to be called as a witness for the prosecution, everyone involved found themselves to be the centre of an unprecedented blaze of publicity. Sir William won his case but the award of one farthing as damages left no doubt in everybody's mind of his guilt. He retired at once to his estates in Scotland and never again attempted to enter Society.

It was whilst these events were fresh in everybody's mind that the Prince of Wales accepted an invitation from Hugh to stay at Lowther to shoot pheasants in the autumn of 1891.

It immediately raised a public outcry. 'The announcement,' one writer declared, 'that the Prince of Wales intends to pay a long visit to the notorious Lord Lonsdale at Lowther Castle serves to set wagging again the tongues of scandal that had just begun to tire of rehearsing the incidents of the great Baccarat Case. . . .' The *New York Tribune* remarked that the Prince of Wales 'seems to disregard evil report and take his own course in associating with pleasant company at the risk of further weakening devotion to the Throne'.

In the end the visit was cancelled the official reason being given as the Court mourning for the Duke of Clarence.

Five years later, on 10th January 1896, the Prince did pay a private visit to Lowther. By that time Hugh was no longer the 'notorious' Lord Lonsdale but well on his way to becoming one of the most popular figures in the country.

It had always been a thorn in Hugh's flesh that the Prince was far more friendly with Lancelot, Hugh's younger brother, and with Gwen Lowther,* Lancelot's wife, than he was with Hugh himself. Gwen Lowther was, in contrast to Grace, one of the most popular young married woman of her day and included in the Prince's most intimate circle of friends. He was godfather to her son Anthony.†

The guests included Lord Curzon, who was shortly to become Viceroy of India, Lord and Lady Churchill, Lord Herbert Vane Tempest, Harry Chaplin who had become President of the Board of Trade, the Earl of Dunraven, Lord and Lady Coke and Lady Gerard to whom Hugh was devoted.

After dinner on the first night of the Prince's arrival, Hugh had given orders for a baccarat table to be laid out in the drawing-room

---

* Lancelot married Miss Gwen Sheffield, sister of Sir Berkeley Sheffield. After her death in 1922 he married Miss Sybil Feetham.

† Afterwards Viscount Lowther and father of the present Earl.

Lord Lonsdale in the garden at Lowther Castle.

iscount Lowther's Hounds leaving Lowther for Fineshade Abbey, Northampton, 1695.
his is believed to be the earliest painting of foxhounds in England.

The Coat of Arms of
the Earls of Lonsdale.

'Wicked Jimmy', First Earl of Lonsdale
(a painting by Hudson).

William the Good, First Earl of Lonsdale by the 2nd creation.

William the Bad, Second Earl of Lonsdale—he twice refused the Premiership.

The Third Earl of Lonsdale, Hugh's father.

St. George Lowther, Fourth Earl of Lonsdale, Hugh's elder brother.

The Countess of Lonsdale, St. George's wife, who later became Lady Ripon.

Grace in her riding habit, shortly after her marriage.

Hugh as a young man in London society.

Lily Langtry.

Violet Cameron in her hey-day.

Hugh in the buggy used in the road-race against Lord Shrewsbury.
The 'speed goggles' were his own innovation.

'Lord Lonsdale's match against time' from *The Illustrated London News*.

Whitehaven Castle.

A view of Lowther Castle from 'Lady Lonsdale's garden'.

An aerial view of the castle. The gardens are out of sight to the right and left of the photograph.

A parade of carriage horses. The stable yard at Lowther.

A parade of cars outside Lowther Castle, 1910. These cars, which all belonged to Hugh, were all painted in the same bright yellow. Here they are led by the Mercedes with Hugh standing by the driving seat.

for the Prince and any of the guests who wanted to play. When he saw the arrangements Prince Edward turned to his host and remarked that he had always understood that Hugh had forbidden gambling at Lowther.

'That is quite true, Sir,' Hugh replied, 'but as your flag now flies over my castle, it is for you to decide whether or not you wish to play.'

The Prince at once ordered the table to be removed and no cards were played during his visit.

If Hugh was jealous of the Prince's friendship with his brother, the Prince equally did not favour Hugh's friendship with the German Emperor.

It was well known that Prince Edward and Wilhelm did not get on at all well together. He resented the close affection which his mother had for her great nephew. The Queen never ceased to regard the Kaiser as a member of her family first and as the head of a rival State second. If German foreign policy appeared to be inimical to British interests, Wilhelm could look forward to a stiff letter from his grandmother and there is no doubt that she exerted a considerable influence over him. Edward had never been close to his mother and felt, with some justice, that she was excluding him from the affairs of State. He resented, too, that she was excluding him from the affairs of State. He resented, too, the dull, heavy Germanic upbringing to which he had been subjected—to the extent that the whole of his life was a revolt against it. Hugh, having no such inhibitions, found Wilhelm a most congenial companion.

Surprisingly, coming from such different backgrounds, the two men had a great deal in common. Both had a passion for detail and a flair for showmanship; both loved ceremonial and uniforms, and both were impetuous with an underlying shrewdness which gave them a similar outlook on life. They even shared the same birth date. They had met in their 'teens and their friendship and respect for one another survived the Great War and the Kaiser's exile at Doorn.

Chapter 13

It is likely that but for the Kaiser's love of sailing Hugh would have given up St. George's yachts. It would no doubt have saved the Trustees a number of headaches. As it was, his interest was limited to attending regattas in Germany as the guest of the Emperor and cutting a dash at Cowes during the fashionable week there immediately after Goodwood.

It was during the second half of the nineteenth century that Cowes started to establish its reputation as the fashionable yachting centre of the world. During Cowes week it was the centre of all social activity. The London Season was over and the rich and famous came to Cowes to relax. Lady Cardigan could be seen being rowed after dinner in her 'gig' playing her guitar and singing. Admiral Beauchamp, nicknamed 'The Swell of the Ocean' because of his vast girth, ruled at the exclusive Royal Yacht Squadron Club which nearly lost its Royal prefix when they threatened to blackball the Prince of Wales's friend Sir Thomas Lipton because he was a grocer. Another of the Prince's intimates, Sir Allen Young, used to bring down all the reigning lovelies to his yacht the *Pandora*, which had the deck covered in to prevent the curious getting too close a glimpse of his attractive 'cargo'.

'Alleno', as he was known to his friends, was an extraordinary character and the Prince's most constant companion. The son of a rich City merchant, he had run away to sea as a boy and served for many years before the mast. He could never sleep in a house with the front door shut. Much to the anguish of the police he insisted on keeping the door of his London house in Berkeley Square wide open night and day.

In the eighteen eighties no Cowes week was complete without a visit from the Kaiser in his magnificent yacht the *Hohenzollern*. It was an occasion for entertaining on the grandest possible scale, each great yacht striving to outdo the other in the magnificence of her hospitality. It was a ready-made opportunity for Hugh to glitter at his brightest.

His first appearance in his yacht the *Verena*, however, was not marked with scenes of great enthusiasm, particularly by the Royal Yacht Squadron, who regarded him as something of a *parvenu*. It was indeed rumoured that if he were to put up for membership he would be blackballed.

Hugh was not prepared to leave the issue in doubt. Learning that the Club was not allowed by its charter to blackball British Admirals he arrived off Cowes flying an Admiral's burgee from the masthead. When his right to it was questioned he replied that as Vice-Admiral of the Cumberland Coast, an honorary rank granted by the Monarch, he had a perfect right to fly the flag. At this show of strength all opposition to his candidature collapsed.

Although he continued to use this title all his life, it would have given his detractors great joy to have known that he had no right to it whatsoever! The title was not in fact an hereditary one, but re-granted by the Monarch on the death of the holder. On the death of St. George, Queen Victoria had reallocated the honour to Hugh's neighbour in Westmorland, Lord Hothfield of Appleby Castle! Hugh, however, was not at all the sort of man to be put off with a small point of detail like that.

The visit of the Kaiser to Cowes in 1895 was to be particularly important for Hugh. Not only that year did his yacht win the Kaiser's Cup, but Wilhelm had agreed to travel north afterwards for a private visit to Lowther.

The announcement of the Kaiser's acceptance of a private invitation from an English nobleman, and the rakish Lord Lonsdale at that, caused a considerable flutter, not least in Berlin, where the Kaiser's friendship with Lonsdale was not viewed in official circles as altogether 'a good thing'. In England the papers referred sneeringly to Lonsdale as 'William's English pal'. Unmoved, Hugh set about making arrangements for the visit with his usual thoroughness and disregard for financial considerations.

That year the entertaining aboard the *Verena* was on a more lavish scale than ever. When the Kaiser came to dinner Hugh had the whole of the deck of his schooner roofed in to form a ballroom for the evening. As the party progressed the *Verena* became literally surrounded by other boats at the regatta, who crowded round to try to catch sight of the Kaiser or the Prince of Wales, whilst at the same time benefiting from the music from the Lonsdale private orchestra to run improvised dances on their own decks. When in the small hours the Royal party decided to leave, they had the utmost difficulty in making a way through the congestion.

The hospitality which awaited the Kaiser at Lowther, however, was to make the lavish feasting aboard the *Verena* seem little more than an alfresco picnic.

For months before the actual date of the visit Westmorland and Cumberland had been in a state of turmoil. The police forces of the two counties had been combed in an effort to ensure that all the best looking and most athletic members of the force were temporarily drafted to Penrith for route lining and crowd control duties. The hunt servants of the Quorn, in full hunting kit, were sent up to Lowther to ride behind the Kaiser's carriage, and the whole of the Cumberland and Westmorland Yeomanry devoted months to ceremonial drilling and kit polishing in the hope of being one of the two hundred to be selected for the honour of acting as Lord Lonsdale's household cavalry for the duration of the visit. An enthusiastic gossip writer of the time remarked, 'Lord Lonsdale is in very truth a prince in his own country.' It was no exaggeration.

The sight that greeted the Kaiser and his retinue as their special train drew in to Penrith can scarcely have been less in grandeur than that of a full-dress State occasion.

Since early the previous day dalesmen and fell farmers had been arriving in the town on foot or by fell pony. The hotels were packed, with guests camping in the corridors, while many thousands got what sleep they could on the pavements outside. At about eight o'clock in the morning the hunting horns of the Quorn huntsmen heralded the approach of the cavalcade from Lowther Castle on its way to meet the Royal train. A wave of applause greeted the procession of landaus, phaetons, shooting wagonettes and even omnibuses and brakes as they passed through the town. On their return, with the Kaiser seated in a dark-blue open phaeton opposite to Lord Lonsdale, the enthusiasm knew no bounds. Every window, roof top and chimney-stack in view of the route held its quota of citizens wildly waving flags bearing the insignia of the Imperial Eagle, and the mounted police fought a losing battle with the crowds which threatened to block the route to the castle gates.

Hugh Lonsdale, in an expansive mood, had once boasted to the Kaiser that on his estates at Lowther he had more 'subjects' than the

King of Wurtemburg in Germany. The remark had not pleased His Majesty at the time, but here was the evidence.

As the visit had started, so it went on. Dissatisfied with the reports of the grouse on his own moors at Shap, Lonsdale had rented the Earl of Strathmore's famous Yorkshire moor Wemmergill for the opening day of the grouse shooting. In four drives there they shot over five hundred brace. At Lowther as an afternoon entertainment he had arranged for many hundreds of wild rabbits to be collected, as he knew that the Kaiser, who had a crippled arm, liked his shooting made easy for him.

After luncheon Hugh casually suggested to his Royal guest that he might like to take a stroll with a gun for half an hour or so. Carefully steering him in the direction of a fir wood he remarked innocently that it might be amusing to see if they could beat a rabbit or two out of it, and, putting his guest in position, he signalled to his keeper to send his dog into the trees. It was also the secret signal for a dozen under-keepers to release the rabbits. Suddenly the peace of the afternoon was shattered as the Kaiser started to blast off in every direction. Rabbits in their hundreds cascaded towards him, almost running between his legs as they raced for the safety of their burrows at the bottom of the hill.

In one hectic half-hour his bag was sixty-seven rabbits.

'There is always an odd rabbit or two in that wood,' remarked Hugh airily when it was all over.

The most elaborate arrangements had been made to ensure that the Kaiser and his staff* should be able to keep in closest communication with Berlin. A private telegraph office was opened in the Castle (which Hugh kept on for many years afterwards for his own personal needs) and a constant stream of couriers plied to and fro between the castle and the German Embassy in London.

The Kaiser was normally something more than a martinet when it came to dealing with his staff, and insisted on seeing every piece of paper personally. At Lowther, however, he had one of his rare

---

* Apart from the aides, secretaries and other functionaries, the house party for the Kaiser's visit consisted of: His Excellency Count Eulenburg, H.E. Lieutenant-General von Plessesn, H.E. Count Metternich, Major-General von Lippe, Professor Dr. Leuthold, Rear-Admiral Baron von Senden, Colonel von Arne, Major von Jacobi and Captain von Chelens, and Her Excellency Frau Wedel, the Dowager Lady Churchill, Major-General Sir Francis Grenfell, Lord and Lady Churchill, Lieutenant-General Marshall, the Hon. Lancelot and Mrs. Lowther, Mr. Henry Wickham and Lady Ethel Wickham, the Marquis of Worcester, Lord and Lady Chesham.

periods of relaxation, even permitting himself the occasional ponderous Teutonic joke. Out riding one morning, Count Eulenburg, who was far from being a great horseman, was allotted a rather spirited mount from which he very soon parted company, falling heavily on his head. The following morning, Grace's sister, Lady Ethel Wickham, was mounted on the same horse, which she managed with the utmost ease and grace. Turning to an aide he remarked, 'Tell Count Eulenburg that I am thinking of introducing a new uniform for my staff officers—a riding-habit.'

Half-way through the visit a large packing-case arrived at the castle, which, on the Kaiser's orders, was rather awkwardly concealed behind a potted palm in the saloon. As the Kaiser obviously intended to keep the matter of the packing-case a deadly secret, everyone studiously ignored its existence.

Each evening after dinner Hugh's orchestra played the same musical programme. It consisted of 'Die Wacht am Rhein', 'Verena' (a tune composed to celebrate the victory of the Lonsdale yacht in winning the Kaiser's Cup), 'Son of Aegir' (the Kaiser's own favourite tune), and 'Ever Welcome', a tune specially composed by Hugh's Master of Music, Mr. Hamilton, to commemorate the visit.

On the final evening of the visit, just before the German National Anthem was played, an imperious signal from the Emperor silenced the orchestra. To the accompaniment of polite gasps of feigned surprise, two aides dragged out the wooden packing-case from its hiding-place, and, bursting it open, displayed a marble bust of the Emperor himself.

'I can think of no better way of showing my regard for you personally, and my appreciation of the hospitality you have shown me, than by asking you to accept this gift as a token of our great friendship,' said the Kaiser, as his aides staggered forward to place the bust in the middle of the room. It was a certain sign of the Kaiser's highest approbation. Hugh's delight in receiving the gift was as great as the Kaiser's delight in giving it. Occasions like these were likely to move Hugh to tears.

Before the Kaiser returned to Germany, he asked the Queen if he might appoint Hugh Lonsdale to an honorary position on his staff. The Queen agreed gladly, taking it as a personal compliment to herself. Thus at the end of August 1895 Hugh Lonsdale travelled to Berlin to attend the Emperor.

*

The honorary post to which the Kaiser appointed Hugh Lonsdale was the near equivalent to Master of the Horse at the English Court. The Kaiser had the very highest regard for his knowledge of everything to do with horses, and consulted him regularly on the purchase and equipment of horses for the German cavalry regiments. He also insisted on his presence at the annual German Army manoeuvres, and even invited his opinion on the suitability of the ground selected for set-piece cavalry charges and other details more usually left to the General Staff. On the final spectacular charge which ended the manoeuvres, and which was led by the Kaiser himself, Hugh Lonsdale rode at his side as an additional A.D.C.

A measure of the Kaiser's friendship for Lord Lonsdale may be judged by a Reuter's dispatch of the 2nd September 1895.

Berlin, Sunday. The city is crowded with people, the influx of foreigners and country residents being enormous. All the principal streets are gaily decorated. The Emperor drove to the castle this afternoon in the company of Lord Lonsdale to whom the greatest attention is being shown. The Emperor has deputed a personal valet and page to wait on his visitor at the Bristol Hotel, and a Court carriage is placed at his disposal. Tonight Lord Lonsdale dined with the Emperor, tomorrow he drives to the great Temple of Parade in His Majesty's own carriage, and in the evening will witness the festival performance at the Royal Opera House from the Royal box.

Lonsdale's popularity with the Emperor made him correspondingly unpopular with the Emperor's advisers, and particularly with the powerful Army clique. Bismarck, however, was astute enough to realize that Lonsdale's real influence in military matters, when it came to the point, was insignificant, but that he might soon have a usefulness in quite a different sphere. He was to be proved right much sooner than he could have imagined.

Before leaving Germany in September 1895, Lonsdale gave an interview to the *Berliner Tageblatt*, which was reprinted in responsible papers all over the world. The statement started with his impressions of the recently completed German manoeuvres. He was quoted as saying:

No army in the world possesses more competent generals, and with them at its head the German Army appears to me to be invincible. Every officer and man was in the right place and each did his utmost to master his task by energy and perseverance. It is impossible to improve on this system.

Only when discussing the German cavalry did a note of criticism creep in.

As regards the cavalry, I think it is as good as other nations, but not better than the English. The training of the men is excellent, the horses splendid, but the cavalry has nonetheless not reached the standard of perfection of the infantry. Their horses are better than the English, for the reason that they are mostly three-year-olds. The cavalry horses are not heavy enough in proportion to the guns. During the march past I noticed that some of them were so 'pumped out' that they could scarcely get along.

But it was for the Kaiser himself that he reserved his unrestricted praise.

The Emperor is an extraordinary man in every respect, and, many as my own friends are—some of them great and notable men—I cannot compare any of them with him. ... His perceptive faculties, his energy, his grasp of everything that awakes his interest, but above all, his foresight, are simply incomparable, and he possesses all these qualities in a degree only met with in geniuses. ...
He is just as excellent a naval expert as he is closely connected with all the details of colonial questions. It is incomprehensible.

Only in the last line of the eulogy can he find any fault with his friend, and this probably because it was being freely said that the Emperor's youth and inexperience often made him act hastily and unwisely. 'If he has a fault,' he remarked straight-faced to the assiduous *Tageblatt* reporter, 'it is his youth, *but in this respect he is improving every day.*'
This unstinted and widely publicized praise for the head of a foreign power, whose intentions were in some quarters regarded with suspicion, was not calculated to make Lonsdale popular with all sections of his own countrymen. On the whole, however, his championship of the Emperor was quite well received by a nation whose thoughts were far from war. As *The Times* commented, 'Strike out half of what Lord Lonsdale says of the Emperor's actions, and still all that he says of the Emperor's talents is deserved. Kaiser Wilhelm is certainly an extraordinary man.'
Within a year, however, the nation was to think very differently of the Kaiser and of the German people, and Lord Lonsdale in his self-appointed role as Public Relations Officer to the Emperor was to

have to stand by the loyalty of his friendship in a very different climate of opinion.

The crisis came when he was attending the German Army man-oeuvres the following year. For some time the British element in South Africa had been at loggerheads with Kruger. Matters came to a head with the famous Jameson Raid.

There can be no doubt, in considering the Raid at this distance of time, that the action of Dr. Jameson and his associates was ill-advised as well as illegal. It was in fact nothing more than an attempt to use force of arms to further private ends—however advantageous those private ends might have been to the British Empire as a whole, it was still a piratical act and not condoned (not openly at least) by the British Government.

Back in England, however, the whole exploit took on the overtones of a great and brave venture, instigated by patriots and worthy of the highest praise. It was a perfect wicket for the jingoists at a time when jingoism was an eminently respectable creed.

As the first shots of the Jameson Raid were fired, Kruger, fearing that the trouble would get out of hand, appealed to the German Emperor for assistance. This was categorically refused, but a wave of anti-British feeling swept Germany when details of Dr. Jameson's action became known.

When news came through that Kruger had defeated Jameson and his band, the Kaiser, reflecting the feelings of his people, sent a telegram of congratulations to the Boer leader which read: 'I sincerely congratulate you that you and your people have succeeded by your own energetic action and without the aid of a foreign power* in restoring order against the armed bands that broke into your country as disturbers of the peace, and in safeguarding the independence of your Government from attacks from without.'

In England this was all that was needed to spark off a wave of anti-German feeling which was principally directed against the Kaiser himself. Queen Victoria wrote one of her characteristic sharp notes and diplomatic tension was stretched almost to breaking point.

In the middle of all this Hugh Lonsdale returned to England from Potsdam to be assailed on all sides about his friendship with the suddenly vastly unpopular Emperor. At first he was inclined to treat the whole matter as of minor importance. 'What if I am friendly with

---

* The original message as drafted by the Kaiser read 'and without the aid you asked for'. It was Bismarck who altered it to 'without the aid of a foreign power'.

the Kaiser?' he would remark with a twinkle in his eye. 'I am also friendly with his uncle the Prince of Wales and nobody seems to think anything of that!'

Soon, however, the whole affair became too serious to be brushed aside with a joke. Hugh decided to make his views clear in a public statement. The opportunity occurred soon after his return, when the Corporation of Whitehaven invited him to address a testimonial dinner given in his honour.

His speech was nothing if not courageous. It was childish, he said, that anyone should imagine that the Kaiser had unfriendly intentions towards this country. Had he not been with the Kaiser when the much criticized telegram had been sent, and had he not heard from the Emperor's own lips of his regard and affection for this country? As for Cecil Rhodes, his Chartered Company and the Jameson Raid, there were no words too strong to express his condemnation of their action. They were playing with the lives of our countrymen to achieve their own ends and increase their financial gains.

Carried away by his oratory the loyal Burghers of Whitehaven cheered him to the echo as his speech swept to its climax.

'When I returned from Germany,' he cried, 'there was not a paper that existed, not a man you met, but said, "What gallant fellows Jameson and Rhodes were. They should have the Victoria Cross." I say that they should have six months' imprisonment and twelve strokes of the cat!'

Next morning the fat was really in the fire. Lowther was besieged by Press reporters, bombarded by cables from all over the world, and inundated by sackfulls of letters, most of them accusing Lonsdale of the most arrant disloyalty and lack of patriotism.

Most of the leading English and German papers devoted leading articles to the speech. German papers, like the *National Zeitung* described it as disgraceful that an English nobleman should appear in the role of spokesman and apologist for the German Emperor. Others objected to a statement in the speech claiming that there was a bond of friendship between England and Germany. 'There can never again be friendship between our two countries,' one German paper stated baldly.

The English newspapers surprisingly were less critical. It was a tribute to Hugh Lonsdale's growing popularity and, perhaps, to a sneaking feeling that he was right.

Only the sabre-rattling armchair brigade in the Pall Mall and St. James's Street clubs were unreservedly censorious.

'Why doesn't Lonsdale stick to his hunting or whatever else it is he is so good at, instead of sticking his nose into things he doesn't understand?' was the general and often expressed view of the die-hard reactionaries.

Unpopular though Hugh may have been in certain quarters, there is no doubt that, in the public esteem, he already stood head and shoulders above most of his contemporaries. The British have always had a capacity for creating heroes in their own image and worshipping them with a peculiarly British dedication. Hugh had all the ingredients of a national idol and his extrovert nature enjoyed every moment of the enthusiasm and excitement caused by his appearance in public.

Even the papers who had made headlines of the real or imagined scandals connected with his name and tagged him as notorious were relenting. 'The Sporting Earl' or 'our foremost sporting Peer' was becoming a more frequent description. To the public, and particularly to his own people in the hunting country and in the North, he was becoming affectionately known as 'The Yellow Man', 'The Yellow Earl', or simply as 'Lordy'.

Part II

The Edwardian

Chapter 14

Hugh was forty-two years old when, in 1899, the grumbling peace in South Africa flared into war. As soon as he heard the news Hugh rushed round to the War Office to offer his services. A few hours later he was on his way to Lowther to raise a volunteer force for immediate service overseas. While others made speeches, shouted slogans and sang patriotic songs, Hugh turned all his attention to doing something practical.

Shortly before the outbreak of war he had been appointed to the command of the Cumberland and Westmorland Yeomanry. In time of peace this could not be regarded as more than a social commitment and, in fact, his first act had been to redesign their dress uniforms to make them the most colourful in the whole British Army.

Now there was more serious business on hand. There was a strong rumour that Hugh would be appointed to command a composite cavalry force raised from picked volunteers from all the Yeomanry regiments. Even in time of war Yeomanry regiments could not be ordered abroad. Only volunteers could be sent and then only if sufficient funds had been raised locally for their equipment.

In England war was still not far removed from the days when the King relied on his Barons for the support of their own private armies.

Hugh at once set himself at the head of the band of volunteers for active service, and poured money and energy into creating one of the best equipped volunteer forces in the country. Certainly none had a finer, more sparkling turn-out than the regiment which soon became known as 'Lordy's Own'.

Whatever visions Hugh may have had, however, of galloping against the enemy at the head of his loyal Bordermen they were soon dispelled by the War Office. To meet the emergency they announced that a mounted force would be raised from the Yeomanry, to be selected for their marksmanship and good riding but they were to be put under the supreme command of Hugh's friend, Lord Chesham. Lord Lonsdale was to be quarter-master general in London, charged with the complete equipping of the force.

Perhaps it was as well. Hugh's military maxim 'When in doubt, gallop!' might not have proved the most successful tactics against the wily Boer farmers.

As it was he threw his whole energy into his new role. Night after night he sat late in his office in St. James's inspecting every item of equipment, testing every piece of harness which was to be ordered.

In the first month he was asked to produce 1,700 horses. The order was given at the beginning of December 1899. By Christmas he had 1,200 horses ready for shipment. It was a mammoth achievement when one considers that scarcely a horse was bought that he had not personally inspected. Having scraped the bottom of the barrel in England, he turned his attention abroad, seeking tenders from all over the world. Eventually he persuaded dealers in Austria to provide first-grade animals at a price of £50 each, delivered to the Cape—a far cheaper rate than home-bred horses. By 2nd January the following year the quota was complete. They were the highest standard of horses to be shipped to South Africa during the whole campaign.

Ever since Hugh's appointment, however, there had been other forces at work. As one of the greatest experts in the country, his appointment by the Government would at first sight have appeared to have been an inspired one, but it had not taken into consideration Hugh's forthright methods or the susceptibilities of some of the more senior Regular officers in the Remount Depot.

Hugh thundered up and down the country, bludgeoning Masters of Foxhounds and other notabilities into parting with quality animals at patriotic prices.

On the day he reported completion of the order for 1,700 remounts, his deputy received a telegram which stated baldly: 'In future, take your orders not from Lord Lonsdale but from me.' It was signed by Colonel St. Quentin, Director-General of Remounts, Imperial Yeomanry.

Furiously Hugh appealed to Lord Chesham but, apart from agreeing it was altogether a grubby way of going about things, his friend was powerless to intervene. The decision had come from far higher up in the succession of armchair soldiers running one of the worst conducted campaigns in our military history.

From the time of Hugh's removal from office at the beginning of 1900 the cost of horses sent to South Africa increased by leaps and bounds whilst the quality deteriorated to an alarming degree.

It was not, however, until after it was all over that the storm really broke. Then Lord Tweedmouth, speaking in the House of Lords, launched a detailed attack on St. Quentin. Speaking of an Austrian contract for 3,800 horses, he declared: 'The horses for which Colonel St. Quentin paid £29-odd in Austria were animals of an altogether inferior type, sadly wanting in stamina in the field. The charge against the Government on this particular point is that these horses cost the taxpayer £111,000, of which certainly not less than £45,000 went into the pockets of four gentlemen who made an altogether undue profit.'

As similar stories flooded in from all parts of the country, a full-scale Government inquiry was ordered. Even supposedly patriotic M.F.H.'s were found to be open to charges of self-interest. Lord Rosebery quoted a case from his own experience whereby 'four screws of the value of £5 apiece, equalling £20, were allowed to be taken over by the officer sent by the Government to buy them at the prices of three for £80 and one for £100, a profit of £320 going out of the pocket of the taxpayer and into the pocket of the M.F.H.'

As is the fate of so many Government inquiries, the findings were obscure and indeterminate, but at least the airing must have given Hugh some personal satisfaction. He emerged from the controversy with greatly enhanced prestige. *The Rambler* declared:

If the matter were not so serious, it might evoke a smile when we hear of all the frauds, follies and wicked waste of public money which ensued from the fact that Lord Lonsdale, one of the best judges of a horse in the world, a man in the prime of life, possessed of great wealth and great ability, willing to give his services gratuitously to his country, was passed over in favour of a respectable but dull old man without knowledge or gumption.

It was a sentiment echoed with slightly less vigour by most of the Press.

In spite of the tensions which existed between England and Germany, both before and during the South African war, Hugh's open expressions of regard for the Kaiser never varied. The Kaiser, he insisted, had the most peaceable intentions towards England and the very highest regard for Englishmen. If there was ill will between the two countries, it was fostered by war-like politicians. Statements of this sort, which he took every possible opportunity of making, did not endear him to the British Government and still less to the German High Command, who were constantly at pains to persuade the German people that their real enemies lay over the English Channel.

In Prince von Bülow, who became Secretary of State at the Foreign Office of Germany in 1897, and later succeeded Prince Hohenlohe as Chancellor, Hugh found a bitter opponent.

Von Bülow during his critical years of power carried the Kaiser along with him in his policy of 'Welt-Politik'. The main plank in his programme was to make Germany strong at sea by building up the German Fleet—a policy which was a direct challenge to Great Britain and one which led to an increasing estrangement between the two countries. Worse, it was a policy which was eventually to isolate Germany, not only from Britain but from almost the whole of Europe as well, and which reached its climax with the outbreak of the First World War.

Because Britain's opposition to his programme of naval expansion was inevitable, von Bülow not only accepted it as a calculated risk but encouraged the German people to regard the British as traditional enemies whose command of the seas represented a deliberate threat to the Fatherland. To achieve this, he put into action a programme of propaganda as intensive as anything Dr. Goebbels was to instigate thirty years later.

It was into these deep political waters that Hugh Lonsdale splashed with all the enthusiasm of a Labrador puppy. Each carefully contrived slight to the British people which von Bülow managed to get the Emperor to throw into the pool, Hugh did his well-meaning best to retrieve. There was no pronouncement of the Emperor's which might in any way alienate the feeling of the British public that Hugh did not cheerfully brush aside or explain away whenever the opportunity offered.

It was bad enough for von Bülow to have Lord Lonsdale's beaming presence alongside the Emperor at the annual Army manoeuvres where his colourful uniform and princely turn-out stole even the Emperor's thunder, but when, in 1901, with the Boer War still undecided, he was appointed yachting representative to the Kaiser in Britain, his antagonism to the now immensely popular sporting Earl knew no bounds. Worse, when in June 1901 Wilhelm decided to replace his famous yacht, the *Meteor*, the show-piece of Germany's naval prestige, he sent Admiral von Eisendecker to England to consult with Hugh at Carlton House Terrace. In a blaze of publicity Hugh rushed the Admiral up to a Glasgow shipyard where the keel for the new yacht was laid! It was a serious smack in the eye for the German boat-builders.

Later in the year, with the German attitude to the Boer War still a nasty taste in the mouths of the British public, the Kaiser sent the Crown Prince to Cowes and afterwards to stay at Lowther with Hugh.

Hugh's omnipotence in the matter of these Royal visits may be judged from one incident concerning the Crown Prince's visit.

As the elaborate machinery for the Prince's reception at Penrith was getting under way, Hugh received a telegram from a station master further up the line proudly announcing that the Royal train was due to pass through his station ten minutes ahead of time. The message spelt disaster to the programme of split-second timing by which the cavalcade of yellow carriages was due to sweep into the station yard just as the Royal train drew into the platform.

Succinctly he wired back, 'Shunt him.'

The Crown Prince arrived dead on time.

In 1902 the Emperor himself paid a second visit to Lowther. The soldiers were just returning to a hero's welcome from the Boer War and the Kaiser was not a popular figure. True, his refusal to receive Kruger when he went to Germany in 1900 had regained for him some of the popularity he had lost in Britain, but he was still regarded with suspicion.

Hugh's stage-management turned the visit into a triumphant success, which was reflected in a rise in the popularity of the Kaiser throughout the country. During the visit the Press rose to new heights of enthusiasm so that excuses were sought even for the indifferent weather which attended the visit. 'The sun did its best,' one paper declared loyally, 'but the gathering of the clouds proved somewhat of an obstacle to the dissemination of its rays.' Even the staid *Yorkshire Post*, in describing a shooting party at Lowther, rose to giddy heights of descriptive journalism. 'The beaters started a fine lot of birds . . . with flying hares as well as fowl on the wing . . .' they declared admiringly, whilst even the humble rabbits were flattered with the description of 'furry scamperers'.

The success of the visit must have made von Bülow hop around with annoyance.

Before he died the Chancellor wrote a gossipy book of reminiscences in which he vented his long pent-up spleen against the man who had unconsciously played such havoc with his anti-British propaganda. 'Not only was this ridiculous Earl, who had bleeding hearts and Cupid arrows tattooed all over his body, a bankrupt, but he did not enjoy the confidence of Edward VII who openly described him as the greatest liar in his kingdom.'

The German publishers were warned that publication in this country might result in a successful action for heavy damages. Lord Lonsdale was cautiously approached. He read the offending passages with great attention. The only part to which he took exception was the reference to bleeding hearts and Cupid arrows. 'I'm tattooed all over,' he protested, 'but I can prove to whoever is interested that I do not have a single heart or arrow on my body!'

In the end he allowed the publishers to print the attack on him in full. 'The statements are so obviously completely untrue that they can only serve to amuse people,' he remarked.

On the whole it was definitely one up to Hugh.

Chapter 15

Hugh's capacity for spending money remained in full flood, but the general pattern of his life was beginning to emerge in more solid form.

He spent the social season with Grace in London. In July after Goodwood he would go to Lowther for the grouse shooting before taking up residence at Barleythorpe for hunting.

If anywhere was the centre of his existence it was Barleythorpe and certainly hunting formed the main interest in his life. The grandeur of Lowther was very convenient when there were Emperors to be entertained but it was in the hunting country of Leicestershire and Rutland that his heart really lay.

His knowledge of hunting and his prowess in the hunting-field could never be called into question. He has been described as the finest heavyweight rider of his day. It was probably true. More extravagantly he has been described as the greatest huntsman of all time, and even this may not be far short of the truth.

Asked once what was the secret of his quite remarkable control of a horse in the hunting-field, he replied that quite truthfully he had no idea. 'It is really a matter of understanding your horse,' he would say. Since his earliest days 'understanding your horse' had been instinctive. Because they had been brought up with horses all the Lowther boys were fine horsemen, but only Hugh had that instinct which made him outstanding in the golden age of fox-hunting.

He rode rather longer than is the custom today with a seat which he described as 'like a clothes peg on a washing line'. Because his leg muscles were immensely strong—he used to claim that he could break a horse's ribs with the strength of his grip—he could practically 'lift' a horse over a difficult jump. If he fell it was because his horse fell which meant that his infrequent falls were serious ones because he never parted company with his horse.

Several of his feats on horseback were astonishing. On occasions he would demonstrate the exact control he had over his mount by placing two plates on the ground on the blind side of a jump. He would then put his horse over in such a way that its two *hind* feet landed exactly in the middle of the plates. It was not trick riding but the result of a precise knowledge of his horse.

Once when out hunting with the Quorn he was taking a line of country he had not followed for some time. Putting his horse at a post-and-rail fence with a shallow ditch at the other side, he was not aware until he was too far committed that another fence, topped with a strand of wire, had been erected a yard on the far side of the ditch. Collecting his horse he cleared the entire obstacle. When it was measured afterwards, the length of the jump was found to be thirty-two feet.

After Hugh's precipitate withdrawal from the Mastership of the Woodland Pytchley in 1884, he virtually gave up hunting altogether for a couple of years. As his finances started to mend, however, he found himself devoting more and more time to it, hunting perhaps three or four days a week with friends all over the country. It was not, however, until the early eighteen nineties that he again thought about taking on a Mastership. It was his ambition to take over the Cottesmore, which from the very earliest days of foxhunting had been the family pack of the Lowthers, and which had been hunted both by his father and his elder brother St. George until he sold them. It was now a subscription pack.

The whole picture of foxhunting had, however, undergone a tremendous change from the days when packs had been the privately owned property of a Master, who kept them as an entertainment for himself and his friends. In those days hunts ranged over vast areas of country, and foxes were few and far between. The famous Mr. Farquharson, who hunted at the turn of the eighteen hundreds, hunted the whole of Dorset with parts of Somerset and Wiltshire thrown in—a country now covered by half a dozen packs. The Beaufort hunted as far afield as Oxford and the Berkeley were known to start a fox where Charing Cross now stands!

With the flood of new industrial wealth and the consequent increase in the number of rich young men looking for excitement and an opportunity to display both their wealth and their courage, foxhunting rapidly developed into the most fashionable of fashionable sports. Foxhunting was no longer a matter of relentless pursuit of the fox. A vast increase in the amount of cultivated land completely altered the scene. There were many more foxes to kill and more country where young bloods could gallop furiously over fences. Soon it became a matter of the greatest social importance to be seen out mounted on the finest bloodstock, and to earn the reputation of being a bold rider to hounds became the highest ambition of a young man who wanted to be thought a good fellow.

Of all the fashionable hunts which came into prominence about this time the Quorn was the most fashionable. In the words of Captain Lionel Dawson, for over the last fifty years one of the great authorities on hunting in this country, 'The doings of the Quorn were, in hunting circles, comparable to the fate of the Government to the general public.' On the other side of the coin a contemporary writer described the Quorn field as 'the most unruly regiment of cavalry in existence'.

Hugh's great ambition to be Master of the Cottesmore was not to be easily satisfied. Mr. Baird (not to be confused with Squire Abingdon), to whom he had rented stables and kennels at Barleythorpe, and who had hunted them since 1880, showed no inclination to give them up, however strong the family claims of a Lowther might be. Hugh even resorted to a most un-Hugh-like strategy of threatening not to renew the lease of Barleythorpe unless Baird surrendered the hounds. Baird retaliated by making arrangements to build his stables and kennels elsewhere, and Hugh gracefully capitulated.

In February 1893 *The Country Gentleman*, discussing the affairs of the Quorn, where the joint-Mastership of Captain Warner and Mr. Paget was coming to an end, confided to its readers: 'It is an open secret that there is in our midst the ideal man, a good sportsman, a fine horseman, of a personal popularity with all classes—the farmers especially—to give foxhunting a new lease of life. It is to our very great gain if he *does* see his way to coming to our help.'

At a General Meeting in the first week of April 1893 under the chairmanship of Lord Belper, Hugh was quietly elected to the vacant Mastership. In the light of subsequent events it appears likely that Lord Belper expected strong opposition to the nomination, for the meeting was not advertised and only twenty-nine people were present out of the many hundreds entitled to attend. Certainly when the hunting season reopened, members were not left long in doubt that the new broom had every intention of sweeping exceeding clean.

As *The Country Gentleman* was to remark '. . . we allowed it to be known that we required a Master of the Quorn, and, by the Lord, we've got one.'

Only the Trustees must have groaned at the news.

Hugh's idea of foxhunting was very different from the ideas of the fashionable young tearaways who flocked to the Quorn meets. He was every inch a countryman. His first consideration out hunting was for the farmers and his second to kill foxes. Neither was held in much account by the supporters of the Quorn, out for a good gallop, who regarded themselves as monarchs of all they surveyed. If they killed a fox—any fox—at the end of it, so much the better.

Hugh could not have had stronger support for his ideas than he had in his huntsman, the great Tom Firr, who had been with the Quorn since 1872.* It was truly a case of the iron fist in an iron glove.

Soon Hugh's 'tick-offs' in the hunting-field were being repeated with glee wherever foxhunting was discussed. 'You shouldn't hunt, sir. Paper-chasing is your line. You'd make a damned good hare,' he would roar at a particularly obnoxious thruster. He was no respecter of persons. When a well-known peer had twice disregarded Hugh's injunction to 'hold hard', Hugh turned to Firr and ordered him to take the hounds home. 'You can do what you like. I'm going home myself,' retorted the disgruntled Lord. 'In that case the rest of us can continue,' replied Hugh amiably.

By the end of the season the Quorn was one of the best disciplined fields in the country. With an air of amazement *The Field* correspondent observed: 'Men and women obey Lord Lonsdale as well as trained wolves obey their instructor, going on only at the word of command.'

Because it was Hugh Lonsdale, it was inevitable that Mastership of the Quorn was inextricably bound up with a sharp rise in his personal expenditure. The revenue from the subscriptions at the outset of his Mastership had been £3,000, but this sum only represented a fraction of what Hugh himself spent. No hunt servants in the country were better turned out, and no detail too small to warrant his personal supervision. Everything was thought of. A critic described his men as 'hung all over with battle-axes, whistles and knives', but everything had a use and woe-betide the most junior member of the establishment who dared to turn out without every

* Tom Firr did not retire until after a bad fall in 1898. It was Hugh Lonsdale's luck to have Firr as huntsman. He has been described as having no equal in England.

item of equipment which it had been decided he should carry. Every second horseman was equipped with a first-aid box containing everything from bandages to needles ready-threaded with surgical gut, and had to have reached a standard of veterinary proficiency sufficient to enable him to give instant treatment to any horse injured in the field. The expense was met largely out of Hugh's pocket. Poor Jim Lowther could protest as he liked. Hugh had got the financial bit between his teeth once more and there was no holding him.

Estimates were cast aside and remonstrances ignored as Hugh poured money into better and better bloodstock, new strains of hounds and more glorious and colourful liveries for the hunt servants. Nothing and nobody could keep pace with his prodigal expenditure.

Under Hugh's Mastership the Quorn became the show Hunt. Huge crowds would gather at the opening meet just to watch and cheer as his yellow carriages pulled up with the utmost dash and flourish. Tom Firr and the Whips were fitted out with immaculate, white leather* breeches and dark-red coats with Lowther buttons— and, of course, they were all mounted on long-tailed, hog-maned thoroughbred chestnut horses.

In vain Hugh's agents reported that the once rich seams of iron ore in his Hodbarrow mines were becoming worked out. In vain Jim Lowther pleaded with him to call a halt for breathing space to allow some of his income to be ploughed back for redevelopment.

Grace, unable to hunt regularly, would watch Hugh's gaily caparisoned army starting off each day and wonder.

Colin Ellis in his book *Leicestershire and the Quorn Hunt* gives another view of Hugh as Master of the Quorn which is well worth quoting in full.

The Duke of Portland had refused the mastership of the Quorn because . . . he had resolved never to put himself at the head of a subscription pack. If Lord Lonsdale had been a prudent man he would have made the same resolution—but if he had been a prudent man, he would not have been Hugh Lowther, and he and the Quorn Hunt would have been the poorer for the loss of a colourful episode. I am bound to say, however, that in the opinion of many people the times in Lord Lonsdale's mastership which were the happiest for all concerned were the frequent occasions when he himself was absent and

* The change from buckskin to leather was remarked on by Tom Firr, 'I have never known what it was to ride in real comfort before!'

his brother, Lancelot Lowther, acted as his deputy in the field. Tom Firr was then allowed to kill his foxes in his own way and it never seemed to be necessary to send hounds home because of the behaviour of the field.

On the subject of sending hounds home Colin Ellis tells the story of how, on one occasion, the hounds ran three times round in the same circle. In this way the leaders on the third circuit caught up with Lord Manners and a companion who were only on the second lap. Lonsdale said they were over-riding hounds and went home. Next day a wag sent him a telegram which read, 'Entirely approve of your action (signed) William R & I.'

On the other hand there were some days when Hugh showed them memorable sport. On 14th December 1894, after a run of two hours and five minutes and a distance, as hounds ran, of twenty-seven miles, only Firr, Fred Earp (for eighteen years first whip of the Quorn), Lord Lonsdale himself and Lady Gerard were in at the finish.

Hugh's six years as Master of the Quorn were in many ways successful in spite of the fact that he made himself unpopular with some of the more fashionable elements.

The great reputation he enjoyed in the hunting-field was founded on the fact that he set out to find a fox and to kill it. A simple enough precept but one to which to this day there is more lip service paid than practical effect given. In Hugh's eyes there was no worse man in the world than a huntsman who would let his hounds into a covert on a true line and simply gallop forward in the hope of hitting off a stray fox. Nor could he stand for one moment the show-off amateur with no eye for a line of country and whose only instinct was to gallop.

His knowledge of how a hunted fox would go was exhaustive. He would sometimes be seen to break away on his own from the hunt, taking some extraordinary leaps in the most unlikely direction. Invariably his line was proved right. This was not entirely the result of some atavistic instinct of the born hunter. Every movement of stock, every sudden turning of a flock of birds told him its own story with the result that if there were a shorter distance between two points he would invariably find it.

Lord Ribblesdale in his book *The Queen's Hounds* pays an eloquent testimony to Hugh as from one great hunting man to another.

I remember hunting with Lord Lonsdale when he hunted the

Woodland Pytchley. One afternoon, latish in the season, we literally rode into an old dog fox in Boughton Woods. He literally jumped up between us. The hounds got right away on the back of the fox and we both started on the back of the hounds. I was riding a handy, quick horse but Lord Lonsdale lost me in three minutes—not because he was riding a faster horse but because of his superior horsemanship and his knowledge of manège riding which to my mind especially distinguished him from other celebrated riders to hounds. . . .

In the middle of the Quorn Mastership had come the visit of the Kaiser to Lowther, followed later in the year by a less lavish, but still expensive visit by the King of Italy.

By 1896 the shortage of money was acute. Towards the end of the hunting season it looked as if Jim Lowther's counsel would prevail. Hugh got as far as offering his resignation. It caused an unprecedented uproar, not amongst the members of the Hunt but amongst the farmers. His successful disciplining of the Quorn rowdies had raised him in the eyes of the long-suffering farmers to the heights of a demi-god. In the days when farmers in the view of the hunting community were less than the dust, Hugh never forgot that he hunted by their permission, and not by right. There was no trouble that he could take for them that was too great and no courtesy that he could not afford. Quite apart from all of which, he liked and understood the farmers far better than he did the Hunt members.

At the end of the meet at Beeby a deputation of farmers waited on him with a petition signed by every farmer in the Quorn country asking him to reconsider his decision. It was a request he was no more capable of refusing than of cutting off his own right arm. He withdrew his resignation on the spot. How he broke the news to Jim Lowther is not known.

Two seasons later, in 1898, the blow fell. The Hodbarrow mines were petering out, and with them went a sizeable part of Hugh's income. Now there could be no question of keeping on the Quorn. He resigned in June, leaving them to find another Master at a moment's notice. It was rather a matter of whether he could weather the storm at all. Once again it was a question of getting Hugh out of harm's way, but first Hugh had to be made to take the first steps to get back on an even keel.

The first step was to sell off some of the horses he had accumulated over the past six years.

*

The Lonsdale sale of horses took place at Tattersall's Auction Ring in Albert Gate on 21st July 1898. The excitement it caused was immense. Long before the bidding opened the ringside was packed with every celebrity in the hunting world. Rich parvenus jostled with the holders of great names like the Duke of Beaufort, Lord Rosebery and Charles Fitzwilliam for the chance of bidding for one—almost any one—of Lord Lonsdale's famous stable. A ripple of excitement ran round the ring when it became known that both the Prince of Wales and the German Emperor had sent representatives to bid on their behalf.

Wedged against the ringside close to the auctioneers podium, Jim Lowther, bright and bird-like in spite of his many years, took in the scene. He expected the sale to make ten thousand guineas. But for Hugh the sale was a personal agony and he wished himself a thousand miles away. It was Jim who had insisted that he should be there. 'They'll bid higher if you are looking on,' he had argued.

When the bidding started it soon became evident that the most sanguine forecasts were to be proved wrong. The Duke of Marlborough trying to buy a hack retired from the running with a look of stunned surprise as the bidding soared above the 200 guineas mark. The Duke of Bedford managed to get an eight-year-old charger for 280 guineas and seemed well pleased with his bargain.

Then came the hunters. The first one went for 300 guineas, the second for 400, the next for 470. 'They must think they are buying bloody racehorses,' remarked one hardened old horse-dealer to another. Even the auctioneer looked a little dazed. The German Emperor had a four-year-old chestnut gelding knocked down to him for 370 guineas. It was one of the cheapest buys of the afternoon. The Prince of Wales's representative put his cheque-book back in his pocket. Top price was for another chestnut, a six-year-old gelding. It fetched 760 guineas.

When it was all over the total for eighty-four animals came to 18,228 guineas. Hugh stood for a long time leaning against the ringside after all the buyers had gone. Then he went home for a quiet supper with Grace at Carlton House Terrace. The congratulations of his friends at the National Sporting Club would have been more than he could have borne.

Highly emotional by nature, Hugh was moved easily to tears, which made him one of the softest 'touches' in the sporting world. When he himself suffered a personal set-back, his first reaction was to retreat from the world until he had recovered his emotional balance. These were the times when he needed Grace most.

The sale of his horses had not only moved him emotionally but the fact that it had been forced upon him had hurt his pride. He knew that Grace would make no more than a passing reference to the affair but that she would understand how he felt and be in sympathy with him. Tomorrow would be another day and his courage would be repaired. The wrath of the Trustees would pass, there would be more chestnut horses and life would once again be such 'lovely fun'.

Chapter 16

Hugh was forty-four years old when the South African War ended. The advent of the war had interrupted the haul back to financial stability planned by Jim Lowther. Hugh had poured money into the war effort. The Kaiser's second visit to Lowther after Queen Victoria's funeral had proved even more expensive than the first, and royalties from the Whitehaven mines were tumbling.

It was a black outlook.

For the second time Jim Lowther decided that the only safe place for Hugh, financially, was out of the country, and once again a fortuitous invitation came to his aid.

Lord Curzon was holding his Durbar as Viceroy of India and invited Hugh to supervise the planning and rebuilding of all the ceremonial carriages for himself and his suite. At the same time he invited both Grace and Hugh to be his guests throughout the celebrations.

It was a task which Hugh with his love of ceremonial and detail entered into with the greatest enthusiasm. It also gave Jim Lowther the lever he required. He would provide the money for the trip only if Hugh agreed not to return to England for at least a year. Hugh accepted the condition readily. The Emperor's flag had scarcely been lowered from the flag-pole above Lowther Castle before he and Grace set sail for India.

For Hugh in particular the Durbar was a magical experience. In the great Indian Princes, he found men after his own heart. The feeling was mutual and soon the Lonsdales were deluged with invitations from every Maharajah of note, each vying with the other to arrange more elaborate and extravagant entertainments for the Viceroy's guests of honour.

Hugh had another reason for making as big a personal impact as possible at the Durbar. His greatest ambition in life was to follow in the steps of his predecessor the third Earl and be appointed Master of the King's Horse. The job given him by Lord Curzon, as well as his honorary job with the Kaiser, were obviously ones which would enable him to demonstrate his suitability for the appointment.

Never was a Viceroy better served than Curzon was by Hugh Lonsdale. His equipage gleamed and glittered—outstanding even in comparison with the glorious displays of the Maharajahs. Indeed His Excellency was only outshone by one person—Hugh Lonsdale himself. As one of the social journals of the day, *Vanity Fair*, remarked, Lord Lonsdale 'was the next best sight after the elephants'.

Perhaps it was this that George V had in mind when he eventually succeeded to the Throne and the question of who should be Master of Horse was being discussed. 'I should really like to have Hugh,' he is supposed to have remarked. 'The only trouble is that I could not possibly afford him.'

After the Durbar Hugh set off on a Royal tour of his own, leaving Grace at the Viceregal Lodge to recuperate from the strain of official engagements. He went shooting to Lalakand, hunted tigers with the Maharajah of Cooch Behar, and visited the Khyber Pass with the Duke of Connaught; then, collecting Grace, he went on to stay with Sir Frank Swettenham, who was then in the middle of his distinguished Governorship of Singapore.

With the knowledge of his promise to Jim Lowther fresh in his mind he discussed with Frank Swettenham which part of the world he should visit next. Swettenham remarked that it was a pity the Empress of China received so few visitors, for the Royal Palace of Peking must surely be one of the most interesting places to visit in the world.

Hugh produced from his luggage an unopened letter which had been given to him some years previously by the great Chinese statesman Li Hung Chang.*

Hugh had first met Li Hung Chang at the Court of the German Emperor, to whom Li Hung Chang had been sent by the Dowager Empress of China to express her regrets over the Boxer murders. Later he visited London to raise a loan to help with his policy of reconstruction.

* The habit of not opening important letters seems to have run in the family. A story is told of how a Lowther, setting out on a protracted journey was overtaken by a messenger, a day's ride from home, and handed a letter which he put unread in his pocket, where it remained until his return two years later. It was to tell him that his house had been burnt down.

As it was not an official State visit, protocol decreed that Li Hung Chang and his retinue could not be accommodated at any of the Royal residences, which raised a considerable administrative problem, as no hotel of suitable status could be persuaded to take the distinguished Chinaman, there being an irradicable belief that the 'heathen Chinese' was not clean about the house.

Hugh Lonsdale came to the rescue by putting Carlton House Terrace at the disposal of the deputation, thereby earning the gratitude of the Foreign Secretary and a warning from him that he would be wise to lock up his valuables. He also put six of his yellow carriages at their disposal. The happy accident of the yellow colour was accepted as a great compliment by the Chinamen, although they did remark that the Lonsdale family crest, which is a winged dragon, was a poor imitation of the Imperial Chinese dragon!

Frank Swettenham had the letter translated, and it proved to be in the form of an acceptance, written for Hugh by Li Hung Chang, of a standing invitation to visit the Royal Palace in Peking. Their problem was solved for them, the letter was sent on ahead and Hugh and Grace set off in high spirits to stay with the Chinese Empress.

Even Hugh was astonished at the welcome at Tientsin. A special train awaited them with a guard of honour lining the platform. At Peking the most exalted mandarins arrived to escort them to the presence of the Empress. Alas, Grace had another of her attacks and had to retire straight to bed, where she stayed for the rest of her visit. Hugh, however, had a truly royal time, being entertained by the Empress to luncheon and being invited to attend a review of the Chinese Army in the company of the Heir-Apparent. It was the first time that an Englishman had been accorded this honour, and Hugh was duly impressed.

From China they went on to Japan and then on to Australia. In Tokio Hugh sampled the delights of the Geisha girls and found them wanting. Their dancing he declared to be boring and their other assets negligible. 'Frankly,' he used to say afterwards, 'if I'd had anything to do with it I'd have had the lot drafted.'

All in all the Lonsdales in their year of exiled wandering proved themselves diligent but uninspired travellers. Grace was unwell for weeks on end. When she was able to go out she spent much of her time taking endless dull photographs, a collection she added to by buying dozens and dozens of souvenir post-cards which she carefully packed away and never looked at again. Hugh collected too—everything and anything from boomerangs to Japanese lanterns. On Thursday Island he met a pearl fisherman who had been a doorman at the National Sporting Club, and bought his whole collection of painted sea-shells. In Australia he made elaborate arrangements, which came to nothing, to ship Australian horses back to England.

It is a measure of their fame that wherever they went they were received in the greatest style. Reporters clamoured for Hugh's views on every subject under the sun, and particularly what he thought of the country he was visiting. He gave his opinions with a ready, if somewhat undiplomatic frankness. He told the Australians that they were ruining their country, overpaying their politicians and starving their workmen. 'The Englishman is far better off at a pound a week than you are at fifty bob,' he told them.

They came home by America, where Theodore Roosevelt received them in Washington. In New York, determined to be unimpressed, Hugh told reporters that American progress was marvellous—but too marvellous to be safe. 'Your iron buildings,' he is quoted as saying, 'will not last fifty years. The iron will corrode and they will fall down.' Diving into the realms of high finance he announced that the rising power of trusts and monopolies was a fleeting phase and one of which no notice need be taken. 'They will,' he declared mysteriously, 'be brought down by their own weight.'

Even Grace was induced to put her views on record. The engagement of the Duke of Roxburghe to the American Miss Goelet had caused the greatest excitement amongst the matrons of the United States. Grace did not approve. Declaring that she had met Miss Goelet, she gave it as her view that there was no future for Anglo-American marriages. 'For one thing,' she announced severely, 'money is not talked about in England as it is in America. I think that as a rule the American girl is far more anxious to get a title than the Englishman to get her money. The list of international marriages will never be lengthened much by marriages between English girls and American men. Our girls will not have your men because they do not like the American life. The life of the American woman of the upper classes is unnatural and useless compared with the life of the wife of an English aristocrat.'

Strong stuff indeed, but the Americans seem to have taken it all with good humour. Hugh and Grace were given a royal send-off as they sailed for England almost a year to the day from the day they left.

Things had a knack of turning out right for Hugh. Jim Lowther's sentence of a year in exile had turned into a triumphal tour. At the same time the financial boat had become steadier and the dark clouds had been blown, at least temporarily, over the horizon. They got back in August 1903, just in time for the grouse shooting. Jim Lowther was invited as usual but he was too ill to attend.

Chapter 17

During the last decade of the nineteenth century Hugh Lonsdale had grown up. The days at the old Pelican Club were behind him. His friendship with the German Emperor, his Mastership of the Quorn, his championship of boxing and the many sporting and charitable causes with which he associated himself had made him one of the best known and most universally popular men in the country.

Now there was scarcely a sporting occasion for which his support was not sought. An organizer who managed to get the Yellow Earl's name on his committee could be sure that the project was already half-way to success. Everything he did he entered into with zest and enthusiasm, while in the background Grace quietly made sure that he maintained the proper social observances. She took her responsibilities with the greatest seriousness. Whilst Hugh spent much of his time with the Yeomanry at Lowther, Grace worked diligently as President of the County Nursing Association. If Hugh was prevented from attending some important meeting, Grace would go along to deputize for him.

Hugh, who scarcely had a day's illness in his life, could not understand illness in others. If he heard that anyone, even a close relative or great personal friend, was seriously ill he would never visit them. Equally he would never fail to send someone else to inquire if there was anything he could do to help. Although his concern was genuine and generosity proverbial he would always keep illness and misfortune at arm's length. During his whole life he never attended a funeral except Grace's and those of members of the Royal Family. If any of his dogs or horses showed signs of failing or being past their prime he would order them to be put down and would never refer to them again.

Grace, on the other hand, who seemed always to be in pain, devoted much of her time to visiting others, and there were few houses on the vast Lowther estates which had not cause to remember her in times of illness or suffering.

Imperceptibly, as the nineteenth century gave way to the twentieth, Hugh's attitude to his great inheritance changed. Barleythorpe began to give way to Lowther as the centre of his existence. Although they both continued to play an important part in his life, his visits to Lowther became more frequent and his interest in his estates much deeper. He now started to go to Lowther on the last day of July where he stayed until the beginning of the hunting season.

This was not to say that he became a better landlord in the way that the Trustees would have liked. He preserved to the end of his days the belief that he was the last of the Lowthers and that nothing should be done to the estates from which he could not benefit in his own lifetime. He did however begin to be disenchanted with the life that London had to offer and find more and more to absorb him in the local life in Cumberland and Westmorland. It was a throwback to the long line of sporting squires from which he came.

In Lowther Castle itself and in the Lowther ornamental gardens he began to take the greatest personal interest—the first Lowther to do so since William the Good had built them.

When Wicked Jimmy had kept his household there in two unconnected wings he had gone so far as to commission Adam to draw up plans for reconstruction. That the plans were eventually scrapped must have been to the bitter regrets of successive generations of servants.

The reconstruction of 1807 had served to join the two wings together again, and in doing so, provided in the new part some really magnificent reception-rooms.

It had achieved little else. On either side of the grand saloon, the picture galleries and the reception-rooms as big as football pitches, the elegantly curving staircases led to rabbit warrens of small rooms. Each one seemed to be on a different level, and such unconsidered items as chimney flues described a criss-cross pattern of such complexity as to drive the most experienced chimney-sweeps to despair.

So remote were some of the bedrooms from the main reception rooms that William the Good, with a rare flash of humour, christened half a dozen of the furthest flung ones Van Dieman's Land. The name stuck, so that knowledgeable guests in Hugh's day, finding themselves allocated to say North Van Dieman's Land No. 4, would spend an hour or so carefully plotting the way to bed. One distinguished visitor, failing to take this precaution, got himself hopelessly lost in the small hours and was found by a maid in the morning fast asleep at the foot of the grand staircase!

No record exists of the number of servants it took to run this vast house in the days before the 1914 War. It is safe to say, however, that they were at least twice as numerous as in the nineteen twenties. Even then they were numerous enough, so it may be interesting to describe the domestic arrangements which existed at Lowther, almost up to the outbreak of war in 1939.

Most of the really big houses in those days had a Comptroller, or the equivalent, whose powers over staff and all matters relating to the household were absolute. At Lowther the arrangements were somewhat different. There was only one person, who, in the opinion of Lord Lonsdale, was capable of directing the whole complicated domestic machine, and that was himself.

Grace's part in affairs was restricted purely to the ordering of meals which she did every morning in an audience with the cook and the housekeeper. For the rest, Hugh, with his passion for detail, and very real administrative ability, kept an eye on affairs.

If there was something he wanted to criticize, his methods were direct and left no room for misunderstanding on the part of the offender, so that life for the staff was a very lively business indeed when his Lordship was in residence. He could be quick-tempered to a degree, and nobody even in the more remote parts of the household was safe from his sudden appearance. If the offence was sufficiently serious and the offender a male member of the staff, he was quite likely to find himself flat on his back as a result of a sharp right-hander to the jaw. His temper was uncertain but it was quickly over. If justice was summary, it was at least just, and he inspired devotion in his personal staff. It did, however, take a lot of getting used to.

On one occasion a newly hired postillion was sent to meet him off the train from London. When they reached Lowther he received such a dressing-down for his handling of the horses that, after being dismissed, he took to his heels, in his livery, and was never seen again!

Hugh had the habit of prowling round his domain at all hours of the day and night, as another newcomer to the household found out abruptly.

This unfortunate was the under butler, whose sole responsibility was to see that the vast amount of silver in the silver-room was kept clean. It was a task comparable with the painting of the Forth Bridge, in that, as soon as it was completed, it was necessary to start at the beginning again. The better to keep abreast of his job he slept next door to the silver vault in the cellars. One night, around midnight, he was conscientiously applying himself to his task when he heard an unknown step outside the door, and stuck his head out to investigate. It proved a tactical error, for Hugh, thinking he had come upon a burglar, laid him out cold with one of his famous right-handers. When matters were explained on both sides, there were no hard feelings. The under butler received one of the ever-ready ten-pound notes, and remained a devoted and loyal servant of the family for many years.

Theoretically, however, responsibility for the day-to-day running of the castle was delegated to the various Heads of Departments, each of whom enjoyed, on paper at least, equal rank.

The male staff were under the charge of the House Steward. This staff consisted of a first footman who was Lady Lonsdale's personal footman and travelled with her wherever she went, a second footman who was Lord Lonsdale's personal man and whose main, and extremely demanding task was to answer Lord Lonsdale's bell (which he found occasion to ring with remarkable frequency), and a third footman who helped to wait at table and assist the other two in their various tasks. Then there was the Head Butler who was junior to the footmen. His prime responsibility was the silver, in which he was assisted by the under butler. The Groom of the Chambers saw that the reception-rooms and writing-rooms were properly maintained, and the Usher of the Hall supervised the laying of the tables and generally looked after the dining-rooms.

The female side of the establishment was the concern of the Housekeeper so far as the maids were concerned, and the Cook on all matters relating to the kitchen. Of the two the Cook was the more important. Her staff consisted of at least three kitchen maids, two stillroom maids and three scullery maids, with an indeterminate number of daily helps who came in to wash up or assist with the heavy work. The Housekeeper had a skeleton staff of seven housemaids, which was added to when big house parties were held, and a sewing maid.

There were also sundry other officials of varying importance. Lord Lonsdale's personal male secretary, Lady Lonsdale's private secretary; Lord Lonsdale's valet and Lady Lonsdale's personal maid, and so on down the scale to minor but essential functionaries such as the house carpenter and the boilerman, and, at the bottom of the scale, the poor pantry boy.

Of course it was quite unthinkable, with a staff varying so widely in importance and standing, that they should lead a completely democratic life below stairs. Protocol was rigidly adhered to and promotion from the rank of, say, second to first footman was as eagerly sought as promotion in the Army.

The Cook, who was not expected to demean herself with preparing breakfasts, was waited on in her own sitting-room by the first kitchen maid, until she took command of her kitchen at nine-thirty. Incidentally, she was always known as Mrs. —— regardless of her marital status.

Whilst the Cook ate in splendid isolation, the other senior members of the staff were served in the steward's-room. Here, at each meal, timed at precisely one hour before meals in the dining-room, the Steward led in the Housekeeper to take either end of the table in exactly the same manner as Lord Lonsdale led Lady Lonsdale into the dining-room. The others followed in strict order of seniority and were waited on by the steward's-room footman even to the extent of whatever wine, spirits or beer they might require.

One degree lower down the scale was the servant's hall, where the footmen and maids followed exactly the same procedure, having the Usher of the Hall as their personal attendant.

Amongst the kitchen maids and stillroom maids, the regimen was even more strict and carefully timed. The first kitchen maid looked after the Cook. The second kitchen maid cooked for the steward's-room and the servant's hall and waited on the first kitchen maid. The third kitchen maid prepared all the vegetables (except potatoes which was a menial task), and looked after the second kitchen maid, and so on down the scale until at the very bottom some junior scullery maid was faced with no alternative but to look after herself.

The whole intricate schedule was geared to the time of the dining-room meals, which were laid down as nine-thirty for breakfast, one-thirty for luncheon, three o'clock for tea, and dinner at eight-thirty in the summer and eight o'clock in the winter. These times were adhered to with a strictness which would appear fanatical today, but the reason for it is easy to understand. If the dining-room were to be late going into dinner, or, for some reason, decided to lunch early, it would cause a dislocation downstairs equivalent to a train smash on a main line. In fact such a thing never happened.

It would be true to say that the real dictator at Lowther was not

Hugh but the clock, and he took the most scrupulous care to see that the dictator was well served. A clock winder would arrive at the castle each week to see that all the clocks were in perfect order and synchronized with the master-clock in the stable-yard.

There was one dreadful day when Colonel 'Poss' Myddelton, later first President of the British Boxing Board of Control, one of Lord Lonsdale's closest friends in the National Sporting Club, was walking with him on the terrace. He glanced at his wrist-watch and remarked that the stable-yard clock appeared to be five minutes slow.

'Nonsense,' said Hugh, 'the clocks at Lowther are *always* correct.'

'I am sure you are wrong,' persisted the Colonel, who should have known better. 'I have just checked my watch with Greenwich time before I left London this morning.'

'In that case, you are obviously unaware,' Hugh observed crushingly, 'that Greenwich takes its time from Lowther,' with which broadside he turned on his heel and strode off puffing furiously at his cigar. Even his closest friends found it all too easy to say the wrong thing!

*

Altogether staying at Lowther was an experience from which some guests did not recover very readily. It was very much a matter, for most of the guests, of staying *at* Lowther rather than *with* Hugh and Grace Lonsdale—and staying at Lowther meant the strictest observance of all the unwritten rules.

When there were guests staying, the whole tempo of life below stairs increased. Virtually nobody who came to stay would dream of arriving without a personal servant. These additional servants were accommodated in the castle and joined in the castle routine. Each servant would be allocated to his or her place in the hierarchy according to the rank and precedence of the persons they served.

When one servant was addressing another it was customary to accord them the rank of their employer. Thus one valet urging his companion to hurry was overheard saying, 'Oh do hurry up, Abercorn! The Curzons went downstairs ages ago.' One lady's maid giving notice to her mistress remarked that she had been extremely happy but she did not want to remain as a mere 'Honorable' for the rest of her life.

Although the greatest precautions were taken to segregate the female sleeping quarters from the male, romances blossomed quickly below stairs—often with far-reaching results. A mistress discovering her maid pregnant by a friend's footman would demand that the man be dismissed. The footman's employer, anxious not to lose an excellent servant would refuse, claiming that the maid was a wanton who had got no better than she deserved, and soon it would become known that Lord A. and Lady B. were no longer on speaking terms.

In the steward's-room the ceremony of dinner was enacted in precisely the same form as it took in the dining-room. If, for example, Lord Lascelles and his wife, the Princess Royal, were staying at Lowther, as they frequently did, the Princess's personal maid would be led into dinner on the arm of the House Steward, followed by Lascelles's valet on the arm of the Housekeeper. The rest then took their places in the same order of precedence as their masters took in the dining-room. The menus, too, took their cue from the dining-room and, of course, the appropriate wines were served with each course.

Amongst the higher echelons of the staff, life below stairs must have been at least supportable!

When there were house-parties the menu in the dining-room varied very little, so the Cook, in solitary splendour in her kitchen quarters, had few sleepless nights thinking up new and exotic creations; the food she did serve, however, had to be precisely to Lord Lonsdale's exacting standards. To ensure this he kept a pad and pencil always to hand throughout a meal and few meals went by without some note as 'peas too hard' or 'not enough salt' later to be passed down to the kitchen.

The meal invariably started with clear consommé, the only soup ever known to be served. It would be followed by some sort of fish (without any sauce, naturally), followed by a joint with boiled potatoes and greens from the Lowther gardens. Then would come chicken, or whatever game was in season, with bread sauce (the only exception to the no-sauce rule) and potatoes. For the sweet course, Hugh would usually have his own little dish of rice pudding, whilst guests were indulged with, perhaps, a fruit flan. A favourite savoury was omelette cooked with spinach, and this was followed with cheese and biscuits and fruit. In fact, an eight course meal.

During the meal Hugh's dogs, which accompanied him wherever he went, would be ranged under the tables round the walls. When the cheese came on they would suddenly and without any apparent signal, troop out and sit around their master to receive a biscuit.

Woe betide, however, any guest who had the temerity to pat any of the animals! Far from being approved of by Hugh for being an animal lover, the offender would earn a ferocious glare if nothing worse. As with his other personal possessions, his dogs were sacred to him alone.

The time for the ladies to withdraw from the dining-room was signalled by a time-honoured ceremony between Hugh and Grace. Catching her eye he would raise his glass and say, 'Mrs. Tommy! The King, Foxhunting and the Ladies!' To which she, with equal gravity, would reply, 'Mr. Tommy! The King, Foxhunting and the Gentlemen!'

The ladies then retired to the drawing-room for an hour of stilted conversation, whilst the port decanter circulated in the dining-room.

Incidentally, when the men did rejoin the ladies it was the signal for the Countess to lead the way to bed, whilst the men repaired to the billiard-room for games and more brandy. The most ladies would be offered after dinner might be a glass of lemon barley water.

Electricity was only installed in the castle in 1926. Until this advance, each guest was equipped by a footman with a candle and a box of matches before setting out for the upper floors. As the vast unheated corridors were apt to whistle with draughts, the problem of keeping this candle alight was a very real one.

One evening, a guest was finding his way to bed with his wife rather late when he slipped on the top step of the grand staircase. In attempting to save the candle he completely lost his balance. The candle crashed to the hall below and in the ensuing darkness his wife listened with understandable trepidation to the sound of her husband rolling head over heels down a whole flight of stairs.

A frenzied search for the candle followed. Hope was almost abandoned when the husband, happily no worse for his experience, spotted it by the light of the last flickering match, firmly wedged between the ears of a vast stuffed grizzly bear which used to stand on its hind legs at the foot of the stairs.

Life at Lowther could be grim and earnest!

*

Particularly as Hugh grew older, he feared loneliness. With Grace unable to accompany him in his more active interests, his inner circle of servants became perhaps as close to him, each in his own sphere, as anybody in his own social circle. This is not to say that they were immune from the rigorous standard of formal behaviour which Hugh exacted from everyone in his employ, but they were men whom he trusted to be on his side to preserve the great illusion.

There was Jeffrey, the head gardener, who had come from Harewood and was one of the most capable gardeners in the country. Together they planned more and more wonderful schemes to beautify Lowther. When one morning Jeffrey dared to suggest that a new scheme dreamed up by Hugh was going to be prohibitively expensive, it was to be greeted with a sharp retort, 'Who is paying for it, Jeffrey, you or me?' Jeffrey, who like everybody else on the estate had a good idea of the true state of affairs, could hardly reply, 'Neither, my Lord, it's the Trustees.'

Haines, Hugh's stud groom who accompanied him wherever he went, was another of his confidants. Haines's life must have been in a constant state of flux. He was in complete charge of the stables at Lowther, Barleythorpe and Carlton House Terrace, with the added responsibility of moving the appropriate horses from one house to another. This was not a job that was ever allowed to be deputed to an underling, so that as he travelled from place to place all over the country, Haines had to go ahead the night before, taking on the train with him Hugh's favourite pony, Merlin, who always had to be available for him from the moment he arrived at the racecourse.

At Goodwood, where Hugh stayed in the Royal house party as the guest of the Duke of Richmond and Gordon, guests traditionally rode round the course in the morning with the King. The finest horses had to be brought down from Barleythorpe and Haines, equally superbly mounted, was expected to ride in attendance. Even if getting the horses to Goodwood had meant two nights being shunted around England in horse-boxes, his appearance in the famous Lowther livery had to be outstanding in its sparkling perfection.

Whilst travelling with Hugh's horses, Haines had to adopt the same panache as if he were the Yellow Earl himself. Before each journey he was required to equip himself with enough ready money to tip every porter and train guard in a lavish manner. Not unnaturally he became one of the best-known figures on the railway. Even when changing trains in some remote backwater in the small hours of the morning, porters could not resist pulling his leg by bowing obsequiously and inquiring if 'his Lordship' had any tips for the following day's racing. Haines, who had a great sense of fun, soon learned to play up to this good-natured ragging and travelled the railways like a grandee, distributing largess with the greatest of *élan*.

Even when there were a few peaceful days at Lowther to look forward to, Haines could not rely on having his sleep undisturbed.

Insisting that he should always be on the end of a telephone, Hugh would ring up at any hour of the night or in the small hours of the morning and order him to saddle two horses and bring them up to the castle. Then they would set off over the fells, and Haines would be lucky if he saw his bed again that night. It went even further than that. Sometimes he would take all his guests up to the top of the fells to see the sunrise, which meant saddling about a dozen fell ponies at three in the morning.

Other members of Hugh's inner cabinet were Sam Robinson, his head keeper, Dick Steel whom he established in the park with a string of coursing greyhounds, and Collins, who, when he was not standing with the dignity of a bishop behind Hugh's chair, hovered in the background to anticipate his slightest whim. Collins had been with him since the age of fourteen, and spent the whole of his life in Hugh's service.

These five made a formidable quintet, each master of his own trade and men of very real ability, whose personalities only became submerged when in the presence of his Lordship. Each played an important part in a régime which Hugh had built up around him and which made him feel secure. With them surrounding him he was monarch of all he surveyed. Nothing must usurp his good content and there was no room for faces that did not fit.

Chapter 18

Jim Lowther died in 1904. He was one of the few people to whom Hugh ever deferred in his life. In spite of their constant battle over money, Hugh was genuinely fond of him. His successor as guardian of the family fortunes was Jim Lowther's nephew and Hugh's cousin, James Lowther.*

Every bit as shrewd as his uncle, he was nevertheless never able to establish quite the same control over Hugh, who had become wily in devising ways and means of extracting financial concessions out of the Trustees. He had in fact several lengths start over his newly appointed Trustee, who, try as he might, never quite succeeded in closing the gap.

It was partly this change in circumstances which enabled Hugh to achieve one of his dearest ambitions—the Mastership of the Cottesmore.

The origins of the Cottesmore are found as far back as 1666, the very earliest days of foxhunting in its present form. The pack was owned by Henry, Viscount Lowther, who took them down from Lowther each year and hunted them from a house called Fineshade Abbey in Northamptonshire. Henry sold them to Tom Noel but William the Good bought them back and hunted them for fifty years until just before his death at the age of eighty-six, when they were sold again to Sir Richard Burton who split the country up between the Old Burton and the Quorn. In 1870 Hugh's father bought them back yet again and hunted them until his death, when St. George took them on. It was a bitter blow to Hugh that he was not able to

---

* Member of Parliament for Penrith for thirty-eight years, he was Speaker of the House of Commons for sixteen years. Created Lord Ullswater on his retirement, he is remembered as one of the most competent and universally respected Speakers in the history of the House of Commons.

continue the tradition. He tried hard to get them from successive Masters but it was not until 1906 that he got the opportunity of again hoisting the Lowther flag over the Cottesmore.

Even then it was touch and go. St. George had sold the hounds to a Mr. Gosling who had presented them to the country. When, just after the turn of the century, the Mastership had been vacant Hugh had put his name forward and been heavily defeated by Evan Hanbury. The reason generally given is that the die-hard hunting fraternity still remembered that Hugh's grandfather had refused to rescue the Hunt when it had been in financial difficulties. It is more likely that the rigorous régime Hugh had instituted in the Quorn country was still fresh in people's minds and the young blood wanted no part of it. His threat to Mr. Baird to withdraw his lease of the Barleythorpe kennels and stables unless he handed over the pack also still rankled with many, so altogether his popularity with many of the Cottesmore followers was not as high as it might have been.

In 1906, however, much of the ill-will had dissipated and he was elected unanimously.

It was the beginning of a lot of trouble.

During Evan Hanbury's tenure of the Mastership, Thatcher had been the huntsman. After his world tour Hugh had hunted with the Cottesmore and found in Thatcher most of the habits he most disliked in a huntsman. On New Year's Day, 1904, he wrote Thatcher a 3,000-word *exposé* of his hunting sins. Because of its lucid dissertations on the science of hunting, it is given as an appendix to this book.* It is also typical of the mixture of kindliness and bluntness with which Hugh was accustomed to express himself.

By the time Hugh came to take over the Mastership of the Cottesmore, Thatcher had gone and Sam Gillson† had taken over. Hugh, repeating the successful formula he had applied to the Quorn, poured money into new strains of hounds and dragooned the members with all his well-known enthusiasm.

The members of the Cottesmore did not conform as readily as those of the Quorn. Within a year all the old animosities had been revived and he had a full-scale war on his hands. Within three years subscriptions had fallen off so badly that the Committee declared that they would no longer guarantee the £2,000 they had originally agreed. Worse, from Hugh's point of view, his methods of hunting

* See Appendix I—'A Letter of Criticism to Thatcher'.
† See Appendix II—'A Letter Reminding Gillson, Huntsman to the Cottesmore, of his Duties'.

came in for criticism. The main objection was to his habit of holding long discussions at the covert side, holding up the proceedings. Furiously he offered his resignation. To his astonishment it was accepted. He withdrew it immediately and called for a vote of confidence. Once again it was the farmers and landowners who came to his rescue. Packing a protest meeting they outvoted the malcontents and Hugh was reinstated for a further year.

Then, in May 1910, he received another body blow.

On the afternoon of 11th May he received a telegram at Carlton House Terrace where he had gone to attend the funeral of Edward VII. It was from his agent at Lowther and it gave him the first news of the disaster at Wellington Pit, one of the great coal-mines he owned at Whitehaven.

The immediate result of this, financially, was that Hugh could no longer afford to hunt hounds on the scale he had become used to. In April 1911 he resigned from the Cottesmore. It had been a short and not altogether happy association, but Hugh was to prove in later years that he bore the hunt no ill-will.

Chapter 19

With the eclipse of the iron-ore mines, the coal-mines at White-haven had become more and more important in the task of providing Hugh with his enormous income.

The original concession, obtained by Sir James Lowther of White-haven from Charles II, was the right to work all the minerals between the high-water and low-water mark. By the second half of the nine-teenth century the advances in mining technology had enabled the Lowther pits to extend their workings further and further out under the sea—and the further they mined the richer the great seams of coal became. At the same time the problems of ventilation and other difficulties, not met with in such acute form in inland mines, increased.

Another snag occurred about 1850, when Ministry officials dis-covered that the Lowther interests were mining a concession to which they had no legal right. All the mineral rights below the low-water mark still belonged to the Crown.

It caused quite a flutter but there was little that officialdom could do about it. The only access to the rich, gassy coal beneath the sea was through the Lowther pit shafts. William the Bad offered to buy all the Crown rights for £5,000. The Crown demanded £100,000. The stalemate lasted for thirty years during which time successive Earls entered into desultory and intermittent negotiations whilst, at the same time, continuing to work the mines with great vigour.

Finally a compromise was reached when St. George consented to regularize the position by paying £50,000. It was one of the greatest bargains in mining history. Instead of fading out as some experts had predicted, the seams became richer and richer, so that by 1910 over 3,000 tons of coal a day were pouring from the pithead conveyor belts.

The town of Whitehaven, laid out so carefully by Sir James

Lowther, fits snugly round its little bay. The streets run down almost into the harbour where the fishing-boats lie protected from the Irish Sea by the sharp outline of St. Bees Head.

Whitehaven Castle, the great house that Sir James built, looks down the main street, and all around—so close that the townsmen in those days could stroll there in the evenings with their wives and sweethearts—was the open countryside of West Cumberland. Only the dark profiles of the pitheads, standing out starkly from their surroundings, distinguished the town, at first sight, from a sleepy fishing village.

A close look at the little rows of stone cottages, and the illusion vanished. Sir James's successors had not followed his example in town planning. In the Ginns district the cottages were built against the hillside, each row separated from the next by a pathway almost too narrow for a pony and cart. The chimneys of the row in front stood level with the bedroom windows of the row behind and the monotony of the lines of dwellings was broken only by the communal privies built obtrusively at intervals along each roadway.

In other districts tenement buildings crowded against one another, their narrow entrances and stone staircases more typical of the notorious Gorbals district in Glasgow than of a small seaside township. Under the skin, Whitehaven was as typically a mining town as Motherwell, Blythe or Merthyr Tydfil.

At tea-time on the afternoon of 10th May 1910 the town was going about its usual business. Barefoot children played about the narrow, chalk-scrawled courts; the housewives busied themselves getting their 'bait'* ready for the miner going on the five o'clock shift or boiling up kettles of water for their menfolk returning grimed with coal dust from the pits. A few stood in groups around doorways and street corners, discussing the news of the death of Edward VII.

Mrs. Bowman, daughter of a miner and married just three weeks to another miner, was handing her young husband his working clothes. One after another she dropped them. There is an old miner's superstition that to drop a man's clothes before he goes to work is certain to bring ill-luck. Barring the door she implored him not to go. 'Well, lass, ta plase tha', I'll stop at hame,' he agreed equably.

---

* Usually bread and jam sandwiches. Because the miners had to walk so far to the coal face, often bent double, the bait boxes in use in other parts of the country were impractical. Instead they had their sandwiches wrapped in paper and carried them in their pockets.

Three doors down the road George Smith, whose wife had left him a widower just over a month before, busied himself getting his six daughters off to bed early. That night he was taking his only son John to the pits for the first time. A shopkeeper out walking met a good friend whom he had not seen for some weeks on his way to Wellington Pit. 'Wey, man,' he remarked, 'I tho't thou was dead.' Grinning, the man walked on.

These were the things that people remembered afterwards about that lovely spring evening.

At about half-past eight a whisper ran round the town that there was something wrong at Wellington Pit. Nobody knew how it started but it ran like a shiver through the houses. Wives hovered irresolutely half in and half out of their front doors. Then, one by one, half ashamed of their fears, they slipped out into the darkness and down the 'broo' to the pithead gates.

Shortly after nine o'clock the colliery manager, called away from his dinner, came down to investigate. All that was known was that there had been some sort of an explosion in Number 3 workings. A team had gone up to investigate and the winding gear in the main haulage way had caught fire and the flames were spreading. Beyond, in the honeycomb of workings, five miles out to sea and 130 fathoms down, 136 men were already trapped.

Within half an hour of this news a second rescue party came back. Knowing only that there was something wrong in the main haulage way, they had made their way up the backdrift in an attempt to find out what had gone wrong. They had not progressed far when they had stumbled across two miners, Wear and Kenmore. They were almost unconscious and it took half an hour to revive them sufficiently to discover what had happened.

Wear and Kenmore had been with the men employed in Number 5 and 6 workings a mile and a half beyond where the explosion had occurred. As soon as he knew something was wrong, the deputy in charge of the working party had gathered his men together and attempted to lead them to safety along the backdrift. All had gone well until they had come to the first of a series of double doors which were kept closed in the old shaft-end, only to be used in case of emergency. Opening them the air was found to be foul, so the party turned back to the uncontaminated air at the coal-face. There they hung about irresolutely until Wear and Kenmore decided to make another attempt to break out. It was obvious to them that unless help was brought soon it would be too late. Wear left his son behind,

Kenmore his brother. They passed through the same doors from which the party had turned back, and struggled through a mile of gas-filled, dust-choked tunnel to the point where the search party had found them.

By the time Wear and Kenmore had been brought up from the pit and a properly equipped rescue operation mounted, the miners had been trapped for over two hours. On the main route between them and safety there now raged an impassable inferno. Attempts to reach them via the return airway were made impossible by the clouds of poisonous fumes which drove back the rescue parties.

Next morning the whole nation, already in mourning for the death of the King, heard that there were fears that one of the greatest pit disasters in the history of British mining was in the making.

All Thursday rescue parties fought to reach the men, hoping against hope that some of them at least had managed to hold out in the diminishing pocket of air. Every train brought more officials and teams of expert rescue men from pits all over the country. Around the pithead hope ebbed from the white-faced, silent crowd who stood and prayed.

Every now and again a new rumour would rustle through the crowd, passed quietly from mouth to mouth. Knocking had been heard in the pit, it was said, and some men had found their way out up the old horse road which came out in the disused working by the cemetery. A connection had been found under the sea with the next-door pit. At this news some of the more hopeful ran over to William Pit to wait there until the rumour was denied.

One old lady had been told by her husband that if she ever heard that he was trapped in the pit she was not to worry. He knew a secret way out of the mine to the sea-bed and from there he would bob up like a cork and come swimming ashore. For a week she sat by the shore, nursing her man's dry clothes, and waiting for him to redeem his promise. Then they led her away.

Adding poignancy to the disaster was the new system they had instituted at the colliery. Under this 'companies' of three men worked together and got paid at the end of the week with a lump sum assessed on the amount of coal the team had dug. The colliery management encouraged 'companies' made up of relations because it meant that there were fewer disputes when it came to dividing up the week's earnings. Now many families were faced with the loss of all the bread-winners at one blow. Trapped in the pit were the three Taggert brothers and the three Brannons. There was Joseph

McClusky and his two sons. There were three M'Courts, four McAllisters; there was the widower Smith and his young son, the Harrison brothers who were both in the Whitehaven bowling team, and so on down the list, the same names recurring with tragic frequency.

At two o'clock on Friday morning the last rescue party was hauled to the surface. They reported finally that the position was hopeless. The men might still be alive but any further attempt to rescue them must mean certain death to the rescuers.

Within half an hour the waiting crowd knew that the decision had been taken to seal off the workings where the trapped miners lay. The mine was to become their tomb. For almost an hour they stood in the pouring rain, stunned and incredulous. Then they turned wearily to their homes.

It was not until that afternoon that the defeated mood of the miners started to change to one of militant refusal to accept the decision of the management. Suddenly every man seemed to have his own plan of how to reach the trapped men. One of the overmen, Charlie Graham, who had worked in the pit for over forty years, produced a plan which immediately gained a great deal of support amongst his fellow miners.

It was known that John Hanlon, the miners' agent, had telegraphed to the Inspector of Mines in London for permission to reopen the pit. He received no reply but hope sprang afresh. Somehow the rumour spread that Hanlon was going to address the miners in the market-place. For half an hour a packed crowd waited for him to appear. Then a collier, Isaac Allen, climbed on to the base of a street-lamp and started to harangue the crowd. 'I have none of mine down there but I'm ready to go down. Is there any will come with me?' The rest of his speech was drowned by cheers.

Headed by Allen the angry crowd marched twenty deep from the market square to the pit, whilst a few hot-heads ran to John Hanlon's house to 'tak him doon wi' us'. Hanlon was not in.

Forewarned of the sudden change of mood the marchers were met at the pit gates by a resolute body of police. For minutes it was touch and go whether the police would be trampled underfoot and the sealed mine stormed by sheer force. Then suddenly the resolution of the miners broke. Secretly they must have been convinced of the hopelessness of the situation. Without a word being spoken they turned and walked slowly back. Many of them were weeping openly.

*

Hugh Lonsdale received the first news of the disaster at Carlton House Terrace on Thursday afternoon. It came in the form of a telegram from his head agent at Lowther, William Little. It announced simply that he was going to Whitehaven to investigate reports of an explosion in Wellington Pit.

The following morning was the Royal funeral. Carlton House Terrace was filled with official guests, accommodated by Hugh at the request of the Foreign Office. News of the decision to seal the pit was handed to Hugh as he left the Abbey after the funeral service. Immediately he made arrangements to get a special train to Whitehaven. Grace was to follow as soon as possible. He arrived in the early hours of Saturday morning just as dawn was breaking over the West Cumberland hills.

On previous occasions when Hugh had visited Whitehaven the miners had turned out to welcome him as they would have welcomed Royalty. Every street had been draped in bunting and the famous Lowther yellow had been proudly sported from the meanest tenements. As his yellow carriages had swept up Lowther Street to the castle they had lined the road and cheered. Now as he made his way on foot from the station to the offices of the mining company, the town was sleeping the sleep of exhaustion.

By mid-morning he had been through every detail of the disaster. He had talked to the experts and to the miners who had been down on the rescue parties. Unsatisfied, he had been down the pit himself, examining the feasibility of Charlie Graham's plan. Then sadly he picked up his stick and hat and walked off alone into the town.

Hugh Lonsdale must have been as moved during the next few hours as he had ever been. Twenty-four hours before, he had sat amongst the great of Europe, the Kings and Queens, Princes and Princesses, each in their proper place of rank and degree, as they had laid His Royal Highness King Edward VII of Great Britain and Ireland, Rex Imperator, Defender of the Faith, by the Grace of God the most powerful Monarch in the world, to rest. Now, twenty-four hours later, Hugh walked alone down the narrow evil-smelling lanes of the Ginns, the district where practically all the miners who worked in Wellington Pit lived. There was not a door in the three long, closely packed rows of cottages where the proudly scrubbed doorsteps and narrow lace-curtained windows did not hide sadness. If some families had not lost a near-relative, there was still a close friend to mourn. None stood outside their door to stare as he moved from house to house. They waited for him to come into their front parlours and then asked him their questions quietly. No, there was absolutely no hope. Yes, he was quite convinced all the men were dead. The officials were right, Charlie Graham's plan would never have worked.

They took it from him as the simple truth. Management and Ministry officials were suspect, but they could believe what Lordy told them.

He learned a great deal in the next few days. Grace joined him and each day they set out separately to visit as many of the mourning families as possible. A distress fund was set up headed by Queen Alexandra, considerate and sad for the miners even in the middle of her own grief.

In Parliament Keir Hardie attacked Hugh Lonsdale. Where a poor widow was prosecuted for stealing a few lumps of coal, he claimed, the Lonsdales had for years lived off the proceeds of stolen coal. They had no right to the coal and they were too mean to install proper safety precautions for the miners who risked their lives in their interests. In the eyes of the Whitehaven miners Hardie had overstepped the mark. Even the local left-wing Press tore him to shreds.

Hugh's sympathy for the miners was real and heart-felt, but perhaps most of all he was warmed by this unexpected loyalty.

During the thirty years he had enjoyed the income from the Whitehaven pits, the miners themselves had been little more than shadowy figures without any real substance. The management of the mines had been the concern of an operating company who had leased the concessions from the Trustees. Hugh's only concern was to get his hands on as much of the resultant income as possible.

If he had thought about the matter at all, he would scarcely have believed that he would have been held in much esteem by the miners themselves whose lot contrasted so vividly with his own. Yet here was the evidence of it. If the first door had been shut in his face, he would have left Whitehaven and never returned. As it was he never lost the regard for the miners which he had learned to have in the days which followed the disaster.

So far as the miners were concerned, the feeling was mutual. Even in the days of tragedy and hardship which followed the First World War they never lost their affection for Lordy. The bosses— the agents and the management—the ruling classes and the Monarchy itself could be at fault, but Lordy could do no wrong.

When the epitaph of the Whitehaven pit disaster came to be

written, the horror was heightened by the knowledge that it need never have happened. If the trapped men had made their way out by the route taken almost two hours later by Wear and Kenmore it is probable that they would all have reached safety. If earlier steps had been taken to quell the fire on the winding gear, all would have been saved. If . . . But all the 'ifs' could not bring back the 134 men who died.

Fifty miners were decorated by King George for gallantry in their efforts to save their trapped comrades.

Chapter 20

Hugh Lonsdale never achieved his ambition to be Master of the Horse. On the other hand, honours were heaped on him from many other quarters.

In the autumn of 1906 five men sat down to dine together at the Badminton Club. They were Sir Gilbert Greenall (later Lord Daresbury), Arthur Evans, Walter Lloyd, John Wimans and their host R. G. Heaton, the well-known hackney judge. At the end of the dinner, carried away with enthusiasm, they sent Hugh Lonsdale a telegram inviting him to be the President of their new project. Hugh agreed by return, and the International Horse Show came into being.

Few new ventures can have got off to such a successful start. The first show was held at Olympia in June the following year. It was attended by King Edward and Queen Alexandra who brought with them the King and Queen of Denmark. America, Belgium, France, Holland, Sweden and Switzerland were all represented by strong entries. The show lasted for six days, and judging of the various classes went on daily from 9 a.m. till ten or eleven at night.

There were classes for every type of horse from officers' chargers to costers' donkeys, and for every form of carriage from governess carts to ladies' one-horse victorias.

From the first the turnout of the costers captured the imagination of the public, so that what had originally been simply one of the trade-vehicle classes to be judged, became one of the highlights of the whole show. On 'coster night' the public turned up in greater force than on any other night, not merely to see the pearlies, but to see the Yellow Earl at his flamboyant best. The King had agreed to become patron of the Show, and most of the big names in the sporting world gave their support, but it undoubtedly revolved around Hugh Lonsdale more than any other, and 'coster night', with the passing of the years, became his benefit night. Ignoring the formal platform erected for the presentation of prizes he would vault lightly into the ring to hand out the awards. One Cockney Donah who had won a prize horrified officials by throwing her arm around Hugh's neck and delivering a smacking kiss. A moment later as the band struck up *If you were the only Girl in the World* they were dancing round the sawdust ring together. The crowd loved every incredible minute of it.

One year a disappointed competitor expressed his disgust, in Hugh's hearing, with typical Cockney vigour. Hugh did not argue. He simply knocked the fellow out, much to the delight of the man's mates who considered him to have been greatly honoured.

His favourite turn was to seize one of the big rakes used to rake over the sawdust after the completion of each item and, emitting huge clouds of cigar smoke, join the team of workmen, applying his rake more vigorously than the most assiduous of them.

The year in which the International Horse Show was founded also saw the inauguration of Brooklands race track. The almost vertically banked track, on which 1,500 men had worked in double shifts for nine months, was regarded in motoring circles as an eighth Wonder of the World. When the Hon. C. S. Rolls had won the Tourist Trophy the previous year at a speed of nearly forty miles an hour, the nation gasped in wonder. Now it was said that Brooklands would become the Epsom of the motor world and that speeds of up to a hundred miles an hour would eventually be achieved.

Brooklands opened in July 1907 with a parade of notabilities round the track. Every existing make of motor-car was in the parade at the new Mecca of the motor-car, with Hugh Lonsdale in the latest of his Mercedes.

Hugh had been interested in motor-cars ever since the Kaiser had put one at his disposal when he visited Berlin in 1901. It was an early Mercedes and he was greatly impressed by the fact that it never once broke down during the whole of his stay. The driver was a young German mechanic called Kieser.* Before Hugh returned to England he had not only arranged to have the Mercedes shipped to Lowther for him but had persuaded Kieser to join his household as driver-mechanic. It was the first of a long succession of motor-cars Hugh was to own, all painted in the family yellow which was to make them as well known through the country as his horse-carriages.

* Now the proprietor of the considerable motor business of that name in Penrith.

When the first Mercedes arrived it proved mechanically up to expectations, but Hugh was horrified to discover from Kieser that the silver-work on the car was not real silver but only chromium plate. It was put on the next boat back to Germany with instructions that all the chromium was to be replaced immediately with silver. The painting of the special bodies with which all his cars were fitted consisted of a minimum of eighteen coats. Although he espoused motoring with his usual enthusiasm he never really trusted the motor-car in the same way that he did a horse. For years he would insist that an identical car to the car in which he was being driven follow behind, lest the first one break down.

He became the first president of the Automobile Association and allowed the Association to use his personal yellow for all its vehicles. It gave him great pride in later years, as the affairs of the A.A. prospered, to see so many of 'his' vehicles on the road.

With the turn of the century and Hugh in his early forties, his life had become very full indeed. He was an inveterate joiner of of Clubs—not the great clubs of the day like White's or Brooks's, but clubs like the Shikar Club which was founded in the interests of big-game hunting, or the naïvely named 'Happy' Club which devoted its short-lived existence to furthering the proposal that everybody should be happy. When other men were content to go on the waiting list to join the fashionable clubs, Hugh was really only interested in clubs which invited him to join as President.

Of all his clubs the one Hugh loved the most was the National Sporting Club.

His historic championship of Slavin and McAuliffe had done much to help boxing appear in a more respectable mantle than in the bad old bare-fist days. Nonetheless the sport was still a long way from achieving universal acceptance. The early days of the National Sporting Club were characterized by a series of scandals which kept the more doubtful aspects of the fight game well in the public eye.

The last fight that John Fleming was to arrange at the N.S.C. was between the American Jimmy Barry and the young English boxer, Walter Croot. It was fixed for 17th November 1897.

Two days before, Fleming had been found dead at the Club. He had passed peacefully away sitting on the lavatory reading a book of fairy stories. Out of respect for the man who, with 'Peggy' Bettinson, was the real founder of the club, the fight was postponed until 6th December. Jimmy Barry won the fight with a knock-out in the last round. Croot never recovered from the blow and died a few hours later in Charing Cross Hospital.

The result of Croot's death was that all the N.S.C. officials found themselves indicted at Bow Street, alongside Barry, for causing a breach of the peace. Hugh Lonsdale and Sir George Chetwynd were called as expert witnesses. The presence of two such illustrious sportsmen seems to have intimidated the prosecution. 'There is no brutality whatever in boxing when it is properly conducted and this match was properly conducted,' declared Hugh. Sir James Vaughan, the magistrate, nodded his agreement, and minutes later the Treasury Solicitor himself conceded that there was no case to answer.

'Peggy' Bettinson and his committee must have breathed more easily—but not for long. Almost exactly one year later, in November 1898, Nat Smith of Paddington, boxing at the club, knocked out Tom Turner. Two days later Turner died, again in Charing Cross Hospital. This time the trial of the club officials took place before a Grand Jury of the Central Criminal Court. Again Hugh Lonsdale gave evidence and again they were acquitted.

That a third death should occur just over a year later would seem to be stretching the bounds of probability too far. The first boxer to enter the N.S.C. ring after Turner's death was a young Scots boy named Mike Riley. He appeared there again on the 20th January 1900, and the improbable tragedy occurred. He was knocked out by another flyweight called Precious and died from the blow. Now the public were really incensed. Precious and the now case-hardened officials of the N.S.C. were charged with manslaughter. Let out on bail they were followed wherever they went by crowds who booed them or cheered them according to the views they held on one of the most controversial topics of the day. The trial took place in a blaze of publicity and again a Grand Jury failed to return a true bill against the accused.

Public opinion was by now so thoroughly aroused that when, a year later, a *fourth* man died in the ring it was quite evident that the authorities would line up the biggest guns they had available to secure a conviction.

The dead man was Murray Livingstone, who boxed under the *nom de guerre* of Billy Smith. He had been leading on points against Jack Roberts in a match at the N.S.C. when he had fallen and struck his head against a corner post. The cause of death was given as laceration of the brain. The prosecution made their case quite clear from the start. They were not so much concerned about the punishment of the ten defendants. They were concerned about the wider implications. Should this type of contest be allowed to continue or not? A verdict against the accused would be a verdict that it should not.

This time the jury returned a true bill and Jack Roberts and nine officials of the N.S.C. found themselves in the dock of the Old Bailey to answer a charge of 'on 24th April last, feloniously killing and slaying Murray Livingstone, otherwise "Billy Smith" '.

Amongst the defendants were 'Peggy' Bettinson, Eugene Corri and the wealthy J. H. Douglas, father of the future test cricketer, J. W. H. T. Douglas. John Douglas had himself been British amateur boxing champion for three years and frequently refereed contests at the N.S.C. It was he who came in for most of the fire from the prosecution. He was a quick tempered, forthright man and it was not long before Counsel for the prosecution had lured him into contradicting the evidence of 'Peggy' Bettinson and others.

Defending Counsel, holding briefs from the distinguished accused, bobbed up and down one after another on behalf of their clients. The defence was about to close when a tall, distinguished figure stood up to adress the jury.

'Gentlemen of the Jury—I appear for Roberts, who is really the principal in the case . . .'

Everyone seemed to have forgotten poor Jack Roberts, the man who had actually struck the blow. Everyone, that is, except Hugh Lonsdale who had briefed Counsel on his behalf. Now the great Edward Marshall Hall was addressing the jury on Roberts's behalf. It was a case after Marshall Hall's own heart—a case where the issues were far from clear-cut and even the law itself was ill-defined. Now he proceeded to goad, tease and dazzle the prosecution with the brilliance of his advocacy. In not pressing their case of manslaughter but relying rather on intricate arguments on the rules of boxing to prove the sport illegal—from which a conviction for manslaughter must surely follow—they had played into Marshall Hall's hands.

He would have none of it. 'Either Roberts is guilty of manslaughter or he is not. We will have no half measures,' he declared. The jury sat up straighter in their seats. Whether boxing should be illegal or whether the men of hitherto blameless character should be convicted of manslaughter were two very different things indeed. Marshall Hall then proceeded alternatively to rag or pour scorn on the case for the prosecution. 'I do not hesitate to tell you,' he confided in the jury, 'that I treat the action of the Treasury in this matter with ridicule. I look upon it as a piece of grandmotherly legislation, inspired by misdirected zeal for public safety, and fortified by a superficial reading of some Scottish rules of boxing, which my learned friend had completely misunderstood.'

Finally he reduced the whole of the prosecution case to farce. Solemnly he declared, 'I suggest that in all future boxing competitions, whether held at the National Sporting Club or anywhere else, the combatants should wear leather jerkins, under which bells should be concealed—electric, if possible. The boxing gloves should be of the largest size and should be plentifully smeared with chalk. For each chalk mark seen on the opponent's doublet the striker should be given a point. But if in the making of that mark he should happen to ring one of the bells, he should be instantly disqualified for unnecessary violence with the intention of effecting a knock-out and be rendered liable to an indictment for manslaughter.'

The jury found no difficulty in returning a verdict of Not Guilty. In discharging the accused the judge, Mr. Justice Grantham, made no attempt to unravel the rules of boxing about which there had been so much argument. The prosecution had not succeeded in proving that boxing contests were illegal. On the other hand, nobody had yet managed to prove that they were legal.

For Hugh the series of favourable verdicts was a personal triumph. The people who held up their hands in horror at his constant appearances in the witness-box and the time and money he spent in fighting battles for such dubious members of the community were confounded. The Cinderella of British sport was fast turning into a Princess—and the Prince by her side was not Bettinson nor any of the other big names behind the N.S.C., but Hugh Lonsdale. It was a situation in which he gloried. The golden age of boxing was about to begin and Hugh was already acknowledged as its Patron Saint.

Alfred de Rothschild once remarked that the finest publicity a man could buy himself was a racehorse. Hugh would certainly not have agreed. In the racing world there were altogether too many wealthy and famous men. The National Sporting Club, by contrast, was not made up of a glittering galaxy of aristocracy. It was a middle-class club run by a group of extremely astute businessmen who realized that boxing, cleanly run and free from scandals, was good business. In the first decade of the twentieth century they established themselves as the arbiters and the ultimate authority on matters affecting the conduct of boxing matches, not only in Britain but all over the world. As their President, the name of Lord Lonsdale lent them glamour in their early days which was returned to him many-fold when their authority had been established and recognized.

Hugh's association with the N.S.C. and the International Horse Show had another effect on his life. They brought him into even greater prominence with the general public.

In the days before popular newspapers, wireless, television and the whole network of instantaneous communications which is available today, there were few national figures outside the Royal Family. Politicians of Cabinet rank enjoyed ephemeral fame, back benchers were seldom known outside the bounds of their own constituencies, and the only glamour in the lives of workaday people was provided by stage beauties, the stars of music hall, and to a lesser extent the sporting figures of the day, such as leading jockeys and boxing champions. There were no film stars, no jazz bands, no international playboys and playgirls variously to entertain, divert, shock or scandalize the public. Inadequate communications even denied the public the vicarious enjoyment of all but a few of the juiciest murders and other excitements, which are now so much part of everyday life.

Hugh had in his nature all the elements of a great showman. It did not require a vacuum for his talents to flourish, but because the vacuum was there his image was thrown into even higher relief. And the public lavished on him all the affection which they are capable of bestowing on their heroes. In their eyes there was no one quite like the Yellow Earl.

The sporting figure who most nearly approached him in the esteem of the sporting public was Lord Derby. Although altogether a much more conventional figure, Derby could on occasions cut just as much dash as the Yellow Earl, and he could certainly match him in wealth and power. On the face of it the two men had much in common. Derby ruled his kingdom of Lancashire in almost the same feudal manner as Hugh ran Cumberland and Westmorland. Both owed their wealth to the Industrial Revolution, and both espoused a life of sport.

Derby, relying on an older Earldom if not as ancient a lineage, described Hugh openly as a parvenu. Hugh, lighting another enormous cigar, would refer to his rival as 'that dreadful show-off Derby'. Neither could or would ever agree to the other's point of view, which made life difficult for people on the several committees of which they were both members. In later years a dispute between them on the question of whether there should be an extra lavatory installed in the 'Ladies' at Newmarket lasted for five years. By that time everyone had forgotten which view either of them represented.

At the National Sporting Club, however, Hugh reigned supreme. An inflexion of his voice, a twitch of his bushy eyebrows, and boxers, officials and members alike leaped to do his bidding. As if to preserve the remoteness of his eminence he never arrived at the ringside with any guests or companions. He always arrived punctual to the minute, immaculately dressed and alone to take his seat of honour at the ringside. However great the occasion, it was never so great that his presence did not cause a stir.

His contribution to boxing was, however, much more real than the mere act of giving his patronage to the N.S.C. and financing boxers in their legal battles. He was playing an active part, from the days of the old Pelican Club onwards, in making boxing a respected sport. There is no doubt that the present rules known as the Queensberry Rules owe their existence in some part to Hugh Lonsdale. He himself, in after-years, always claimed that he in fact wrote the Queensberry Rules and that but for his modesty they would have been called the Lonsdale Rules! This was not true, but it is true that he had a greater part in the framing of the Rules and the putting of them into practice than did Lord Queensberry.

The ninth Marquis of Queensberry, with whose name the rules were associated, was not altogether a very pleasant person. The way in which he treated his wife and children gave little indication that his name would go down in history associated with sportsmanship and fair play. He was cantankerous, narrow-minded and dictatorial, with little thought for anyone but himself.

It is said that the original Queensberry Rules were worked out by the ninth Marquis on a trip to America with the British lightweight champion Arthur Chambers, who went there in quest of the American title. Chambers won the American title in 1872 and did not retire for another five years. If he and Queensberry did frame the original rules, he certainly never fought under them. One of his fights in 1873 ran for one hundred and thirty-six rounds.

It is undoubted, however, that in the beginning of the eighteen-seventies, long before Hugh could have been taking an active interest in the game, a set of rules was drawn up by Queensberry. They had nothing to do with professional fighting, but laid down that a fight between amateurs should consist of three rounds of two minutes each. They also ruled as illegal such professional tactics as holding, throwing, hitting on the ropes, and so on.

It was the Pelican Club who first adopted these rules and applied them to professional fights held on the club premises. In this Hugh Lonsdale, as Chairman of the Pelican Boxing Committee, played a leading part, and when later the 'Queensberry Rules of Endurance', on which the modern professional rules are based were drawn up, there is no doubt that Hugh had considerable say in the matter and Queensberry none other than by virtue of his original contribution.

The real originators of the rules of modern boxing were probably that intrepid pair John Fleming and 'Peggy' Bettinson, who took the gentlemanly rules of the Pelican Club and moulded them to a formula of their own forged in the fire of their experience in making the N.S.C. a paying proposition.

If Hugh can take much credit for the part he played in the development of the Queensberry Rules, he can probably take less than he is usually given for originating the Lonsdale Belts, which have made his name famous all over the world. In fact nobody really knows to whom the credit should go for first thinking up the idea of the belts. Only the reason why they came into existence is clear.

Bettinson had been extremely sagacious in seeing the shape of things to come in 1890 and in backing his hunch. It had paid dividends for almost twenty years, but towards the end of the first decade of the twentieth century the red light was beginning to show for the N.S.C.

With the indulgence shown by the law and the immense rise in popularity of the sport both here and in America, boxing was becoming less the private property of the N.S.C. Rival establishments were springing up everywhere, so that it was no longer necessary for the cream of the profession to stand cap in hand outside the door of the N.S.C. and beg for permission to show their paces for a consideration of a few guineas. Now there was competition for their services, bigger fees could be commanded and for the first time the voice of the promoter was being heard in the land. Not only were the promoters anxious to pack arenas like the White City with capacity crowds, but the boxers were equipping themselves with managers who knew what their boxers were worth. Slowly the prestige value of appearing at the N.S.C. was being eroded; if there was no prestige there was certainly no inducement in the value of the purses the club was able to pay. The quality of the boxers appearing at the

N.S.C. started to drop and this was rapidly reflected in the sharp decline in subscriptions.

It was in this atmosphere of crisis that somebody dreamed up the idea of making up for the inadequate purses by offering the prestige of a belt. The final touch of genius was given to this sound piece of marketing thinking when somebody suggested that the belts should be called the Lonsdale Belts.

The first reaction of the committee of the club was not enthusiastic. They still felt that the vogue for the mammoth purses and the taking of big arenas was a passing phase. However, something had to be done and the idea was put to Hugh who agreed to put up the first belt, to become the sole property of the holder if he successfully defended it three times. It would also entitle him to a pension for life of £50 a year. Firmly the N.S.C. declared that the belt could only be fought for in the ring of the N.S.C. and the holder would be regarded as the champion of his weight in England. Only British-born boxers could compete.

Hugh deputed the firm of Mappin and Webb to design the belts at the cost of about £250 each,* and the first one was contested at the Sporting Club between Johnny Summers and Freddie Welsh in November 1909. The fight raised little interest in the Press. They missed history in the making. When Hugh stepped into the ring to fasten the belt round the waist of the Pontypridd lightweight Freddy Welsh, it was the beginning of a new era in British boxing. Henceforward to win a Lonsdale Belt was to be the greatest ambition of an English boxer. It was an award which was to carry with it international recognition far more valuable to the winner than a large purse.

It had also saved the bacon of the National Sporting Club.

* They are today worth approximately £1,000.

Part III

The Georgian

Chapter 21

Hugh was fifty-seven when the 1914–18 War broke out. The exuberance and puckish sense of enjoyment which had endeared him so much to the public seemed to have grown stronger rather than declined with the years. Hunting several days a week had kept him as fit as an athlete in training. When he was not hunting there was scarcely a day when he did not walk several miles, not in a conscious effort to keep in training but because he enjoyed it.

As he neared sixty his auburn hair was losing some of its colour and starting to recede, but otherwise he showed few signs of age. He had never been good-looking, but there was a charm in his expression which became more benign and kindly with the passing of the years.

Time had dealt less generously with Grace. She had never been very attractive, with a too-low hair line and eyes which were set too close together. By the time she was sixty she had become stern and rather forbidding—an appearance which was added to by her refusal to use either powder or other cosmetics. She dressed with severe neatness, rarely wore jewellery and generally presented to the world an impression of grim disapproval which only her courtly good manners did anything to relieve.

They were both at Lowther preparing for the annual grouse-shooting party when they heard that war had been declared. Already one of Hugh's old loves, Lydia Kyasht, who was also a friend of Grace, had arrived with her husband; so had Lancelot Lowther's son Anthony,* who would one day almost certainly inherit the Lowther estates. Hugh hurried at once to London to report to the War Office. It was a disruption of the even pattern of existence and

---

* Within a few months, at the age of seventeen, to be in France with the 10th Hussars.

therefore rather a bore but little else. Nobody really thought it could take very long to deal with the Germans.

Hugh was Vice-President of the Empire Service League and his first job was to recruit a composite Colonial Force from amongst the thousands of resident Colonials who wanted to serve.

There was of course no such thing as conscription. War was still very much of an amateur affair. It was a 'good show' for young men to volunteer to help out. Their country, the War Office assured them, would be grateful to them.

The general attitude to the proposed Colonial Force was that it was a jolly good idea and very sporting of all the volunteers to offer to join—but there was no equipment for them, and no fund from which they could be paid. It was a situation which Hugh thoroughly enjoyed. With the help of a few wealthy men like Lord Glenconner, Lord Rothermere and Sir Ernest Cassel, he set about equipping, clothing and paying a Colonial Force of 500 men. Within a few weeks the job was done, and the new force snugly housed on Hugh's orders at the White City. Then, stuffing his cheque-book back in his pocket and dressing himself up in his uniform of Colonel of the Cumberland and Westmorland Yeomanry, he set off back to Lowther in search of new fields to conquer.

He found that plans for a recruiting campaign were well advanced and indeed that the Border Regiments were already embarrassed with the numbers of volunteers. Nine battalions had been raised and every day more and more young men were flocking to the colours.

It was not nearly good enough for Hugh. His own 'kingdom' must lead the country with a display of their patriotism with Hugh Lonsdale in the van. He decided to issue his personal call to arms. Shutting himself in his study, he set to work to draft a poster which would carry his own message to every corner of the two counties. Some hours and quite a few cigars later he emerged and sent for the leading printers in Penrith. Soon thousands of Hugh's posters were rolling off the presses. It was a fantastic document. Printed in his racing colours of yellow, white and red, its message was nothing if not direct, as can be seen by the reproduction opposite.

Soon the gaudy poster was stuck up on every village noticeboard, at every road end and in every country shop for miles around. It caused a furore in more ways than one. The Mayor of Whitehaven, thinking it was directed exclusively at the lack of patriotism of the people of his Borough, drove furiously to Lowther to protest. Hugh

ARE YOU A MAN

OR

ARE YOU A MOUSE?

Are you a man who will for ever be handed down to posterity as a Gallant Patriot,

OR

Are you to be handed down to posterity as a Rotter and Coward?

If you are a Man,

NOW

is your opportunity of proving it, and ENLIST at once and go to the nearest Recruiting Officer.

REMEMBER

if you can get 15, 30, or 60 of your Comrades to join, you can all ENLIST together, remain, train, and fight together.

THE COUNTIES—CUMBERLAND AND WESTMORLAND—HAVE

ALWAYS

BEEN CELEBRATED FOR THE FINEST MEN, THE GREATEST SPORTSMEN, AND THE BEST SOLDIERS.

NOW IS YOUR OPPORTUNITY OF PROVING IT.

HURRY UP!

Please take my humble Advice before it is too late.

THE COUNTRY HAS NEVER BEEN IN GREATER PERIL.

LONSDALE,
Lowther Castle.

R. SCOTT, PRINTER, "OBSERVER" OFFICE, PENRITH.

was too busy designing uniforms, appointing officers and ordering ammunition and weapons for his private army to see him.

Typical of the letters which poured into the offices of the local Press was one from a Cumberland vicar.

'Sir—I scarcely know whether amazement or disgust were more predominant in my mind when I read Lord Lonsdale's extraordinary call to arms. If it was a hoax, which I was at first inclined to believe, I offer to Lord Lonsdale sincere apologies for the comments I am making; if it was really written by him I offer no apology. It is fatally easy to recline in an arm-chair after a seven-course dinner and urge your dependants to fight. . . .' and so on.

'Whilst in full sympathy with all legitimate measures for obtaining recruits,' wrote another angry citizen, 'I should like to point out that there are many young men preparing for their future careers whose prospects would be marred and perhaps ruined by rash enlistment. . . .'

'I don't give a hoot for Lord Lonsdale and care as little about empty titles as the man in the moon,' wrote another.

The protests may have been vociferous but they did not reflect the growing tide of patriotism which swept the dales. Recruits flocked to join the new battalion which Hugh proudly christened 'The Lonsdales'. Because the wiry dalesmen who crowded into the recruiting offices were very often under the required height, Hugh wired to the War Office for permission to enlist men under the statutory five feet eight inches. By return he received an agonized wire, 'Stop repeat stop collecting recruits.' Blandly he announced that any man over five feet six inches would now be accepted.

With a committee of all his neighbouring landlords he set about ordering special uniforms in hodden-grey for his army which soon numbered over a thousand strong. Undeterred by the lack of official support, which meant no financial support, he made his committee finance each pay day out of their own pockets. Overnight he promoted a retired army captain to colonel and put him in command.*

He held a giant rally in the grounds of Lowther Park with free beer for recruits and all the fun of the fair. The only music available was the band of the local Temperance Society. The band leader objected furiously when he found that their stand was just outside the beer tent. 'Outside the beer tent, you said?' Hugh asked. 'That's splendid. One of your fellows can hand out the free beer tickets,' and, pushing the books of tickets into his hands, he strode off in high good humour.

* Captain Machell of Crackenthorpe Hall, nephew of the Captain Machell who had managed St. George's racing stable.

It was Lordy at his best and his immense enthusiasm infected everybody around him.

Finally the War Office, seeing that there was no beating him, wisely decided to join him. He was allowed to keep the name of the Lonsdale Battalion but authority drew the line at the hodden-grey uniform. In the end the Lonsdales had to go to war dressed in khaki like everybody else.

Hugh was never happier than when he was playing at soldiers. Brass bands, waving flags and colourful uniforms could bring tears to his eyes. No Yeomanry Regiment had a more splendid annual camp than the Cumberland and Westmorland Yeomanry whilst he commanded them. If his approach to the whole business was rather amateur, his men loved him all the more for it. One of the most prized possessions amongst the rankers was one of Lordy's cigars. On one occasion when the Regiment was drawn up for inspection by a visiting General, Hugh, getting tired of waiting, calmly lit up. He had just had a first contented puff when a voice from the ranks behind him urgently stage-whispered, 'No smoking on parade, my Lord.' Like a naughty schoolboy caught in the act he surreptitiously tossed the cigar over his shoulder. A moment later there was almost a riot as half a dozen men in the front rank dived on the treasured trophy.

It was always Hugh's boast that he liked to share the hardships of camp life with his men and he would make much ado about retiring to his tent at the end of the day's manoeuvres. After all the lights were out he rode back to Lowther Castle for a comfortable night in his own bed!

The atmosphere of gay adventure which surrounded the outbreak of war was not to last very long. Soon reports of mounting casualties started to fill the columns of the Press and the public began to wake up to the horrors of modern warfare with modern weapons.

Hugh, although too old for active service, found himself deeply involved in the war effort. Firmly placing the bust of the Kaiser in a prominent place of honour on the grand piano in the saloon at Lowther, he set about the business of fighting the German Army with all the great energy of which he was capable.

War still very much involved horses. Tanks had still to make their first massed appearance three years later at Cambrai, and the mechanization of other arms was far in the future.

It was perhaps typical of the British that as the casualty list lengthened enormous public concern should be expressed about the treatment of the many thousands of horses drafted to the front. To meet growing criticism General Birkbeck appointed Hugh Lonsdale to tour the remount depots of England and France and report to him what he found. It was a task after Hugh's heart. '. . . It is very consoling to have so great a judge of the horse as yourself satisfied with the performances of the remount depot. They all said, as they did at the Advanced Veterinary Depot abroad, that you and your comments have been of the greatest assistance to them. . . .' wrote General Birkbeck after Hugh had put in his first report. And again two months later, 'I am so glad that you went to Maidenhead. I don't think you can realize the pleasure your visits give to these depots, and the good they do.'

On 23rd November 1915 the Lonsdale Battalion left their comfortable quarters at Carlisle for active service. After a few preliminary skirmishes they found themselves at the end of June 1916 in Authille Wood. A Corporal wrote in a letter home, 'I think most of us are tired of the so-called rest and are really glad to get into the front lines where we have a chance of knowing our daily work and how much rest we are to have.'

On 1st July the Lonsdales climbed out of their trenches in the wood and mounted a daylight attack on the enemy.

It was the beginning of the first Battle of the Somme.

A reporter who interviewed one of the survivors took down this account verbatim:

Aye, it was half-past seven when we started, sir. 'Twas kind of a bit of a wood, you know sir. We was the third line like, B and C Company being afore us. Ye see, we could see them movin' in the open like, past the wood, till the fire caught them and they went down like grass. I was beside the Colonel in the front trench. I carried the bombs, ye see. The Colonel he was to go with the last line after us. But when he sees the second line cut down that way an' our time come, 'Oh, damn!' says he—just like that—an' he ups an' over the parapet. 'Come on, lads,' he said—like that—an' just at that moment he was hit an' kind of staggered, an' before we could get to him like, he fell backward into the trench again. I doubt it killed him. But we had to go on. I had me bombs you see. We was singing John Peel like mad an' cheerin' to raise the dead. . . .

I got a bullet in me arm directly I was on the parapet an' somehow it made me stumble like and I fell. But I went on as quick as I could; me havin' the bombs. But ye'd have wondered to hear how loud our lads were singin' an' cheerin' like at a football match. . . .

The words they sang to the tune of 'John Peel' as they advanced into the teeth of the German machine-gun fire were of their own composing:

> D'ye ken Lord Lonsdale, that sportsman true?
> D'ye ken his charger of chestnut hue?
> D'ye ken that battalion of Cumberland true
> Who will march to Berlin in the morning.
>
> 'Twas the sound of the bugle woke me from my bed
> And the call to parades has me oft times led
> In the glorious battalions of Cumbrians true
> Who will march to Berlin in the morning.
>
> Yes, I ken Lord Lonsdale, and Machell too,
> Yes, I ken that charger of chestnut hue,
> Yes, I ken that battalion of Cumbrians true
> Who will march to Berlin in the morning.

Within a few minutes of the attack being launched the twenty-eight officers and eight hundred men who had gone into action were reduced to three officers and two hundred and eighty men. Colonel Machell was to have left the following week to command a brigade. He was killed instantly.

News of the disaster was a shattering blow to Hugh Lonsdale. With Carlton House Terrace as Grace's headquarters for her war work (for which she was awarded the C.B.E.), and Barleythorpe on loan to the King of the Belgians for the duration to house all the Royal carriages and horses, Hugh redoubled his efforts to raise money and equipment for the front.

To the intense irritation of the R.S.P.C.A., he set up the Blue Cross Fund to provide special veterinary aid for the British, French and Italian armies. He established three fully equipped animal hospitals whilst the R.S.P.C.A. spent valuable money taking advertising space claiming that they were the only body entitled to raise money by public appeal. Public opinion laughed them out of court and the Blue Cross flourished. It was not until Hugh became a vice-president of the R.S.P.C.A. after the war that the breach was healed.

In the middle of it all he could not resist a thrust at his old rival Lord Derby. Writing to his agent at Lowther, he remarked, 'I see Lord Derby has given a hundred acres of his park to be broken up for Food Production, but that is the sort of stupid thing he would do as he is entirely out for advertisement and never loses an opportunity to advertise.' Later he gave orders for Lowther to follow Lord Derby's lead.

Towards the end of October 1915 Colonel Hall-Walker (later Lord Wavertree) sold his famous Tully stud in Ireland to the British Government as well as his training stables in Wiltshire at Russley Park. He added to the sale an outright gift to the nation of his brood mares and stallions valued at over £70,000.

The Government accepted the gift on the grounds that the breeding of high-class bloodstock was in the interests of maintaining a high standard of horses for the Army, and Hall-Walker's gift was placed under the control of the Ministry of Agriculture. Most of the bloodstock at Russley Park was sent to Ireland for breeding purposes, but the two-year-olds were kept in training in this country. It was the foundation of the National Stud.

Because the financing of a racing stable was rather outside the province of the officials of the Ministry of Agriculture, a sponsor had to be found. In consultation with the War Office, it was agreed to offer all the horses in training of the National Stud to Hugh Lonsdale with the agreement that they should run under his colours. Hugh was captivated by the idea. He had always had a few horses in training, but, partly because he was not particularly interested in winning races and partly because he knew very little about breeding racehorses, he had never had any very marked success. This did not mean to say that he did not dream of leading in a Derby winner. Nothing would have given him greater pleasure. Now, with the fine horses of the new National Stud racing in his colours, he had, at one blow, made himself one of the most important owners in the country.

That the whole thing was rather in the nature of a Greek gift may have worried the Trustees, but Hugh never gave it a second thought. The arrangement was that he should pay all the training fees and hand two-thirds of his winnings to the Chancellor of the Exchequer. That this ensured that he would have to stand a serious financial loss did not deter him from espousing his new role with the greatest enthusiasm. It is doubtful if anyone else would have taken it on.

In the midst of the increasingly grim news from France, the public and the Members of the Coalition Government permitted themselves a smile at the news of this strange new partnership. 'To whom in the War Office does one now go to get the best tips for the Derby?' one Member wanted to know. 'Whose colours will they run in—the Coalition's or the Prime Minister's?' asked another. 'Lord Lonsdale's,' replied the Under-Secretary for War, unamused.

Amid all his other jobs, the Committee of the Cottesmore came to Hugh more or less on bended knee to ask him if he would resume his Mastership until the end of the war. When they had last parted company in 1911 the atmosphere had been rather more than chilly on both sides. Now that the Hunt was short of funds, fodder for the horses and food for the hounds, and in danger of folding up altogether, Hugh Lonsdale no longer appeared to them in the green, baleful light of the Demon King. He was now the Fairy with the magic wand. He accepted this *volte-face* with equanimity. He was incapable of bearing a grudge and from 1915 onwards poured out money and energy in keeping the Hunt going at full pitch until the end of the war. When he gave up for the second time, he never hunted again. In answer to criticisms that the maintenance of hunting was not essential to the war effort he would reply with devastating conviction, 'What on earth are officers home from the front going to do with their time, if there is no hunting for them?'

That there were some officers in Britain's wartime army who had never even seen a fox was something right outside his comprehension.

Chapter 22

Hugh was over sixty by the time the war ended. Grace was sixty-two. Neither had spared themselves in the war effort. Hugh had headed the Sportsmen of Britain in raising funds to buy ambulances and as a full Colonel in the army had travelled back and forward to France in the interests of the Blue Cross, as well as undertaking all manner of other duties. His efforts on behalf of the National Stud and the Cottesmore, therefore, strenuous though they were, had to be squeezed into his spare moments. Grace had had a full-time job with the Red Cross as well as fulfilling as many engagements as she could, entertaining convalescent soldiers, collecting war comforts and joining in the many patriotic activities where her presence or active help could be most useful.

Surprisingly, of the two of them, Hugh felt the strain the most. By the end of the war, for the first time in his life, he had lost some of his exuberance. Only his capacity for spending remained unimpaired.

His cigar bill alone was £3,000 a year and there were no arguments the Trustees could use to make him pull in his horns. In the interests of wartime economy he had dispensed with his private orchestra and cut down drastically on his stables, but these were the only economies he was prepared to make.

With the onset of peace his role started to change. He now played the part of elder statesman in the sports he had once adorned. The old power of the National Sporting Club was passing to the British Boxing Board of Control, but Hugh sought no part in the new management of affairs. When he gave up the Cottesmore, he bowed out as a Master of Foxhounds, but remained as a wise counsellor to his successors.

As a result of his connection with the National Stud he had been elected a Steward of the Jockey Club and racing had become his main active interest. His life became largely governed by the Racing Calendar so that he knew exactly what his programme would be as far as a year ahead.

With Grace he would take up residence at Carlton House Terrace in May until Goodwood Races in July. He would always take a house for Ascot week near the course and it became traditional for him to drive down the course in his yellow carriage on the opening day behind the King and Queen. He had a house in the main street of Newmarket, with a garden which backed on to the sale ring to which he had a private entrance. It was a small house which he decorated with rose chintzes and papered throughout with rose patterned wallpaper. All the prominent names in the racing world used to come to this little house for dinner, and George V himself was a frequent visitor.

At the end of July he would usually go to stay with the Princess Royal in Yorkshire until the time came for him to go to Lowther for the grouse shooting. From there he would visit all the northern meetings, and especially Doncaster where he would take a house for the St. Leger meeting. In Edinburgh for the Scottish meetings he would take over a small hotel completely for himself and his guests.

It was not an economical way of life. In each of his large houses, including Barleythorpe where he still went in the autumn and the spring, a housekeeper held sway with a skeleton staff. A few days before the appointed date for him and Grace to take up residence, grooms, valets, lady's maids and household officials would go ahead to make everything ready.

Whenever he went to Lowther the first department to be favoured with his special attention was the stables. The stable-yard at Lowther was a religion with him. It was the holy of holies, only to be entered by the authorized staff or by Hugh Lonsdale himself. Only by his express invitation was any visitor ever allowed to view the stable-yard, and then never unaccompanied. It was one of the unwritten laws which everyone was expected to observe. For an offender to plead ignorance was no excuse. It was most unlikely that he or she would ever be asked to Lowther again.

Any economy in the stables was unthinkable. Every day the thirty-odd stable hands would be busily occupied polishing and grooming to a standard of perfection which was almost unbelievable. Each morning the complicated design of the Lowther coat-of-arms would be reproduced in powdered, coloured chalks on freshly laid sand in the yard. It was a work of the most meticulous and painstaking detail. There it would remain until the time came for Hugh's morning inspection, when his dogs would joyfully romp over it and ruin the picture. The following morning the first task of the stable lads would be to re-create the masterpiece in all its perfection.

The highlight of each week was the Sunday inspection which took place immediately after luncheon. As Hugh walked into the yard followed by his favoured guests, one groom would hand him a freshly laundered pair of yellow gloves; another would carry behind him a basket of chopped carrots pulled that morning in the Lowther gardens. Then, followed by a retinue of guests, he would visit every horse in the stable to feed it carrots from his own hands.

If really distinguished guests were staying, Hugh would sometimes order a review of all his horses. Positioning his party in the yard, he would order the horses and ponies to be trotted out in turn with a groom holding the bridle. On these occasions he was not above arranging that all the horses were shown twice. His meticulous attention to standards made his horses so alike that even the most knowledgeable had difficulty in tellingo ne from another. By this device he was able to show to his duly impressed guests a stable twice as large as he actually possessed.

From time to time, too, he would call for a review of all the gundogs on his estate. The keepers stood in line with their yellow labradors at their heels. As Hugh passed by, each dog was supposed on a word of command to sit down and stand up again after he had passed. The show was rather spoiled during one review when one of the dogs instead of sitting down sat up and begged!

Second to the stable-yard his great interest at Lowther was the gardens, although he hardly knew the name of a single flower. When he inherited Lowther, the gardens at the back of the castle extended for a mere hundred yards or so. Moreover they were dull gardens. Only the great avenue of yews which dated from A.D. 927 lent any interest. They were planted by the first Lowthers to live on the site in order to provide wood for their bows. Today the yews are amongst the oldest in the world. Some are over a hundred feet tall with spans of over eighty feet.

When Hugh first inherited, the park which surrounded Lowther was vast, but it was not big enough to satisfy Hugh, principally because his neighbours, the Howards at Greystoke Castle, had a larger one. By dint of flattening the fences of twenty farms he enlarged it until it was the biggest in the country—bigger than Windsor Great

Park, and certainly very much bigger than Greystoke, until then the largest private park in England.

Hugh lavished money on the new gardens he created. To the south-west of the castle a natural terrace runs high above the Lowther River. This was developed into a mile-long border of trees and ornamental shrubs. An old watering-place for cattle known as Jack Croft's Pond he converted into an exotic ornamental lake. Two miles of beautifully trimmed yew hedges were a feature of a garden which he created in the image of the gardens at Versailles. Each year thousands upon thousands of annuals were bedded out to form a blaze of colour in August and September in the borders between the yew hedges and the wide, exquisitely manicured grass pathways which ran between them and which radiated out from a central hub like the spokes of a great floral wheel.

A rock garden, dotted with lily ponds and all manner of arbours and bridges, was created for the Alpine plants and dwarf trees which Grace collected avidly on her travels all over the world, and which was her special province. In another corner of artificially created waterfalls, sheltering behind tall shrubs, every conceivable sweet-scented flower was concentrated in lavish profusion; beyond, and equally hidden away, a Japanese garden was constructed where, in addition to the masses of Japanese water-lilies and irises set among tiny islands and hidden paths, there were, at every turn, life-size bronze birds, scarlet lacquer bridges and Japanese stone shrines.

The *pot-pourri* had been created by Hugh from a wasteland of rocky scree. He went on adding to it year by year as some new idea took his fancy until his gardens extended to well over a hundred acres. Nor was he content for very long to leave anything in one place. On a whim, the rose garden would be uprooted of its twenty-five thousand rose-bushes and twenty-five thousand new ones planted in their place, while the Trustees, who had been trying to get some money spent on a tenant's farm or a new afforestation scheme, wrung their hands in anguish.

His views on trees was odd to a point of eccentricity. He liked what he chose to call 'dark green trees'. When he started to visit Lowther in the winter he was depressed to see the fine avenues of hardwoods without their leaves. The estate workers were occupied next winter with cutting them down and planting yews or fir trees in their place. As a result of this idiosyncrasy he cut down a wonderful beech avenue which ran right through the park.

As has been remarked earlier, Hugh's relationship with the Trustees had undergone a considerable change since the days when old Jim Lowther could call him to order. Distinguished body of men though they were and headed by James Lowther, whose presence as Speaker dominated the House of Commons, they found Hugh increasingly impossible to manage. He resented bitterly, as a small boy resents authority, that he should have to ask the Trustees for anything. He regarded them as the enemy to be bamboozled and deceived on every possible occasion. He resisted with all the power at his command the constant pressure put upon him by them to spend money for the improvement of the estate. Nothing was to be done from which he could not benefit in his own life-time. Every penny that could be spared must be given to him to keep him going in the style in which he considered he was entitled to live.

On one occasion he persuaded himself that nobody would notice if a Rubens, which was a family heirloom and therefore under the control of the Trustees, were to find its way on to the market. 'Sell it to anybody except Duveen,' he instructed. 'He has a reputation I hear all over London of buying for too little and selling for too much.' It was eventually bought by a firm of distinguished dealers for about a quarter of its value. Unfortunately for everyone concerned, the Trustees did find out and the purchasers were ordered to return the picture. As it had already been resold to France, a compromise was reached whereby the purchasers paid a similar sum to the Trustees as they had paid Hugh Lowther. In this way they got the picture for only *half* its value, Hugh kept his money and the Trustees had to be satisfied.

They did not do even as well as that when Hugh discovered that for years they had been running their own fire insurance whereby the Trustees had accumulated a reserve fund out of income. So successful was this operation that the fund amounted to almost a quarter of a million pounds. When Hugh discovered this secret hoard he made their lives so miserable that they eventually closed the fund and handed him the kitty.

To Hugh the Trustees were the Great Enemy. Anybody who had anything to do with them was suspect. Between him and the agents appointed and paid for by the Trustees a state of cold war existed. On the surface he treated them with politeness, even with consideration, but beneath the surface he watched, like a cat watching a mouse, for them to put a foot wrong. They were the people who were out to spend his money on things he did not approve of, and everything that could be done to spike their guns must be done. With the royalties from the coal-mines steadily diminishing and the end of the wartime boom in agriculture in sight, money was becoming shorter and shorter in supply. Every penny that was available was needed for himself.

Like an embattled medieval baron, Hugh gathered around him his own retainers whom he could trust to support him in his fight against the Great Enemy. They were men he could rely upon to carry out his orders and to watch after his interests when his back was turned. On the other side were the Trustees and their agents.

In 1921 the first light went out in the Lowther empire. Whitehaven Castle was sold. It was bought by the mayor of Whitehaven and presented by him to the town as a hospital. It was the part of the Lowther inheritance which Hugh cared about least. He scarcely ever stayed there for there was little fun to be had in a great rambling place which had now become almost completely encircled by the industrial growth of the town.

The sale of Whitehaven Castle meant that more money could be released for Hugh's private purse. Part of the Trustees' responsibility was the upkeep of the official Lowther residences, and Whitehaven had for a long time been a considerable drain on their resources. Now, in theory anyhow, they could consolidate the position at Lowther. In spite of their efforts, however, the minimum amount of money found its way into improving the estate.

For Hugh and Grace life went on at Lowther much as it had always done.

*

Mrs. Lowther,* wife of Hugh's nephew and heir presumptive, Anthony, was a frequent visitor to Lowther in the inter-war years. She has written this first-hand account of the experience:

Punctually at 9.30 a.m. when we were all assembled in the dining-room, Hugh would stride in through the door from the main hall, exuding energy and fresh air, carrying his hat and walking-stick which he would place on the sideboard. The impression he gave was that he had just returned from a long tramp around his estates.

I watched his timed-to-the-minute entrance many times before it occurred to me to question (to myself of course) whether he had in fact been outside the front door. In his later days at Lowther, anyhow, I am sure that his entrance was a bit of showmanship and that he had, in fact, come straight from his bedroom.

* Now Muriel, Viscountess Lowther.

Breakfast was a substantial meal, which we helped ourselves to from a row of silver dishes on the side-table. Hugh's breakfast was rather different to the rest of us.

First he would heap his plate indiscriminately from several of the dishes available, seat himself at the head of the table and proceed to feed each of his dogs in turn from his plate. He himself ate practically nothing. When this performance was over he would light a cigar and, returning to the sideboard, drink, at one gulp, a claret glass of brandy. He would follow this immediately with half a bottle of white wine, much in the same way as people nowadays take pills and medicines, and then bid everyone a bright good morning, explaining that he must deal with his correspondence. I believe he never drank a cup of tea in his life. He said it upset his insides.

As Lady Lonsdale never appeared until lunch-time, the guests were then left to their own devices to employ themselves as they wished.

During breakfast, particularly when there were important guests staying, there would always be tremendous activity visible from the breakfast-room window. Hugh had brought Sam Armstrong's father Bob Armstrong to Clifton, where he had set up his racing stables, and strings of horses could be seen exercising in the park. The impression one gained, of course, was that they were all Lonsdale's horses but, in fact, most of them belonged to other patrons of Armstrong and anyhow morning gallops would have taken place long before any of the guests were out of bed. They had to parade just the same.

Solemnly pacing up and down the terrace, too, would be the various heads of departments, like Jeffrey the Head Gardener and Sam Robinson the Head Keeper, waiting to be interviewed by his Lordship. Sometimes they would have to wait an hour or more before he would see them.

Unless there was a shooting party or a large number of people staying in the house for some reason or another, meals were extremely plain, although of course beautifully cooked and served. In fact, even on the most important occasions, the food itself was extremely simple and under no circumstances were sauces permitted. Nor were aperitifs or cocktails of any kind ever served at Lowther. People asked for luncheon or dinner were expected to arrive precisely at the moment stated on the invitation and to go into the dining-room within minutes of arrival. To be late was to be never asked again and an offender amongst the house guests was likely to find his or her bags packed the following morning. Even so the food was never really hot as the kitchens were about two hundred yards from the dining-rooms.

When just by themselves or with close friends the luncheon menu might be simply roast chicken or a cutlet, followed by rice pudding which was Hugh's favourite dish, but, however simple the meal, they seldom left the dining-room before three in the afternoon.

The time until tea-time was usually devoted to going round the gardens, which were magnificent and about which Grace was extremely knowledgeable. After that they would disappear again to their own quarters which were a sort of sanctum sanctorum to which only the most intimate of their friends were ever invited, and then only on the rarest of occasions.

Tea was served to the guests at five in the afternoon in the saloon, a ceremony over which Lady Lonsdale usually presided, after which everyone retired to their rooms to prepare for dinner, for which they must parade in the prescribed dress, dinner jackets or tails, at five minutes exactly after the second gong had sounded.

Conversation at dinner was apt to develop into something of a monologue by Hugh, usually on the subject of some of the achievements of his past life, the details of which were fantastic in the extreme. Because most of his closest friends were inclined to be sycophantic and seldom dared to contradict him, his stories were apt to get wilder and wilder.

Ever since the aftermath of the Whitehaven pit disaster when Hugh had tramped through the streets and got to know the miners and their families at first hand, his attitude towards his great possessions in the north had changed. Or, to be more accurate, his attitude to the people who dug his coal and farmed his farms had changed.

Criticism of tyrannously small wages, of appalling housing conditions and other social evils was laid at the door of the managers, the agents, and the Trustees. Hugh himself was above criticism. 'Ar, if only Lordy knew about that. He'd soon sart 'em,' they would say about anything that seemed to be unjust or unfair. But they seldom appealed to him direct any more than few people ever appeal direct to the Throne.

It was in this atmosphere of mutual good-will that Hugh began to take a greater and greater interest in the everyday life, outside his own park gates, which he had ignored for so long.

His appearance at Grasmere Sports had for many years been one of the highlights of the sporting life in the North. There from his private stand he had by custom held open house, dispensing hospitality on a fine scale to all and sundry. Farmers, Cumberland wrestlers, fell runners, trail-hound handlers from all over the North would talk the year round about what they had said to Lordy and what Lordy had said to them—and the tales lost nothing in the telling.

With the passing of the years and the closer Hugh grew to the people the more fantastic the tales became of his early exploits. Up in the remote dales and isolated farmhouses, in the country pubs and the miners' cottages, there was no subject more likely to get people talking happily than if anyone mentioned Lordy. There was always some new tale of how he had played a trick on some fell farmer or how he had knocked out a groom who had cheeked him.

There was one retired shepherd who was never seen without a bowler hat perched incongruously on his head. It was green with age and so battered that, when it rained, the water poured through the holes in the brim. It was his proudest possession because it had been given to him by Lordy.

He used to love telling the story of how he came by it. It happened that he was out early one morning feeding his sheep with some corn he had managed to purloin from Lordy's stables. Suddenly his Lordship loomed up from nowhere, although it was scarcely daylight.

Asked what he was doing he replied with great presence of mind that he was just feeding his sheep up a little to get them ready for the Penrith Show, adding cunningly that he would not like to put in any animal reared on one of his Lordship's farms which would not win a first prize. Completely disarmed, Hugh promised that he would buy him a new hat if he won. He kept his promise, even if the headgear was hardly suitable for a sheep farmer.

Hugh's love of prowling round at night was an eccentricity that many a poacher discovered to his cost. Every night when his valet laid out his night clothes he was also required to lay out his complete riding-kit in case at some late hour he decided on a visit to one of the several shooting boxes which he had built all over his estate. In remote Martindale, one of the last private deer forests in England, he constructed a luxurious lodge equipped with every modern comfort. It was an hour's hard ride from the castle but he would think nothing of making the journey at all sorts of strange hours.

Rumour had it that these nocturnal adventures were to keep assignations with various local ladies. Substance was added to this gossip when, after his death, the contents of one of the shooting lodges were put up for auction. The initials of one of his lady friends were found to be emblazoned on all the bedroom china, including the chamberpots!

It was on his way back from one of his moonlight expeditions, so local legend has it, that Hugh met his match for one of the few times of his life. Coming across a tramp sitting on the roadside suspiciously near one of his pheasant coverts, he strode up to him and demanded to know what he was doing.

The tramp told him to mind his own business.

'I am Lonsdale and you are on my land,' Hugh protested.

'I sit down where I please, and if you don't like it you can take this!' replied the tramp, with a haymaking punch to the jaw which set his Lordship firmly on his behind.

It was, however, Lordy who was usually the hero of the stories they told about him in the dales. There was the time he met a tenant from one of the more remote fell farms fishing by the side of one of the deep hill tarns which are scattered over the Cumberland and Westmorland uplands. The man had not shaved for several days and it was evident that the long winter had passed without his making a close acquaintance with soap and water.

Lordy said that he had not seen him for some time, and the farmer replied that he had been snowed up all the winter. 'As a matter of fact, your Lordship,' he said, 'I was intending to call in at the estate office this week to ask about putting sanitation in at the farm.'

'Well you had better have a bath before you come,' Hugh retorted, pushing him into twenty feet of ice-cold water.

Chapter 23

However wonderful the stories told about Hugh Lonsdale they were not nearly so wonderful as the stories he used to tell about himself.

The great advocate F. E. Smith used to say that the thing he liked about Hugh Lonsdale best was his ability to exaggerate even the most trivial of incidents into a story worth listening to.

Not everybody took the same view. Whether or not von Bülow had quoted Edward VII correctly when relating that he had described Hugh as 'the greatest liar in my kingdom', it is certain that the Prince was amongst those who were not so amused by Hugh's congenital inability to stick to the unvarnished truth, particularly where it concerned his own exploits.

The more remote the incidents in terms of time the more vivid were his recollections likely to be. His favourite setting for his more extravagant tales was at the head of his own dinner table, with Grace presiding at the other end, and the impassive Collins standing behind his chair. He would then regale his captive audience of guests with traveller's tales which would have put Baron Munchausen to shame.

When he had perpetrated a whopper of such dimensions that even he felt it might strain the credulity of his listeners, he would half turn to Collins and say, 'Is that not so, Collins?' Without a flicker of emotion Collins would incline his head slightly and reply, 'It is, my Lord.' The truth of his statement thus confirmed beyond any reasonable doubt, he would continue blithely with the next story.

On occasions Grace would be used as a court of appeal. 'Isn't that so, Gracie?' he would ask, his blue eyes gazing innocently up the table; and she with the slightest flicker of a smile would reply, '*You* said so, Hugh.' She would have made a marvellous wife for a diplomat.

Grace's manners were in every respect impeccable. She would

flatter even the most tedious of guests by listening to every banality as if it were a pearl of wisdom. Not a great conversationalist herself, guests would extol her wisdom and intelligence because of her ability to punctuate their monologues with 'yes' and 'no' in exactly the right places. Only very occasionally did this formula let her down. It happened once when they were entertaining some South African Air Force officers shortly after their return from a South African tour.

The young officer sitting next to Grace was all out to impress his distinguished hostess with the people he knew in South Africa, as well as to demonstrate to her that he was well abreast of the current popular slang in England. Everything was 'quite spiffing', and everybody was a 'good old fruit'.

Grace was quite bewildered, particularly as none of the names he mentioned meant anything to her, but she managed to keep up the appearance of paying the greatest attention. Finally he hit on the name of somebody she had met, and she took the opportunity of putting her guest at his ease by using what she hoped was the correct slang. Inclining towards him with the greatest dignity, she exclaimed enthusiastically, 'Oh indeed, Mrs. Dawson, I remember her well, such a jolly old tart!'

Most of Hugh's tales were based to some degree on fact. He loved to tell of his buffalo hunting in Wyoming and of his trip to the Arctic, but the plain truth was never good enough. One of his favourite anecdotes was of how he had saved the Cheyenne stage-coach from outlaws and, with the passing of the years, he left nobody in any doubt that he had in fact been to the North Pole.

'People who haven't been to the North Pole,' he would declare airily, 'always imagine that the snow there is white. They are quite wrong. The snow is pink. Also it is not generally known that there is life at the North Pole. Believe me, there are mosquitoes as large as the top of this wine-glass!'

It was whilst he was retelling this story to a distinguished dinner party that the young Mrs. Anthony Lowther, goaded beyond endurance by the sycophantic credulity of the other guests, exclaimed, 'Only as big as the top of your wine-glass, Uncle Hugh? Why, in Africa I've seen mosquitoes as big as this soup plate!' For a moment there was a horrified silence as the gaze of the entire dinner party turned on the newest member of the Lowther family. Then Hugh burst into roars of laughter and the situation was saved. Ever after that he called her Mosqui.

It was one of his proudest claims that he had discovered Klondyke on his travels in Alaska. 'Not having any need for more money myself,' he would say modestly, 'I reported the matter to the Governor-General for Canada with the results that you all now know.' Alas for the truth. When he was interviewed by the San Francisco *Record* he was specifically asked what he thought of reports of rich mineral deposits in the North. He replied, 'I came across a few scattered nuggets but there is nothing there worth the cost of developing.' What was true was that he had walked right over the site of the Klondyke gold strike.

Events had only to appeal to his romantic nature for him to believe that he had played a part in bringing them about.

When he was eighty he was prevailed upon to write his memoirs for *The People*. One of his most vivid passages concerns his meeting with Rasputin.

Remembrance of the Arctic always calls to my mind the picture of Siberia; Siberia of Russia and my unhappy friends the Tsar and Tsarina, whose kindness and hospitality I had so often enjoyed. These two fated persons were indeed among those of the Royal blood whom I particularly respected and revered and whose special friendship I had the happiness to enjoy. . . .

I wished to go and see Siberia and to wander round some of the penal settlements and convict camps. Part of Siberia is a lovely country. Its limitless plains have a marvellously bracing, exhilarating effect on a man; the atmosphere is such that ailing folk who go there find themselves in no time strong and hearty.

On my way to the Lena River I went only to a certain number of camps; and before I reached the Lena I went to stay with one of the Governors of the penitentiaries, or whatever the places are called. The Governor said he thought I would be acting unwisely in going on, despite the fact that I had all the necessary passes from the authorities and letters from the Emperor himself.

While I was staying with the Governor in this particular village, I became very friendly with him. He told me during our conversation that there was just then in captivity in the village a mysterious person who seemed to possess uncanny powers. The man, he said, had been arrested nearly a year previously on a charge of horse stealing and murder. It appeared that the prisoner had been for some time in the neighbourhood before the police had swooped on him, and that nearly all the local people, especially the women, were attracted to this man in the most extraordinary way. And this despite the fact that his appearance was positively forbidding. He wore his hair, which was matted and dirty, all down his back, and he was dressed in the shirt and blouse of a peasant. He could, they said, cure all sorts of ailments in women simply by making them look at him. The women seemed to regard him as an almost divine personage. But I was naturally not much impressed by what I had heard about him.

That man was Gregory Efimovitch Rasputin, the strange religious fanatic who was destined in the years that followed to wield such power at the Russian Court that his slightest word could change the fate of millions throughout the Russian Empire.

What was my chief impression of this strange creature? When the Governor took me along to see him my greatest feeling I remember was one of the utmost revulsion at the sight of his moist, red lips. They made such a contrast with the queer swarthiness of his features and his peculiar light-coloured eyes. As long as I live I shall never forget those lips. His eyes? They said, all those who wrote and told of their meeting with Rasputin, that his eyes were mesmeric, compelling, fearful. Yet they did not have the slightest effect on me.

When I went to see him in his prison he smiled at me, a strange sort of smile, and began to mutter quickly a long string of unintelligible words in Russian dialect; and we left him alone in his cell. . . .

Years later I again met Rasputin. This was at Breslau, when I went there at the time of the murder of the Russian Ambassador. Again I looked upon the sinister features of the charlatan adventurer. It seemed to me that his mesmeric eyes were trying to convey to me knowledge of my previous encounter with him. But whether they were or not I never knew. . . .

It was all stirring stuff and a great story, with the weakness only that he had never been to Russia in his life.

The fashion was just beginning to develop amongst newspapers of publishing the reminiscences of the famous in a more objective way than would have been thought either possible or good for circulation a few years earlier. Actresses and big names in sport were beginning to find a lucrative sideline in 'telling all' in the popular Press. Even the remote bastions of the aristocracy had been breached. Viscount Castlerosse in the *Sunday Express* was giving a weekly eagle's eye view of life in high places, whilst in the *Daily Express*, Tom Driberg, under the name of William Hickey, was developing the forceful, sharply written type of column which was to be the prototype for gossip writers of the future.

The public appetite for inside stories and backstairs gossip was insatiable and the papers which provided it put up their circulations by leaps and bounds. Hugh, now secure in the affections of the public as 'the greatest sportsman of our time', with a name that was a byword for straight dealing and fair play, was a 'natural' for circulation building, if he could be persuaded to co-operate—and particularly because almost all his life his name had been tainted with scandal.

Practically every popular newspaper and feature agency made an offer at some time or another. Some used the now well-worn 'you-owe-it-to-posterity' theme in their approaches. Others, more practically, relied on weight of money with mention of sums of up to £10,000 being freely bandied about.

At about the same time Gordon Richards, who was the champion jockey, was enjoying similar attentions. Having just received a particularly sumptuous offer Gordon Richards decided to ask Hugh Lonsdale, as the doyen of the Turf, what reply he should give. Hugh considered the matter for a few moments, and then gave his opinion with typical bluntness. If Richards wanted to ruin his career, to publish his life story was the correct way of going about it. And who the devil did he think he was, anyway—a damned film star or something? Modestly Richards accepted Hugh's advice.

Six months later *The People* proudly announced they had secured exclusive rights to publish in serial form the life-story of Hugh Cecil Lowther, 5th Earl of Lonsdale, K.G., G.C.V.O.!

It duly appeared, running for twenty-eight weeks—surely a record in Fleet Street. It resulted in the greatest rise in circulation of that celebrated paper, or in any other, until many years later when they broke their own record with the publication of the life-story of Errol Flynn.

It also created another record which made Fleet Street gasp. They paid Hugh £16,000.

Chapter 24

Hugh Lonsdale seemed to have the secret of eternal youth. He was seventy-three by the end of the nineteen twenties, but his immense zest for living remained unabated. Most of his battles were over and he was riding high on a wave of popularity. Now there was not a newspaper which did not praise him nor a sporting event where his appearance did not cause as much excitement with the public as the presence of Royalty.

Just before the Great War he had intervened personally for the last time in the struggle by the boxing fraternity for legal recognition. Before their featherweight title bout due to take place in Birmingham, Moran and Peerless Jim Driscoll had been bound over to keep the peace. Once more the big guns had gone into action. Again Hugh had dug into his pocket to brief Marshall Hall for the defence. Eugene Corri, Sir Claude de Crespigny and Hugh had appeared as evidence for the defence. Oddly the defence failed and the fight did not take place,* but it was the last time that the authorities were to try to prove that boxing was prize-fighting and therefore illegal. The long battle had been won.

After the war the big promoters had moved into the game—C. B. Cochran (later Sir Charles) had emerged as a big-fight promoter, so had H. D. 'Huge Deal' McIntosh. The N.S.C. had started to shrivel and die. By 1928 it was to all intents and purposes dead. Lord Lonsdale remained as a momument to all that had gone before. From his seat at the ringside, his gardenia gleaming white in his buttonhole, his cigar always looking miraculously newly lit, he epitomized the spirit of fair play and sportsmanship which had transformed what had been a seamy, sordid excuse for gambling into a national sport.

* It finally took place a year later at the N.S.C. After a disappointingly dull fight Driscoll won on points.

The presentation of the Lonsdale Belts was eventually taken over by the British Boxing Board of Control, but the lustre which surrounded them remained connected with his name. There was not a boxer in the country whose dearest ambition was not to win a belt, nor a boxer in the world who would not have been proud to shake the hand of the man whose name was linked with them.

When he gave up his wartime Mastership of the Cottesmore in 1919 he passed into the history of foxhunting, but the war had already set him on a new throne from which he could glitter. The wartime policy which had created the National Stud was continued and expanded, and its horses continued to race in Lord Lonsdale's colours. A rather better financial arrangement had been arrived at whereby Hugh could keep two-thirds of the winnings. It was still not a money-making proposition but it gave him a big stake in horse-racing to which he had previously paid only desultory attention. Once again he had come in, as it were, on the top rung of the ladder.

On 9th September 1922 the colours of the Lonsdale Battalion were laid up with impressive ceremony in the family church at Lowther. Hugh invited every survivor of the disbanded Battalion to the service, paying for all their train fares and superintending every detail of the great reunion with his usual administrative ability. Grace cut the yellow ribbon of the commemorative gates to the church and the gallant Battalion marched past for the last time.

The following Monday he left for the St. Leger meeting at Doncaster, where Princess Mary and her husband Lord Lascelles were amongst his guests to see his two National Stud entries Diligence and Royal Lancer compete in the big race.

On Tuesday morning, as he inspected the course with his distinguished party of guests, the miners in the new Haig pit at Whitehaven, which Hugh had named after the Field-Marshal, were commencing the day's operations. The first charges were fired; a moment later there was an explosion of such severity that it rattled the windows in the town.

At first it was feared that the disaster was on an even greater scale than the Wellington pit tragedy. As it turned out, it had occurred in the deepest and most remote workings, which had the effect of localizing its effects. As more and more workers struggled to the surface it was realized that only the comparatively small number of men working at the coal face were involved—but for them there was no hope. A mile and a half out to sea thirty-nine men had been blown to smithereens.

Next day the race crowds at Doncaster erupted in a tumult of cheering as young R. A. Jones, riding a superb race, won the St. Leger by two lengths on Royal Lancer against odds of 33 to 1. Unfancied, Royal Lancer left his stable companion Diligence well down the field to score the first Classic win for the Lonsdale colours, for the National Stud and for 'Bobby' Jones who was at the beginning of a long and successful career. When the Yellow Earl left the Royal Box to lead in the winner the great crowd rose to their feet and cheered and cheered again.

In Whitehaven all through that afternoon a single bell-note sounded as each battered, charred body was brought to the surface. It was the signal for a dwindling group of women to file through the grim improvised mortuary at the pit-head. One young wife identified her husband by a darn in his sock, a mother her son by a patch on his trousers. It was all they could be sure about. Young Sammy McLintock, whose shape was found blasted into the coal face, had had a pound 'on the nose' Royal Lancer. His widow paid the winnings into the distress fund.

Should Hugh, when news was first brought to him on Tuesday, have abandoned his plans and travelled at once to Whitehaven? It is certain that the idea was not even suggested. The truth of the matter was that such a course would not have been quite unheard of. His life and Grace's, and the lives of everybody around him, were as immutably fixed as the planets in their courses. Once a programme had been embarked upon nothing could be allowed to change it. A feature of the 'spacious' days of the Victorians had been their utter inflexibility. Everything had to be done to the minute and the pattern of living had to be planned for months ahead. It was a feature which Hugh perpetuated. It was never possible to make a decision at lunchtime to visit the shops in the afternoon. Orders would have to be given the night before, so that the necessary staff and horses would be available. Even to take a stroll around with a gun to fill in an idle hour presented almost insuperable difficulties. A keeper would have to be summoned by messenger from a distant cottage. The man who looked after the gun-room would have to be found and the appropriate gun and ammunition produced. A valet would have to be ordered to lay out the correct clothes.

In a life geared to gracious, trouble-free living, nothing was simple. Even to order a fire in the drawing-room in an afternoon in May which had suddenly turned chilly presented its complications. During the winter months all the fires would be lit in the morning and maintained throughout the day as a matter of routine. Then, on a given date, all the steel fireplaces would be burnished and the fires replaced with an elaborate arrangement of pleated paper fans. Not until the day ordained in the autumn when fires could be lit again, could the orders be varied.

In all the big households it was the machinery which had been set up which was the despot and everybody else its slave. Only a Royal Command or death could break its bondage.

Hugh did not share in the general emancipation which the motor-car and the telephone were bringing about. Urgent matters were dealt with by telegraph. Cars were just another form of horse transport and to be used with just as much consideration. If a guest was asked to dinner he was expected to stay the night even if he lived only a few miles away. Nobody could be asked to unstable their horses and drive them home at a late hour. When, in later days, they arrived by motor-car it made no difference to the rules.

For Hugh the end of the war was the beginning of his own personal war against all the forces which were conspiring to break down his private world. It was his last great fight. In an age where everything was change, he gathered his forces around him and prepared to resist to the last ditch. The enemy were on all sides. Even the railways, which he had for so long regarded as his personal conveyance, were showing signs of restiveness. When some of his dogs were travelling by first-class sleeper from London to Lowther, a traveller complained that their barking had kept him awake all night. The railway company deferentially passed on the complaint. Furiously Hugh wrote:

I would rather give up the rights I have always had for trains to be stopped for me at my own station at Clifton than have the travelling arrangements of my animals interfered with. I would point out, with the greatest respect, that the dogs complained about were my own personal dogs travelling on my express orders. It is well known to everybody, including some of the greatest dog experts in the world, that my own dogs are always perfectly behaved.

The greatest enemies of all were, of course, the Trustees. They controlled the money which was the ammunition Hugh needed to fight his battles. The Trustees had long given up the unequal struggle of both trying to improve the estates and keep Hugh happy. They were busy men in their own spheres and they were getting older. All they hoped to do now was to keep Hugh off their backs by giving him

The famous yellow coach used by the family on State
occasions standing outside Carlton House Terrace.

A Spy cartoon of Mr. Speaker
Lowther, Hugh's senior trustee, who
later became Viscount Ullswater.

Below: Jim Lowther, the only man
Hugh would listen to.

Hugh Lonsdale, Master of the Cottesmore during the Great War.

The Cottesmore hunt servants and second horsemen. Haines (Hugh's stud groom), second from left, Sam Gibson, fourth from left.

A photograph showing Hugh's jumping feat. The distance measured 32 feet from take-off to landing.

Lancelot Lowther, Field Master of the Quorn and the Cottesmore to his elder brother. Later he became the 6th Earl of Lonsdale and is the grandfather of the present Earl.

Hugh in his butt shooting grouse. Notice that he uses *three* guns with *two* loaders! Another keeper is in the foreground.

Right: Grace in her butt.

A grouse-shooting party up on the fells. Left to right: Lady Lonsdale, unidentified gentleman, the Hon. Francis Egerton, Mr. Crackenthorpe, Lady Gerard, Poss Myddelton (President of the Boxing Board of Control), Hugh, the Hon. Anthony Lowther (father of the present Earl), Lady and Lord Mar and Kellie.

A house party at Barleythorpe. Edward VII and Hugh are standing on the right, Lady Lonsdale seated in the centre, with the Dowager Countess (Pussy) on her right.

Hugh enjoying the tea ceremony during his visit to Japan.

Hugh Lonsdale as Sultan of the Atlas Mountains.

Below: Grace on board ship, bound for Cape Town.

Hugh on his famous pony Merlin, outside Carlton House Terrace, 1928.

Hugh with Fred Darling at Ascot.

The Prince of Wales presenting the cheque to Hugh at Olympia, 26th June 1928.

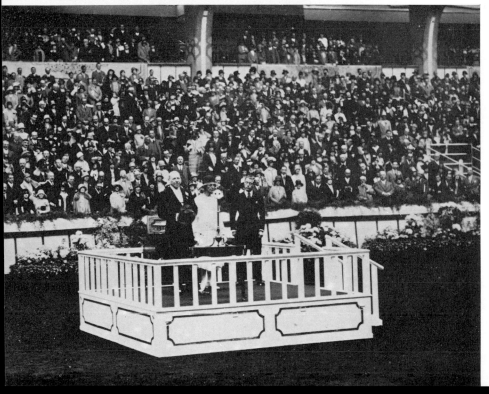

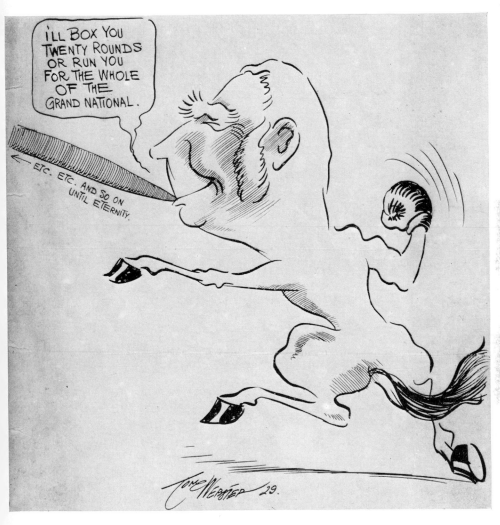

Cartoon by Tom Webster on the front of the menu at the British Sportsman's Club Dinner 1929.

Left: The Golden Wedding gift display in the drawing-room at Carlton House Terrace. The gold casket presented by the nation is in the centre.

Jem Mace, the great English boxer.

Hugh Lonsdale settles a dispute in the ring at the National Sporting Club, 1930.

Sandown Park, April 1930.
Hugh Lonsdale with
Ras Prince Monolulu.

The opening of Bertram
Mills Circus, Olympia,
21st December 1930. The
Duke of Kent and the
Lord Mayor of London
are with Hugh.

Hugh at Patterdale sheep dog trials talking to 'Candy', a well-known candy vendor at local sporting events.

The keepers at Lowther with Hugh's yellow labradors. Third from right: Charles Robinson, Headkeeper; second from left: his son Sam, who succeeded him.

A portrait of Hugh in his study at Carlton House Terrace.

"Limelight"   by Lynwood Palmer

SANDRINGHAM.

26th Dec 1935.

With warmest thanks for the
globe which you have so kindly sent me.
I heartily reciprocate all your good wishes
for 1936.   I am so sorry that
you have had to close down Lowther,
which I know you & Lady Lonsdale
will feel very much.

G.R.I.

Christmas card from George V to Hugh and Grace.

every penny that could be spared. It was still a considerable sum, but it was never enough.

For a time, however, it was enough to preserve the illusion. Hugh could still flap his wings and crow his defiance.

It was at Lowther that he found the greatest scope for living on a grand scale.

Because his friend Lord Sefton had a fine kennel of coursing grey-hounds, he imported the best trainer and an even finer lot of dogs and established them in the park as well. The following year his trainer, Dick Steel, carried off the blue riband of coursing, the Water-loo Cup, with Latto. Hugh was sitting on the top of another sporting tree.

Above all he turned his attention to all the local Cumbrian sports. Soon he had set himself up as the patron of hound trailing, a pastime unique to the district. Hugh set about organizing it, presenting cups and prizes and judging at meetings. There were few miners or fell farmers in the game whom he did not know by their Christian names. Whenever he could escape from the rigid routine of his life he would be out on the fells or with his miner friends, talking about their hounds, expounding his views or laying down the law. With them he was more at home than anywhere else. The circle was completing a full turn from his days in the stable yard at Asfordby.

His friends amongst his own social equals contracted rather than expanded. In the house-parties at Lowther the same names were repeated year after year. Princess Mary and Lord Lascelles were amongst his most regular visitors, so were Lord and Lady Mar and Kellie, Sir Noreen and Lady Bass and Lord and Lady Jersey. Year after year the same names appeared for the grouse-shooting parties, the pheasant drives, the local race meetings. For the rest Grace's family descended with unfailing regularity, singly or in clusters. By contrast with the long ago days at Orton Longueville, he was now the rich relation, the source of all bounty. Of the Gordon boys only the old Marquis, who had once preached so severely to Grace, had survived. In his old age he was becoming increasingly eccentric. Money was in chronic short supply and the difficulty he had in mak-ing both ends meet was common knowledge.

On one occasion when the Marquis was staying in the country, a mysterious visitor arrived to see him and was immediately taken off for a long walk. Although immensely curious everybody was too polite to ask what it was all about. It was only when the visitor called at the estate office to inquire whether it was in order for the old gentleman with the white moustache to sell him all the woods in the park that the secret came out!

The shooting parties at Lowther were conducted with the same rigorous discipline as Hugh imposed on the hunting-field. All the keepers and under-keepers were turned out in suits of Lowther tweed, and each man carried a laid-down inventory of everything from string to cartridge extractors. On the big days armies of beaters would be employed from first light, driving in the outlying coverts until the area to be shot over was literally seething with birds.

Some of the finest shots in the country came to shoot at Lowther. Sir Harry Stonor, who, with Lord Ripon and King George V, was among the finest game shots of the day, was a frequent visitor. Where the average gun would be mightily pleased to kill two birds out of a covey of driven grouse swirling over the guns, Stonor, shooting with three guns, could kill six. It gives an idea of the speed required to achieve this feat when it is realized that he would probably have four dead birds in the air at once.

Although the bags were as high as anywhere in the country—two or three thousand pheasants in a day—Lowther was not one of the shoots where the performance of the guns was of major importance. Some of the regular guns were merely competent, some simply bad. Hugh, himself, could have been a very good shot but he never took his shooting seriously. He was much more interested in the mechanics of the shoot and its social aspects. Sometimes he would merely puff away at his cigar and watch the other guns shooting whilst the birds streamed over his head.

After one grouse drive Lord Sefton, who was an extremely good and very keen shot, noticed that where everybody else had a dozen or more birds laid out behind their butts, Hugh had only two.

'Good heavens, Hugh. Is that all you shot?' he remarked.

Hugh said nothing, but the following day as Sefton walked past Hugh's butt there were thirty or forty birds laid out in rows. Astonished, he picked up one of the grouse to find it was stiff and cold. 'Oh, I say, Hugh, that's not playing the game; these birds were shot yesterday.'

'Nonsense,' retorted Hugh. 'Don't you know I always shoot with chilled shot!' His delight at pulling Sefton's leg knew no bounds, and he chuckled over his elaborate practical joke for days.

Once, on one of the rare occasions when Grace was out with the guns, Hugh shot a fox. Grace, in common with most people dedicated to foxhunting, considered the shooting of a fox as one of the greatest crimes in the calendar. Hugh, who had no such inhibitions, pulled her leg without mercy when the damning evidence was 'discovered' where Hugh had instructed one of the keepers to find it —right behind Grace's stand.

In order to have perhaps twenty days shooting in the year, the overheads which had to be met were colossal. Sam Robinson controlled a staff of eighteen full-time keepers all of whom had to be housed on the estate. Thousands of pheasants were hand-reared every year and on shooting days up to fifty beaters were employed to drive the birds. The only dividend which was received for all this outlay were the birds supplied to the castle. The cost could not have worked out at much less than £50 a brace.

The whole question of food supplies to the castle was also bound up with unchangeable tradition. Every week a game cart would be sent to Whitehaven, thirty miles away, for fresh fish. All the meat and game had to be provided off the estate. If by any chance a miscalculation in the amount required had been made, there was a frightful scene. In no circumstances could meat be ordered from the excellent local Penrith butchers. It had to be telegraphed for to London and collected off the train. Nobody quite knew why this was but it was a tradition which was never questioned.

The amount of food consumed each week was vast. Even if Hugh and Grace were alone, there was a staff of at least fifty in the house who sat down to four meals a day. If there were house guests the numbers could be well over a hundred. It could never be a question of managing with a few lamb chops. Whole sheep had to be provided, and if not required they would find their way out of the back door to someone who could use them. This was not a dishonest practice. It was simply that the food would have gone bad if it had not been disposed of.

The supply of drink was on an equally liberal scale. Beneath the castle and running the whole length of the building there were vast cellars where every type of drink was kept. On one side there was rack after rack of wine, on the other side vats of whisky and gin, and barrels of beer for the benefit of anyone who might call at the castle. This custom, which dated from the days when spirits were as cheap as ale, never altered with the times. Any tradesman or estate worker who had occasion to call could ask for what he liked, a fact of which many of the local stalwarts were quick to take advantage. Collins, who was in charge of the cellars, never had to refer to anyone when ordering. His only responsibility was to see that there was always enough. By the same token the head cook had complete authority to order all supplies for the kitchen. If she erred on the liberal side it was only a natural precaution against the unforgivable sin of running short.

Neither Hugh nor Grace had the slightest idea of what anything cost. Gin might still have been a penny a glass and a baron of beef five shillings. The only money Hugh handled himself was the money he carried with him for the purpose of distributing largess. For this practice he carried a quantity of half-crowns and pound notes. In principle the half-crowns were used to reward small services like opening a gate and the pound notes for everything else, but they could be interchangeable. It was purely a matter of convenience. If he handed anybody a tip it was usually a pound note. If it was thrown out of his car or carriage it was invariably a half-crown because pound notes could not easily be thrown. On very rare occasions when an actual purchase was made, change was never required. It is very unlikely that he ever had in his possession any pennies, sixpences or shillings. They were simply coins of no value for him.

Grace, on the other hand, although she knew nothing of the day to day economics of living, never lost her respect for money and the meticulous attention to money matters which she had acquired in her early days. Gravely she apportioned out her income, allocating so much to charity, so much to family presents. In the midst of Hugh's prodigal expenditure she lived almost parsimoniously. If, by chance, a stamped envelope was not used, she would carefully steam off the stamp and keep it for another day. From the little private money she had she gave generously to charity, even if her guinea here and half-guinea there must have looked mean in comparison with Hugh's flamboyant gestures.

Occasionally even careful Grace got caught. Every day the mail brought bundles of begging letters. For the most part they were addressed to Hugh, but Grace came in for her share. One that particularly touched her heart was a masterpiece of the gentle art of writing begging letters:

My dear Countess,
    I am a little girl that has hurt my back. My daddy was killed in the same accident. He was a doctor and now I have to lie on my back all day long.
    Please, dear Countess, a lady had shown me how to make this pretty doily, and I have made it lying down. Will you please buy it. The price is one shilling. We are very poor now Daddy is dead. Mother has to

work for us all. She writes short stories. There are four younger than me and sometimes Mother's stories are sent back. When Father was alive someone used to send us a Christmas hamper, but we shall not have one this year now, and my little brother Leslie cried when Mother said we should not have a turkey this year, and then Mother cried all night. He is only four and he did not know any better.

I wanted to sell enough doilies to give Mother enough money to buy a turkey with but I shall not have time now. It has taken me a fortnight to make this one and I have only four shillings. I think mother can perhaps get a pudding and a cake for the children with the four shillings.

Please, dear Countess, I have never written to a Countess before so if I have made a few mistakes will you please excuse me. I have had to write a few lines at a time lying down. I do hope a shilling is not too much, dear Countess.

Mother knows nothing about it. Only my sister Dorothy knows. She is giving me the penny for the stamp. Her teacher gave it to her.

I am, dear Countess, your obedient little friend,
Gwennie Errington.

P.S.—If you please, Dorothy and I hope the Earl is quite well.

Grace at once sent 'her obedient little friend' a gold sovereign in a registered envelope. Eventually the writer was exposed as a middle-aged lady of substantial means. She must, however, have been a lady of talent. She had used quite different, but equally brilliantly conceived stories to get money from everyone from the Duchess of Westminster to Lord Rothschild.

Hugh received an enormous number of begging letters, all appealing to his reputation as a sportsman. They came from abroad from home-sick Cumbrians asking for the price of the fare home, from men who claimed to have served in the Lonsdale Battalion, from broken-down boxers and jockeys, and, of course, from every professional begging letter writer in the country. Many, and the most difficult of all to deal with, came from old acquaintances and distant relatives. Typical of one from the last category is the following:

Dear Lord Lonsdale,
I do not suppose you remember me but I feel I knew *you* well enough in the past to be sure that you will not be offended with this letter. We met a good many years ago at those jolly little dances at the Savoy and quite often riding in the Row. . . .

Hugh dealt with all his begging letters conscientiously. Unless they were obvious frauds he would go to the greatest lengths to check up on their stories and if the case was a deserving one he would help in whatever way he was asked. For years he gave away about £5,000 a year.

As the nineteen twenties turned into the 'thirties, however, the financial noose was getting tighter. . . . More and more frequently the never-ending demands for money were turned down out of hand. There was just not enough money to meet them. 'I am sorry,' he wrote to an old friend, 'but I am completely bust. Under different circumstances I would have been only too pleased to have helped you but the Government has taken all my money. I do not know what is going to happen to me.'

But so far as the public were concerned the image was never allowed to crack. As the Trustees endured the permanent winter of Hugh's discontent, his yellow carriages never glittered more brightly, nor did the splendour of his retinue abate by a farthingsworth.

'I believe,' remarked one of his footmen wryly, 'that if he could have painted *us* yellow, he'd have done it.'

The appearances in public remained as splendid as ever. At Ascot in the large house he took each year he entertained lavishly. At Epsom the entertaining was on an even grander scale. For days before the Derby an army of men scoured the fields around Lowther to collect hundreds of plover's eggs which were served up by the bowlful in his private stand. At Newmarket, Doncaster and Edinburgh it was the same story.

In 1926 he became Senior Steward of the Jockey Club and the most powerful figure in the racing world. It was the signal for even greater expenditure. Whenever Royalty were present he insisted on his right to park his yellow Daimler next to the Royal car. On one occasion he found that Lord Derby had forestalled him. Furiously he strode into the Stewards' box and told his rival in no uncertain terms what he thought of him. He was 'king of the castle' and nobody must usurp his rights—least of all Lord Derby.

The strictest disciplinarian, he was still loved by everyone connected with the Turf and by none more than the racegoers in the Silver Ring. Instinctively they knew that everything he did was in the best interests of the sport.

One famous story about him that gained currency was of when he detected a trainer feeding a lump of sugar to his entry just before a race. There was one of the periodical doping scares on at the time, and all Lordy's suspicions were aroused.

'What was that you gave your horse?' he demanded swooping down on the offender.

'It was only a harmless lump of sugar,' protested the trainer, taking one or two lumps from his pocket. 'Taste one, your Lordship, and you will see for yourself.'

'You eat one first,' ordered Lordy, still suspicious.

Eventually both men had a lump and, honour satisfied, Hugh stumped off puffing at his cigar.

Later, when the trainer was giving his jockey last-minute instructions, he told him to hold his horse in behind the leaders until the last two furlongs, before going to the front.

'You are as good as home,' he said. 'If you hear anything coming from behind, don't worry. It will be either Lord Lonsdale or myself.'

It is a story which has since been repeated about other personalities of the Turf, but if it happened at all, it would have happened to Lordy!

Chapter 25

Barleythorpe was sold in 1926. It was a necessity forced on Hugh by his increasingly difficult financial position, and the cost of being Senior Steward of the Jockey Club. He contracted his household into nearby Stud House explaining that, as he was hunting less frequently, his old establishment was too big for him. Not for a moment could he bear for anyone to think that he had a financial care in the world. It would be letting the enemy see a chink in the protective armour he had maintained so assiduously all his life.

Everything had to be thrown into the breach to get capital to replace his dwindling and now hopelessly inadequate income. The money he had extracted from the fire insurance fund had served only to keep the bonfire burning brightly for a few years. Now it was all gone.

Finally there was nothing more that could be sold. The main estate was protected from him by chains he had forged for himself when he had sold his reversion and there was not another penny that could be squeezed out of the Trustees.

There was just one more trick to be pulled and in the end he managed to bludgeon them into agreeing to it. Covered by a vast and expensive life insurance, he commuted all his income for the next ten years in return for a capital sum. Repayments were at the rate of £20,000 a year, which meant that his income would be reduced in the future to negligible proportion. It was a desperate throw, but as the foundations of his life crumbled, Hugh's public image flared more brightly than ever.

The golden age of British boxing was already drawing to a close. The frail little Welshman, Jimmy Wilde, was still illuminating the last days of the N.S.C., but most of the glory was gone. Perhaps it had died that night in the early days of the war when the Frenchman,

Georges Carpentier, had demolished the once great Bombardier Billy Wells in seventy-three seconds at the National Sporting Club, where people had paid up to £75 for a seat to see the Englishman win.

After that fight little Jimmy Driscoll had leapt into the ring hysterically shouting, 'Coward!' at the defeated Bombardier. Only when Hugh Lonsdale put his arm round the little man and led him sobbing back to his seat did the boos change to cheers. England was still England while the Yellow Earl had a say in affairs.

At race meetings his popularity was phenomenal. He knew everyone from Old Kate, who used to sit by the roadside on the way to the course selling her selections, to 'Prince' Ras Monolulu, colourful and resplendent in his nodding plumes, who was one of his special friends. For everybody he had a smile, a word, or a pound note concealed in a hastily given handshake.

There was the famous occasion at Epsom when the bank holiday crowd almost rioted when the stewards called off racing for the day. It had been raining steadily for days past and, as the horses came round Tattenham Corner during the first race, there had been a dangerous fall. The turf was just not fit for racing and it would have been madness to continue.

When the decision was announced there was complete uproar. The crowd had been saving up for this day for weeks past and they were not going to be cheated out of their fun. Sticks, hats and umbrellas were thrown on to the course. A few hotheads, ducking under the rails, started to harangue the crowd.

Then suddenly everyone was silent. Pushing his way through the crowd, mounted on the Starter's white pony, was the Senior Steward, Lord Lonsdale. Putting the pony into a beautifully controlled canter, scarcely moving in the saddle, he rode down the centre of the course to Tattenham Corner. As the crowd recognized the figure in immaculately cut morning clothes, a cigar jutting like a naval gun from under the beautifully brushed top hat and holding incongruously in one hand an umbrella to protect him from the sleeting rain, they erupted into cheers.

Even when Hugh returned, waving to confirm that racing was over for the day, the immense good-will of the crowd remained undissipated. They had come for a show and they had got one. Long after the disappointments were forgotten, they were to remember how Lord Lonsdale had won the day in a one-horse race.

Perhaps Hugh loved the crowds even more than they loved him.

Perhaps he knew that when they stopped cheering his life would be over. In any event he was going to keep the party going no matter what the cost.

Relief from his critical financial state came from an altogether unexpected quarter.

The twenty-seventh of June 1928 marked Hugh's and Grace's Golden Wedding anniversary. In December of the previous year a Mr. Charles Howard of Coombe Park, near Whitchurch in Oxfordshire, had put forward the idea to the *Sporting Chronicle* that a subscription list be opened to honour Lord Lonsdale whom he described as 'the Admirable Crichton of Sport'.

The whole project was presented in the vaguest possible terms. It was thought that perhaps subscriptions should be limited to a guinea. If the fund reached sizeable proportions it might possibly be used by Lord and Lady Lonsdale to found a convalescent home for incapacitated sportsmen, or be put to some similarly appropriate use.

It says much for the vision of Mr. Howard and the *Sporting Chronicle*, who first publicized the idea, that from the very first their thinking was never petty. The use to which the money would ultimately be put may not have been very clearly defined, but they never seemed to have any doubt that the amount would be substantial. The fund raised after the great pit disaster at Whitehaven had reached over £30,000. It was never doubted that for a nationally loved institution like Lord Londsale the response might be expected to be just as great.

Within a few weeks of the inauguration of the appeal the *Sporting Chronicle* was able to announce proudly that their expectations looked like being realized. 'That there should have been a most gratifying response to the modest appeal for a limited subscription is what was expected,' they reported. 'There is now every prospect that the idea of founding a convalescent home for incapacitated sportsmen ... is within the sphere of practical realization.'

The fund stayed open for six months and each month it gathered greater and greater impetus. For newspapers all over the world it was a good story. Suddenly everybody wanted to play a part. Yacht clubs and racing clubs, boxing clubs and golf clubs all over the world opened subscription lists. Commercial firms, regimental associations and trade unions followed suit.

Soon the original idea of one guinea limit was forgotten. Indian

Maharajahs weighed in with munificent donations. European Royalty followed on a more modest scale. King George V sent five guineas, so did the Prince of Wales.

Above all, swelling the fund every day with an avalanche of postal orders, half-crowns carefully wrapped in tissue paper, and even pennies, the contributions poured in from ordinary people all over the world. Boxers and circus performers, costers and coal-miners wrote their carefully worded tributes and sent their shillings. A ninety-four year old Crimean veteran who had stormed the guns at Sevastopol sent two shillings, a backwoodsman from Canada five and sixpence.

An old Irish sportsman wrote, 'Although I have never had the pleasure of seeing Lord Lonsdale, writing this is a pleasure. We all have, over in Ireland, tremendous admiration for him. There has been no one like him a bit that any of us can remember; this gracious Victorian figure unconsciously making others around, in whatsoever society he appears, seem mere dwarfs in comparison. Alas! This kind of sportsman is not bred now.' A Hunt servant from the Cottes-more sent his contribution with his tribute, 'A juster and kinder master no man ever knew.' A Master of Foxhounds sending a guinea remarked, 'Some of us who have to make a box of fifty cigars last a year look with benevolent envy on his Lordship.'

By 11th April it was clear that the most sanguine forecasts were hopelessly inaccurate. The fund topped £100,000 and the money was still pouring in from all over the world. Charles Howard had taken on the job of honorary secretary to the fund. Within weeks the task had become an overwhelming one. Batteries of secretaries moved into his country house, Coombe Park, to deal with the sacks of mail which arrived each morning. As the closing date approached the spate of contributions showed no signs of abating.

The town of Penrith sent a gold loving cup. All the members of the family who bore the name of Lowther gave a model of Henry VIII's tall ship the *Marie Rose*, fashioned in silver-gilt.

By the end of May it was known that the Prince of Wales had agreed to make the presentation to Lord and Lady Lonsdale at Olympia during the International Horse Show Week.

The *Sporting Chronicle* announced that the fund had now reached such proportions that not only could the convalescent home be built but it could probably be sufficiently well endowed out of the surplus to make it self-supporting for all time. Rich and prominent sports-men gave immense personal donations and spurred others on to greater efforts. 'Only the foundations of the fund have been laid,' announced Lord Dewar. 'A huge sum will be required to build such a home as is contemplated, equip it as it should be equipped and provide capital sufficient to relieve the minds of the Trustees or Governors of any anxiety as to its future maintenance.'

The sportsmen of the world needed no urging. Soon it was being reliably reported that the fund was reaching the staggering sum of a quarter of a million pounds. Nothing like it had ever happened before. As a demonstration of one man's popularity it was almost unbelievable.

The presentation took place before a crowd of ten thousand people. As a tangible token of the affection of thousands of sportsmen all over the world the Prince handed over a solid-gold casket. Eight panels in bas-relief depicted sports with which Hugh had been closely connected—hunting, steeplechasing, yachting, coursing, shooting, boxing and stalking.*

'In addition to this casket,' said the Prince, 'there is a considerable sum of money—the amount of which I am unable to announce at the moment—which has been subscribed to be handed over to you to distribute to charity, in whatever way you think fit.'

As Hugh stood to reply the crowd rose as one to cheer him. It was five minutes before Hugh could get a hearing.

For once the famous cigar was gone. White-faced and near to tears he murmured his thanks into the microphone. 'Anything I have done for sport has been done because I loved it and because I maintain that the greatest friendships both national and individual are made on the field of sport. I do not know what the final sum will be, but I can think of no better use for it than to provide a home for men who have deserved well of sport and who have fallen on evil times.'

Then, as the Prince of Wales patted him on the back, Hugh and Grace stepped down from the presentation platform and made their way back across the ring to their box. As they reached the centre of the arena, Hugh impulsively put his arm around Grace and kissed her—the crowds cheered and cheered again.

The following evening Hugh and Grace gave a private dinner party at Carlton House Terrace. Almost the entire Royal Family were there. The King and Queen attended, the Queen dressed in a gold evening gown in honour of the occasion, the Prince of Wales, the

* The casket is now on loan from the present Earl of Lonsdale to the reconstituted National Sporting Club and is reputed to be insured for £20,000.

Duke and Duchess of Gloucester and the Princess Royal with her husband the Earl of Harewood. It was probably the first time a private citizen had been so honoured in his own house.

Long before the distinguished guests were due to arrive, Carlton House Terrace was packed with people cheering the coming and going of the telegraph boys bringing telegrams of good wishes from all over the world, the florists with van loads of flowers and private individuals leaving cards and messages of congratulation.

Inside, the great mansion had been transformed for the first big party to be given there for over fifty years. On the lawn at the back a marquee had been erected with a parquet floor and decked in Hugh's racing colours. A fountain had been installed in the centre of a specially created lily pond filled with goldfish. In the great drawing-room the golden wedding presents were laid out in dazzling array with the gold casket in the place of honour in the centre.

About forty guests sat down to dinner, while the band of the Metropolitan Police played background music, being careful to include the King's favourite tune 'Indian Love Song' from Rose Marie.

After dinner there were no speeches, but Hugh typically had a surprise for his guests. When the gentlemen went through to join the ladies, the whole party was ushered through to take their seats in the marquee and a moment later the long-legged lovelies, Carl Hyson's Follies from the fashionable Embassy Club, were high-kicking across the floor. It was the first time the Royal Family had ever seen a cabaret.

Jack Buchanan and Cecily Courtneidge, who were playing at the London Hippodrome, did a rush change and dashed over in time to appear in the last act singing their hit songs which were sweeping the country, such as 'That's a Good Girl' and 'Fancy our Meeting'.

It was a daring innovation in Royal entertainment and it came off triumphantly. The King and Queen loved every minute of it.

As the party broke up and Hugh started to show his guests to the door, his every appearance was greeted by the waiting crowds who struck up with 'For he's a Jolly Good Fellow'. The unconsidered second son who had had his education in the stable-yard in Asfordby had come a long way.

In September 1928 it was announced that his Majesty had been pleased to appoint Lord Lonsdale to the Most Noble Order of the Garter. He and Grace were invited to stay at Windsor for the investiture but Grace was too ill to accept. Hugh went to Windsor alone. It was sad that she could not be present to see the final accolade of respectability bestowed on Hugh.

Although Grace had lived her life out of the limelight, her influence on Hugh was very real. It was she who had steered him round the pitfalls which his way of life made inevitable. She had made a compromise in their relationship, within the terms of which Hugh had been able to live his colourful, extrovert life without letting the side down.

From being almost unacceptable to Victorian Society he had become the doyen of the aristocracy with a public image which had done much to make the aristocracy acceptable in a world of changing values.

The subscription to their Golden Wedding had been a spontaneous public tribute to the usefulness of his life. That he himself was almost totally unconscious of the good he was doing did not matter. He lived his life by instinct and his instinct was unerring. The award of the Garter set the seal of Royal approval on his merit already recognized by the public, but Grace's part in earning it was undeniable.

In telling the story of Hugh Lonsdale's life it is easy to lose sight of its real worth. In time of war, with much of the tinsel and glitter with which he loved to surround himself cut away, he emerges more clearly.

He did not, however, shirk his responsibilities in time of peace. When Whitehaven was raised to the status of a borough, Hugh was its first Mayor and was unanimously elected to a second term of office. His flamboyance in presenting a Mayoral chain second only in value to the chain worn by the Lord Mayor of London is apt to be remembered long after the useful work he performed while he held the office is forgotten.

He was Lord Lieutenant of Cumberland for seven years and proved to be one of the most effective in the history of the county. His interest in the Territorial Army was not restricted to time of war, and again it is unfair to remember only the splendour of the uniform he introduced or the magnificent style in which the Territorials lived during their annual camp.

There were few charities which did not benefit from his generosity at one time or another and many which enjoyed his active support. Although it was characteristic of him to boast outrageously about what he imagined were his personal achievements, he seldom thought it worth mentioning the onerous work he undertook for good causes.

One of the few references in his private correspondence to this side of his life is contained in a letter to Mrs. Anthony Lowther, written in the summer of 1930 after he had returned to London from opening the new infirmary at Cardiff:

... I have had a strenuous week in Cardiff and been busy each day from 8 till 1.30 a.m. each day. But I got a wonderful reception! and during my stay a collection got £25,000 for the Infirmary. Every class of sport was represented. Dog-racing, Donkey Derby, wrestling, bowling, running, cricket, football. We went from one to the other and round the Stock Exchange, and they were all too kind for words. The whole town decorated with white, yellow and red [his racing colours]. I do not understand it! Never shall.

We had one day: lunch 545 people, tea 376 (all ladies), dinner 728 and the next day almost the same; but the object of the Infirmary seeking aid from various sports was attained and they got £5,000 more than they expected. ...

Hugh claimed he did not understand it, and that was nothing more than the truth. He enjoyed his immense popularity but he could not understand how it had come about.

If his achievement had been limited to what he did for good causes and the undertaking of certain conventional offices, however, it would have been little more than might have been expected as the proper responsibilities to be undertaken by anyone of his wealth and position and certainly would not have distinguished him from his peers.

It was his showmanship—the very failing which Victorian Society most deplored in his make-up—which made his career such a remarkable one. If Britain had wanted to appoint an Ambassador Extraordinary to represent them throughout the world they could not have found a better one than Hugh Lonsdale. Wherever he went he epitomized the spirit of fair play and honesty of purpose of the typical Englishman.

His natural courtesy and distinction made friends for Britain abroad at a time when the country needed every bit of prestige it could muster. His habit of presenting cups, to be competed for in various sporting endeavours, remains a permanent memorial to him in small and large communities all over the world.

There is an extraordinary story about Jack Jonson, the Negro

Heavyweight Champion of the World, at the outbreak of the 1914–18 War which demonstrates the high regard in which Hugh was held by all manner of people.

Jack Jonson was one of the most mixed-up men ever to win the World Heavyweight Championship. He had a colour complex and all sorts of other complexes as well. He gave the impression of disliking the world and the world in general returned the compliment. At the outbreak of war this strange man was in Russia where he was engaged in a mysterious business with another Negro named Thomas; It was probably espionage in some form and it was probably on Thomas's business that Jonson came to England in the first few months of the war.

While in London he was set upon and robbed in the street by unknown men. Knowing nobody and mistrusting authority Jack Jonson could think of only one person in all England to whom he could go to get a square deal—Lord Lonsdale. He had never met him, but his reputation as a fair and honest man had impressed even Jonson. When he found that Lonsdale could not do anything for him he took it as final and left England for Havana, where he lost his title to Jess Willard.

In the General Strike after the Great War, Whitehaven, in common with all the other industrial towns, was at a standstill. It was a time of great suffering and privation amongst the workers, and the street-corner orators found it easy to whip up feeling on the subject of the evils of capitalism and the sins of the idle rich. Yet Tom Cape, the great Labour leader, gave it as his opinion that the only man in the country who would be trusted by the workers to effect a settlement was Hugh Lonsdale. Cape even approached Hugh, but Hugh turned the suggestion down, no doubt feeling that territorial loyalty and affection had caused Mr. Cape to put too high an estimate on Hugh's reputation outside Cumberland. It seems a pity, nonetheless, that Hugh did not try.

These are just two examples of the high reputation which Hugh held, not only in this country but abroad. He captured the public imagination to such an extent that by the time of his Golden Wedding he was probably the best-known Englishman after the King. The image he projected of someone above party politics, concerned only with the free-masonry of sport and common standards of fair play made an immense contribution to presenting a benign image of the aristocracy at home and of the 'typical Englishman' abroad. That the whole effect was achieved almost by accident does not detract from the fact that, of all the Lowthers in their thousand years of history, Hugh's name was to make the greatest contribution to his country's fame and to add the greatest lustre to the ancient line. It was no mean achievement for someone whose only conscious ambition was probably to be Master of the Cottesmore.

In his private life his achievements were less impressive. Consumed by the idea that he was to be the last of the Lowthers, he cared nothing for preserving, let alone adding to his inheritance. In fact, had it not been for the bonds which he had created for himself by selling his reversion, there is no doubt that he would have destroyed the estate completely. As it was, the only good he did was accidental.

For years he had agitated for the Trustees to buy a small area of moorland to improve his grouse shoot. Eventually and reluctantly they agreed. Today this, one of the few pieces of land added to the estate during his life-time, is reaping rich dividends—it is the site of a prosperous lime works.

If he had devoted his energy to improving his estate, or at least encouraged the Trustees to do so, he would have handed down fabulous rewards for his successors. Where more sagaciously run estates followed a policy of diversification, spreading their accumulated wealth into the industrial developments of the twentieth century, Lowther stood still. Every penny available had to be used to maintain the golden image that was Hugh Lowther. What was the family's loss was the country's gain.

Hardest of all to assess in Hugh Lowther's life is the extent of his personal happiness. That both he and Grace suffered grievously through their inability to have children cannot be doubted. Although he is credited with a series of love-affairs discreetly conducted, there is equally no doubt that their affection for each other increased rather than decreased with the passing of the years. A strength they both had in great measure was loyalty. Loyalty to each other, to their friends and to the standards by which they lived. Hugh could be despotic and demanding with those who surrounded him, but it was tempered with a strange mixture of kindliness and consideration.

Accused in his early years by his contemporaries of letting the side down, he remained loyal to his standards long after the fashion in standards had changed. In the end it was he who was the upholder of the old values and the bulwark of the Establishment. He never abandoned his old loves either in people or things. Perhaps it was this that finally gave him his greatest satisfaction.

If the criterion of the value of a man's life is whether he did well or badly according to the sum total of his doings, Hugh Lowther's balance sheet must show a sizeable credit.

Chapter 26

The General Strike of 1926 had created a serious position for the Lowther mines at Whitehaven. The basis of the Whitehaven coal trade had been built on the coal they exported. When the strike closed down the mines, all the export trade was lost and it was never recovered.

Although the seams of coal under the sea were immensely rich and produced coal of the highest quality, the cost of producing it was also high. While the mines were not being worked they still had to be kept dry from the sea-water which constantly seeped in and threatened to flood the workings. In addition the problems of ventilation at the coal face, which was as far as five miles from the pit-head, could only be solved by heavy expenditure.

For many years the Lowther family had not operated the pits themselves but had let out the concession to operating companies on a royalty basis. By 1926 the concessionaires, crippled by the effects of the General Strike, decided that they could not carry on any longer. When their lease came up for renewal they elected to let it lapse with the result that the Trustees found themselves with the mines untenanted, and the whole cost of keeping the empty galleries in good working order devolved on them.

It was not until 1930 that the Newcastle company of Priestman were persuaded to take on the concession, and then only after the Trustees had agreed to plough back all the royalties into the mines. From 1926 onwards, therefore, the golden goose was to all intents and purposes dead. With the iron mines at Hodbarrow now producing a fraction of their once immense output, it meant that most of the income from minerals which had sustained the Lowthers for so long, had dried up.

It was a desperate situation but one which with a little foresight need never have occurred to such a drastic extent. Hugh had seen to it that no reserves whatever were built up for a rainy day, and where other coal owners had spread their interests into other fields Lowther had contracted.

It could be argued that this was the fault of the Trustees and, in fact, different Trustees might have reacted differently to the circumstances. The ultimate responsibility, however, was Hugh's. Indeed although the Trustees were autonomous once they were appointed, it was Hugh who had the power of appointment. The whole situation degenerated into an undignified tug-of-war with most of the weight on Hugh's side. That they tried to carry out their duties by their lights is undoubted, but they were all busy men in their own spheres while Hugh had little else to do but think of ways and means of out-manoeuvring them.

In the end they had to resort to the most rigorous methods to control him. In a letter to the head agent at Lowther, they undertook to settle Hugh's bills only to the extent of £6,000 a year and not a penny more. The penalty for failure to carry out these instructions to the letter was instant dismissal. It was, however, easier said than done.

Hugh's own retainers, like Collins, Jeffrey, Sam Robinson and his personal secretary Clarke, were only concerned with preserving the image, while the estate office staff were under orders to keep expenditure on the gardens, the shooting and entertaining down to the minimum.

George Howard, a kinsman of the Duke of Norfolk who stayed a night at Lowther alone with Hugh during this period, loved to relate a story which illustrates Hugh's own determination to keep his flag flying.

At dinner Hugh asked him if he would like a keeper to take him out shooting the following day. George Howard replied that there was nothing he would like more but that he had not brought his gun with him.

'That is easily remedied,' replied Hugh turning to Collins in his usual position behind his chair. 'Send for my armourer.'

Gravely Collins left the room to return ten minutes later with the report that inquiries had revealed that it was the armourer's night off. Not by a flicker of an eyelid did he let it be known that the official was only a figment of Hugh's imagination.

The situation was not a very comfortable one for anybody, but perhaps the person in the most difficult position of all was Lancelot's son Anthony who acted as a sub-agent at Lowther and who one day might have inherited the whole estate.*

As an agent he worked hard to improve the estate, only to find his good intentions frustrated. That he remained immensely popular with everyone, while carrying out an almost impossible task, is immensely to his credit. On one occasion his assistant took two retainers to an agricultural show in Edinburgh. When asked on his return how he had got on he replied, 'I think everyone enjoyed themselves. When I left ―― and ――, one of them could walk and couldn't talk and the other could talk and couldn't walk!'

Although the staff had been curtailed and the stables at Lowther were filled with Fell ponies instead of carriage horses, Hugh managed to entertain on almost as lavish a scale as previously.

His close friends who came to Lowther year after year were either relations—mostly Grace's—whom he could dominate, or couples such as Lord Lascelles and Princess Mary and Lord and Lady Mar and Kellie. Sibyl Mar was probably the closest friend he and Grace had in later years. Her husband was almost stone deaf and referred to by everyone as 'little Mar', but wherever the Lonsdales went the Mars were sure to go. Hugh even took them on a protracted tour of South Africa and there were few house parties at which they were not present.

In accordance with the agreement they had come to so many years before, nobody was ever asked to stay at Lowther of whom Grace did not approve. Lady Gerard had been the most regular visitor and she had died at the end of the war. She was a friend of Hugh's whom Grace was prepared to accept, and in fact Mary Gerard became one of her closest friends. After that Hugh's girl-friends were perhaps more in his imagination than in reality, although he continued to have his bedroom on the ground floor at Lowther with a private staircase which ascended to a guest room above and which could only be locked from Hugh's side of the door!

Shooting parties were held on a grander scale than ever, although in later years guests were by no means certain of a day's sport no matter how elaborate the arrangements had been. Hugh would never admit to feeling in the least below par. If, however, he did not feel up to the exercise when he woke up, he would find some reason for putting off the day's sport. It was usually the weather. Even if the day was fine and sunny he would announce that it looked like

* In fact he did not outlive his father, and the estate passed direct from Lancelot to his grandson, the present Earl.

rain and he felt it would be wise to postpone the start until he saw how the day turned out. It meant that there would be no shooting that day and fifty beaters and half a dozen keepers would have a long wait on the top of Shap Fell for guns who never came.

Sometimes he would be taken with a different whim and waken all his guests at an unearthly hour with the information that, as it was such a fine morning, he had decided that they would breakfast on the moors. The sleepy party would then be mounted on ponies and face an hour's ride to one of his shooting boxes. There they would be regaled with a sumptuous breakfast served by a staff of a dozen servants, all looking as unruffled as if they were serving a normal meal in the castle. Goodness knows at what hour those servants would have had to rise to achieve this miracle. It would, of course, have all been carefully planned in advance, and if the weather had been bad another set of servants would have served breakfast in the dining-room and no mention made of the other meal which was spoiling out on the moors.

Although Lowther had become much more the centre of his existence than at any other time in his life, he was still there for only a few months in the year. His duties as a Steward of the Jockey Club and his National Stud interests kept him busy attending all the principal race meetings in the country. Of them all perhaps Doncaster gave him more pleasure than any. At Doncaster he was king and shared the limelight with no one—not even Lord Lascelles whose territory it really was. That Doncaster is such a popular meeting today is in part due to the time and money Hugh lavished on making it so.

If the Trustees had imagined that their severe financial strictures were going to stop Hugh living the life of a grandee, they must have forgotten the vast sum subscribed by the nation for his Golden Wedding. True he had made some half-hearted attempts to set up a 'strong committee' to look after the fund, but, in the end, the task had proved too much for him. Beset on all sides he forgot about the committee altogether. So far as the fund was concerned he could claim with Andrew Lang:

> I am the batsman and the bat,
> I am the bowler and the ball,
> The umpire, the pavilion cat,
> The roller, pitch and stumps and all.

Perhaps he reflected, looking back at his own oratory, that here was at least one sportsman who had deserved well of sport and for whom no provision had been made. However he argued it, the result was the same. By 1935 the whole of the £300,000 had been sunk without a trace.

Chapter 27

It was at the beginning of December 1935, when Hugh was seventy-eight and Grace a few months short of her eightieth birthday, that the axe finally fell.

Mr. Rigby, the Trustees' agent in London, put the matter succinctly in a letter to Mr. Nanson, the head agent at Lowther:

18th December 1935

My dear Nanson,

In regard to the inquiries over the telephone you had yesterday, I ought to have informed you that owing to the financial state of affairs Lord Lonsdale had consented to give up residing at Lowther and also at Carlton House Terrace, and to make his headquarters at the Stud House, Barleythorpe, early in the New Year, by which time it is hoped that the available income which will be coming to him from the Trustees will meet his requirements. He has taken the Trustees' ultimatum very well indeed and has realized that without the necessary money it would be foolish of him to try to carry on at Lowther and Carlton House Terrace. I am very sorry for both of them but as he says 'it can't be helped' and 'I am only like a great many others'.

His Lordship is arriving in London this evening. I don't know exactly what he is going to do about Christmas but I fancy he will if possible return to Lowther. I do not know what her Ladyship's arrangements are but, if possible, I think she will go to Lowther as well. . . .

Hugh and Grace did go to Lowther for Christmas. They spent it alone in the great echoing rooms of the castle. Nothing was changed. The servants were all in their places. The family crest was still etched out each morning in the sand in the stable-yard. Jeffrey, Robinson and Steel came up to the castle for their orders and in the

232

stewards-room the housekeeper went gravely into dinner on the arm of the House Steward.

Everything was just the same except that there were no guests. On 27th December Lady Mar arrived for a three-day stay. She left on the thirtieth. She was the last visitor ever to stay at Lowther.

On 1st January 1936 Hugh's yellow Daimler swung through the castle gates. The gatekeeper saluted for the last time and then walked sadly back to the castle to lower Hugh's flag. It hardly seemed possible that the rumours which had been circulating were true— that Lordy had left Lowther for the last time. On his desk lay the correspondence he had been dealing with that morning, his clothes hung in their cupboards and the freshly ironed blotting-paper marked the place in the great silver-embossed visitors-book for the convenience of the next guests.

But it was all perfectly true. Neither Hugh nor Grace ever set foot in Lowther again. Each week the clock winder came up from Penrith to wind the clocks to tick the hours away unheeded until his next visit.

As the country drew closer and closer to another war, Hugh's visits to Carlton House Terrace became less frequent. By the time the first sirens sounded over London, he and Grace were living in their own world at Stud House. At Lowther, where in 1914 Hugh had reviewed his 'Lonsdales', a village of Nissen huts now stood. Around the miles of park wall high screens were erected behind which one of the most secret training operations of the war was carried out. Thousands of acres of parkland were ploughed up knee-deep in mud by the tracks of Britain's new mechanized Army. Lowther was doing its part again in yet another war. But for Hugh all wars were over.

At Stud House, there were few callers and still fewer occasions when Hugh, as immaculate as ever, ventured out to a public engagement. Even the last few years he had cut down his public engagements to the minimum. One of the events he never missed was the opening of Bertram Mills Circus, of which he was President. There for a few short hours each year he would appear beamingly in the Royal box adding his own distinction to the spangle and glitter of the Big Top. To the end Hugh Lonsdale was 'the next best sight after the elephants'.

At Stud House all the habits of a lifetime were carefully perpetuated. Each morning Hugh would appear dressed as if he were going out for a day's shooting. His brandy and his white wine stood ready

on the sideboard. Each evening he would gravely lift his glass to
Grace at the other end of the table and give the time-honoured
toast, 'Mrs. Tommy, the King, Foxhunting and the Ladies,' and
Grace sitting erect in her straight-backed chair, would incline
slightly forward and reply, 'Mr. Tommy, the King, Foxhunting
and the Gentlemen.'

In September 1942 Grace died. Her maid found her in the morning dead beside her bed. Grimly Hugh travelled to Lowther to stand
by her graveside and then take the next train home. He scarcely
spared a glance for the great castle which overshadowed the tiny
family graveyard.

He hated funerals or anything to do with sadness. Grace's was the
only funeral he attended all his life, apart from State ceremonies. He
refused to have her buried in the gloomy mausoleum which had been
built by his father because all the available space in the family church
had been taken up by past generations of Lowthers. Instead she was
laid to rest on a green mound in the churchyard which overlooked the
Lowther River, her grave marked only with a simple cross of granite.

As R.A.F. planes droned overhead on their way to Germany from
the airfields around Oakham, Hugh spent his days dreaming by his
fireside or pottering around in his garden.

Just occasionally there was a flash of his old spirit. A favourite dog
running over a flower-bed got its paw caught in a mole trap. Furiously Hugh demanded to know who had set it.

'I did,' confessed the old gardener who had been with him for
many years.

'Well, you will leave my employment this minute,' Hugh growled.

'In that case, before I go, you can take this!' retorted the old man
throwing a punch at Hugh with sufficient vigour to knock him down.

For a moment the two old men glared at each other. Then Hugh
held out his hand. 'Help me up,' he said. 'I suppose I'd better keep
you. Can't get anyone else.' Pushing one of the now rare fivers
into the man's hand, he continued his round of morning inspection,
smiling to himself and secretly highly delighted with the whole
incident.

Occasionally there would be callers. One of his great nephews on a
hurried leave from the Army, or an ex-girl friend with whom he
could talk over old times, would come to stay the night. Within his
means his generosity remained unabated. After Grace's death he
wrote to most of her old friends asking them whether they would
like a piece of Grace's jewellery.

Once when an old friend who had been a bridesmaid at their wedding called to see him, he asked her what she would like. She said she would like a diamond brooch Grace had worn on her wedding day. Hugh sent for the jewel-case and finding the piece in question missing asked what had happened to it.

'I believe you gave it to the cook last week, my Lord,' replied the butler.

'Well, get it back from her. The cook had better pick something else,' snapped the Yellow Earl.

One of the last letters he ever wrote was to his nephew's wife, Mosqui, who had stood up to him so long ago.

... Life has been such lovely fun. There is nothing much I can do now, but they can never take my memories away from me. ...

To the end the 'they', who were trying to destroy his fun, haunted him.

Late one night his steward found him in a coma in his armchair by the fire. Gently he picked up the once massive frame now so shrunken that he hardly felt the weight. As he carried him upstairs Hugh awoke to the indignity of being helped. 'Put me down, damn you!' he said.

They were the last words he ever spoke.

*

In spite of the difficulties of wartime travel, people flocked to the funeral of Hugh Lonsdale from all over the country. In accordance with his last wishes he was buried alongside Grace, his grave marked with a cross of Westmorland granite. He was carried to his grave by the servants who had served him so long and so well. As a last tribute Jeffrey had lined the grave with yellow daffodils packed bloom to bloom so that no newly turned earth showed. It was a tribute he would most certainly have appreciated.

Among the wreaths sent to the church was one from his old friend 'Prince Monolulu'. The card, which summed up the feelings of so many of the people there, read:

LORD LONSDALE

Great Britain's Greatest Ambassador of Clean Sport,
Boxing, Wrestling, Swimming, Yachting,

All Ball Games,
Man's Friend, the Dog his delight.
'A Horse, A Horse.' The Pillar of the Turf.
'A Horse, a Horse.' The Friend of the Friendless.
An African Negro prays that your Spirit, like
John Brown's song, will go marching on
'In Glory, Glory Hallelujah'.
That all Mankind will be Brothers through
Clean Sport

RAS PRINCE MONOLULU

All over the world Hugh's death made headline news in a Press preoccupied with other things. He would have appreciated that, too.

Family Tree and Appendixes

LOWTHER FAMILY TREE (ABBREVIATED)

Lowther cum Darncourt	940	Edmund
Lowther cum Bromflett	965	Edgar
Lowther cum Roohsbye	985	Ethelred I
Lowther cum Quaile	1015	Ethelred II
Lowther cum Mowbrey	1038	Harold
Lowther cum Burnett	1064	Edward the Confessor
Lowther cum Lascelles	1090	William Rufus
Lowther cum Stapleton	1116	Henry I
Lowther cum Stuckland	1146	Stephen
Lowther cum Viponte	1171	Henry II
Lowther cum Moulton	1199	John
Sir Gervase de Lowther cum d. of Baron Ross de Kendal	1221	Henry II
Sir Hugh de Lowther cum L'Engleys	1232	Edward I
Sir Hugh de Lowther cum Moresbye	1247	Edward I
Sir Hugh de Lowther cum Tiliol	1300	Edward II
Sir Hugh de Lowther cum Lucy	1373	Capt. Carlisle Castle, M.P. Cumb. 1324
Sir Hugh de Lowther (wife not recorded)		M.P. Westm. 1377
Sir Robert de Lowther cum Strickland		M.P. Cumb. 1392, died 1430
Sir Hugh de Lowther cum Darentwater	1426	at Agincourt 1415, M.P. Cumb. 1426
Sir Hugh de Lowther cum Lancaster	1475	M.P. Cumb. 1449, Sheriff 1456
Sir Hugh de Lowther cum Curwen		Sheriff Cumb. 1516, 1543 and 1567

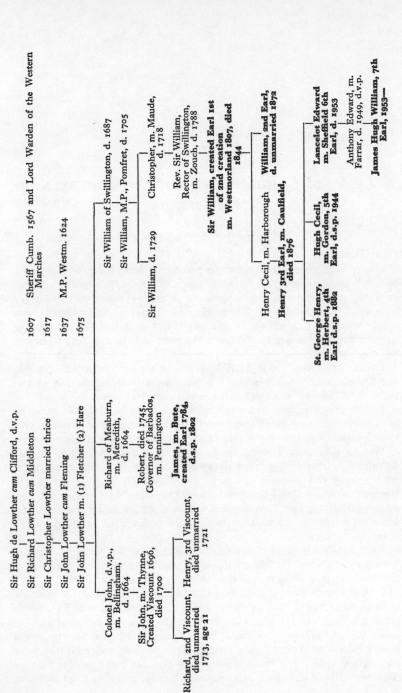

A Letter of Criticism to Thatcher, Huntsman to the Cottesmore

Private and Confidential and for you and myself only.

Dear Thatcher,

I have been meaning to write to you for at least three weeks, but I had diffidence in doing so, for two reasons: Firstly, I do not think that anybody has a right to interfere with, or express opinions to another man's servant. Secondly, I thought that it was quite possible you might naturally say, although you might not wish to express it owing to your personal courtesy, 'What right have you to say this, I am not your servant?'

I therefore asked you if I might write you a private letter, and you very nicely said 'yes'. I said, 'I hope you will understand it in the right light,' and your answer was equally kind and nice.

I wish you therefore to understand that I am writing this letter to you, not in any way in your capacity as a servant, but as between two men interested in the chase, and with a desire for your welfare.

Having said this, I write freely and fully, and shall only be too delighted to answer any point that you take exception to, or discuss it with you, or you to come over here and dine with me quietly and talk the matter over, when I will get Mr. Richardson, Mr. Chaplin and one or two knowledgeable men to meet you, and we could discuss the thing amongst ourselves without anybody outside knowing anything at all about it.

I am anxious in your own interests, and I am also anxious that the Cottesmore should be looked upon as one of the first-class packs of England, instead of, as it is at the moment, held up to ridicule.

On my return from India I went to the Turf Club, and I was asked if I was returning to Barleythorpe. I said, 'Yes, and I hope to have some good hunting,' and I was surprised at the number of gentlemen— some ten or twelve—who said, 'Well, you won't stand hunting with the "headless huntsman" very long; people are very sick of it now; the calculation is that he never hunted any one fox last year for twenty minutes without changing or going to a hulloa, and they are talking of

getting up a memorandum to the Master to ask for a change of huntsman.'

I immediately took up your cudgels, and said I thought it was a most
extraordinary thing to do, and most unfair thing to do; that the huntsman's duty was to carry out the wishes of his Master, and therefore the
Master was to blame and not the huntsman.

I came down here, and I regret to say that before I had been here a
week I was entirely of the same opinion as what I had heard all over
London. I saw your hounds out, and you had 22½ couples. Within
twenty minutes you had changed your foxes three different times, and
you wanted five couples. On another occasion, at Woodall Head, we
went away from there and ran down a lane for three hundred yards.
The wind was blowing south-west. You held down to Edmondthorpe,
which was virtually upwind, and let everybody go down the lane right-
handed, which was the first ground that you ought to have made good,
which showed that what was really in your mind was getting away
forward and jumping fences, instead of thoroughly hunting and
pursuing the fox. You then went right on into the covert, and went
away on the west side towards Edmondthorpe, and then into the
Spinney at the top of Wymondham.

Had you heard the remarks and criticisms of the field you would
have felt that you had committed some frightful crime and had it not
been for me I think there would have been very strong representations
at the moment that you had done what no huntsman had a right to do.
You had gone into the covert without a true line, and were simply
galloping forward on the off-chance of hitting off a stray fox.

That is not foxhunting, and I therefore quote you the words of Lord
Henry Bentinck to Goodall, who eventually became one of the greatest
huntsmen of the day.

In the year 1845, Goodall did exactly the same thing, and Lord
Henry Bentinck, who is admittedly the greatest authority on foxhunting that ever lived, wrote as follows:

26th October 1845: 'Goodall, after today's performance, you will
kindly make such arrangements as to deliver my pack over to the First
Whipper-in on 1st November.'

Goodall's reply: 27th October. 'My Lord, I beg to acknowledge the
receipt of your Lordship's letter, which has enveloped me in mystery.
Should be exceedingly grateful if your Lordship will give the reasons
for such sudden dismissal, which is ruin to me and to my two young
children.'

Lord Bentinck: 'Goodall, I require a huntsman. A huntsman is a
man who pursues the fox, and who works his fox and his hounds to the
detriment of the animal, not changing from fox to fox or from holloa to

holloa, but who pursues one animal unto death; and who can be trusted by his employer to maintain the rules of foxhunting, which rules, though unwritten law, are the most important rules to honourable men. They are as follows: "Unless you have a good line into a covert you should never let your hounds go in, and, even then, having a line up to the covert an artist should stop his hounds and make good the outside of the covert before letting his hounds enter it where they have identified the line in, for you must remember that where you are not on a line you have no right to pursue a strange fox into another country." You seem to be devoid of a huntsman's honour, for I saw you do this twice today, added to which, if you allow hounds to go from a line which they have identified and take up the line of every fresh fox you traverse, your pack soon becomes deteriorated to such an extent that the venery of foxhunting is lost and it simply becomes a brainless chase. I have seen you now five days cubhunting. You have always gone away with the first fox that left covert, which is most brainless, the most useless, and the most detrimental style of foxhunting that can be possibly imagined, causing friction amongst occupiers of land, causing annoyance to the graziers of stock, and, what is far worse, the absolute ruination and destruction of your hounds, and, under any circumstances, you cannot make your hounds now to hunt like a pack of foxhounds until November year.'

Goodall's reply: 'My Lord, I have never realized quite the value of what your Lordship has written. If your Lordship will give me another chance I will try and bear your wishes in view. Will you kindly reconsider your notice?'

Lord Bentinck: 'I omitted in my last letter to point out that you seem to think, beyond what I have already told you, that it was your duty to gallop about jumping fences. You must remember that you have never seen a great huntsman who ever jumped a fence when he could open a gate, for the reason that, if he has his hounds in hand and he goes through the gate, he takes the pack with him. If he jumps the fence only one hound can get through the aperture at a time. The consequence is that before he has gone three hundred yards, he has a string of hounds instead of a pack of hounds in the palm of his hand. I will give you until 1st January to see if you have head enough to improve your present methods, and therefore I withdraw my present notice, and will give you until 1st January.'

Goodall's reply: 'My Lord, I beg to thank your Lordship for your kindness. I will do my best to carry out your wishes, but I was under the impression that the gentlemen liked galloping, and looked more upon galloping after hounds than foxhunting as their pleasure.'

Lord Bentinck: 'Your last remark has evidently arisen from the detrimental interests of a huntsman, namely, newspaper reports. Take my advice and never read them, but remember this that the very men who encourage you to gallop and jump unnecessary fences are the very men who will bring you to your doom. Your hounds are hunting like drag hounds, not like a pack of foxhounds, and remember that no artist had ever tired his horse yet, and I have seen you tire two horses in a day, which of itself proves want of science and want of knowledge, and want of proper intellect and observation of the chase. Let me see no more of it.'

When Tom Firr went from the Pytchley to Lord Eglinton's, the following letter appears to have passed between them: 'I have great complaints as to your mode of foxhunting. Your chief desire seems to be to gallop after foxes, and to make yourself the laughing stock of the public. Unless this changes before 1st November I give you notice for 1st February (signed) Eglinton.'

On 26th December there was a very long run, and after hunting his fox for an hour and twenty minutes Firr went to a holloa, got on to a fresh line, and hounds went away, and at seven o'clock in the evening fourteen couples of hounds were missing and they were eighteen miles from home. Lord Eglinton went up to Firr and said, 'Firr, how come you to overreach that horse like that?' Firr got off to look at the horse and said, 'He is not overreached, my Lord.' Lord Eglinton said, 'Give me the horse a minute and look at this hind leg.' As soon as he had the reins in his hand he trotted straight home, leaving Firr to walk home and collect his hounds, saying, 'You have overreached your fox as well as your horse, for your horse is well-nigh cooked. Collect your hounds and walk home.' Firr has often told me that he suffered agonies during that walk home, but he collected seventeen couples of hounds before he got home, and he told me that from that time until the time of his death he never stopped a horse in his life, neither did he care what the gentlemen or anybody else said. He always did his best to stick to one fox, and that was the real making of him, and he also told me that he had never read one single criticism about himself from that day to this.

Now, I mention all these facts because they are really applicable to yourself, and I confess that I have been very much surprised at the way people are talking of you at the moment. You are now known all over England as 'the headless huntsman', and I can assure you that, if anything happened to Mr. Hanbury, I believe it would be an impossibility for any Master succeeding him to take you on as huntsman, for the feeling in the country is so strongly against you, and the ridicule that is caused by your manoeuvres (which are far from a huntsman's point of view) would make it impossible.

I most sincerely trust and believe that there is no likelihood of a change, but personally I sincerely trust that you will take all this to heart and think it over.

You will find it very difficult to get a situation as huntsman were any change to be made from here, and I am absolutely certain that no Master could take you on, because the feeling is so extraordinary at the present moment against your system that I have determined to write and tell you exactly the position in which you are.

Your hounds are probably one of the greatest disgraces in England at the present time. They hunt like drag-hounds, not like foxhounds. You have no idea when you once start with a fox of identifying your line, whereas you ought to be able to see whether your hounds take up a fresh scent or not, and you ought to have stopped your hounds three times on 12th December and gone back and identified your line, when you could have killed your fox. But your hounds cannot identify a fox for you, and that I realize.

You recently wrote to a huntsman and said, after describing your start: 'I gave the gentlemen a good gallop, and there is none of them know whether we hunted a fox or not.' This is the greatest mistake you ever made in your life, for, though a great many of the gentlemen know more of riding than of the pursuing of the fox, yet the majority here think far more of your adhering to one fox on the chance of sport than you are aware of, and everyone of them complain that you go from fox to fox and fox to fox, and that since you have been huntsman here they have not had a really genuine foxhunting day of any sort or kind except by accident owing to good scent. You go from holloa to holloa; you leave your line at angles that show you don't grasp the position. You neither watch the flight of birds, which are the greatest signposts to foxhunting; you pay no attention to the position or attitude of sheep or cattle, and when once you are at fault, instead of working out your line and making your ground good, you gallop away on the off-chance of hitting some strange line, which is ruination to your hounds, and one has only to be out a few minutes to realize the terrible state into which you have reduced the pack.

I doubt if there is any man, other than Charles Isaacs, who has so small a sympathy in the hunting world as yourself at the moment, and I do sincerely trust for your own interests that you will think this over and read it carefully, and see if you cannot try and hunt a fox instead of galloping promiscuously over the country.

Any day you like I will arrange a dinner for you, and come and dine with her Ladyship and myself and Mr. Harry Chaplin. I will get Mr. Richardson to come, and we can talk of foxhunting, and do our best to explain exactly the position I mean, but you must remember that, if you accept this invitation, we shall tell you exactly what we think, not from a wish to criticize or to hurt your feelings, but with a view of improving your position in the eyes of the public.

I will now only refer to one more subject, which was Adam's Gorse the other night. The rent of Adam's Gorse, and virtually the management of it to a certain extent, are dependent on myself. You lost your fox on the top of Burrough Hill, where it turned to the left and went to ground, which was as plain as plain could be. You held your hounds right down to the bottom and all along the bottom, and if the fox had gone into Adam's Gorse you must have hit the line off somewhere there. I heard people making very unsatisfactory remarks, and I came to you as a friend and asked you not to go into the covert, for you must remember that you were five couples of hounds short, that we had been running the whole day, and that no sportsman or sensible man at three twenty-seven in the evening would wish to start off on the line of a fresh fox disturbed outside the covert. You kept the upwind side of the covert and turned to your right hand and began blowing your horn, and you must, if you thought for a moment, have known that any hounds coming up behind you would turn upwind to the sound of the horn, which would take them all into the covert. This showed either enormous ignorance on your part, or at least a distinct wish to start a fresh fox coming up the chase of your hunted fox. To start a new fox under the circumstances and at that time of night showed a monstrous want of knowledge of venery, and a very wrong thing to do on the principles of foxhunting law.

Let me assure you that this letter is written entirely and solely in your own interests, and there is nobody in the world except my confidential secretary, Clarke, who is aware that I have written or said a word to you. But the fact of my remonstrating with you has saved you an enormous amount of trouble in the future, because it was all over Melton and London that I had pointed out to you that it was a wrong mode of procedure, and everybody says, 'Now Lonsdale has told him, probably he will never do it again.'

I should not have said all this if I did not like you as a man, and if I did not think you capable of far greater things, and it is for this reason solely that I wish to point out to you that, if your system continues as it is and any change takes place in the Cottesmore Hunt, it would be impossible for you to be recognized here, and, I very much doubt, anywhere else.

I know perfectly well that there are plenty of people who are ready to pat the huntsman of any pack on the back and say that he is a remarkably fine fellow, and then, when he is gone, 'crab him': but there are few who will really write to a huntsman and say what they think and stick up for him when other people are 'crabbing' him.

Let me wish you and yours the very happiest of New Years, and let me beg of you to use your brain, for you have plenty, and your observation, of which you have much, and to try during the next two months to retrieve a character as huntsman, which, I regret to say, at the moment is very severely criticized all over the world.

If you do not care to answer this letter, do not hesitate in leaving it alone. You have plenty to do without writing, but if you care to say that you will come and meet Mr. Chaplin and myself and her Ladyship alone, do so, and I will send over for you one evening, give you plenty of notice, and send you back home at night. And if you can spare the time I will take you down to Badminton in the spring, where we can have some good talks with the most remarkable man in foxhunting in the world—the Duke of Beaufort—who you will see stop hounds four or five times on a run to recover his original line and kill his fox, and kill sometimes four or five foxes in a day by doing so.

Believe me,

Yours very truly,

(*Signed*) LONSDALE.

A Letter Reminding Gillson, Huntsman to the Cottesmore, of his Duties

Dated 24/5/08. Lowther, Penrith.

My dear Gillson,

It is now over a year since you took over the position of huntsman to the Cottesmore Hounds, and I think that perhaps it is time for me to make any remarks that may convey to you my ideas. I hope that you will when reading this letter fully realize that it is written entirely in the interests of yourself and myself and the pack, which means *Sport*.

(a) *The pack.* You came on 1st May and took over a very moderate pack of hounds from the point of looks, hardly a single hound straight. They were possessed of good hunting qualities that they had not for the last few years been allowed to develop. There were many that were full of vice that ruins a pack, and it was difficult to see a pack hunt less for themselves or even keep their heads down; they could not draw properly, they were full of tricks, but the worst fault to my mind was that any sound—a halloa, a train whistle in the far distance, any sound—drew their heads up immediately, just when they should have been down. This was due to a system that to my mind is '*the most fatal system on earth*'—galloping from fox to fox, changing every ten minutes, and not legitimate hunting at all, but a huntsman's attempt at point-to-point under the impression that nobody knew.

Remember this: there are always plenty of gentlemen out who know far more than is imagined. So long as you are with me, and I hope at any time, never play tricks. I have never seen you do so, and I hope never shall. There was only one day when you were inclined to jump off to 'new halloa' and that was close to Cold Overton Wood, and the result was that you did the hounds no good—or yourself either—and missed catching a fox that should have been caught. But you improved the style of hunting. You made your hounds hunt and very well too. Your hounds were as fit as hounds could be and looked it too, and I have not the slightest hesitation in saying *nothing* could be better than their production in the field, and their look in the kennel. They did you credit, and you fully deserved the credit you got. The only hound management fault I *have* and *had* to find was that often the hounds went too fast to covert and you were late. This is a fault and the very greatest fault and must not occur again. I know that it will not, and I know how anxious you are to fall in with my views, but it is almost a '*most essential point*' and of vital importance for *men*, *hounds* and *horses*: 6½ to 7 miles an hour is the greatest rate of speed hounds should be slowed and set to go to covert.

Your system of feeding is excellent. Your management of men is very good. Your interest in all that goes on in kennel is worthy of all praise. Your breeding of hounds showed you are an artist at the game, and therefore I have no hesitation as far as hounds are concerned, yourself and subordinates, everything was perfect up to the day of cubhunting. The only fault I have found was that instead of taking care of new horses, young and just from Ireland, you treated them more as machines for your hard work, rather than as young horses that had to be broken to hounds, and were not fit for long road distances.

Now, remember this: to be a good huntsman means to be observant and thoughtful to a degree, nothing should miss the eye or brain of a really brainy observant man, and he should study his horses as well as his hounds. You thus put sixteen horses out of the list for hunting, owing to over distancing them, splints, etc., being the result. This must not occur again, under ordinary circumstances, for they were all fresh, green young horses from Ireland and selling races. But that is no reason why you should not observe. It was their first year and had you changed to ½ exercise time it would have been more reasonable, more thoughtful and more observant, and you settled £2,000 worth of horses for the season. However the value is not the question, my point being observation and thought—so ends that.

(b) *Riding.* I have no reason to find any fault with you beyond the fact that I would like to point out in the best of spirit that you are very light and that a light man tires his horse more than a medium or heavy-weight. I think often because the light man takes too much for granted and does not, or is not strong enough, to hold his horse together in the deep, and he always allows (this is particularly noticeable in your riding) his horse to over stride himself at every stride when galloping. Secondly, when first you came to the Cottesmore country you never gave your horses a chance of swinging out of their strides or even jumping out of an ordinary pace. Remember this: the art of riding over fences in Leicestershire is timing them, steadying going to them, and *it is the last two strides* well timed and stride well placed that crosses the country to the credit of horse and man, and with ease to the horse. To trot and walk at a fence is childish and ignorant. You must convey to your horse what you want to do, and further than that you must realize that the horse understands before you try, whatever it is. I know you came out of a bank country, and as the season improved you improved to a vast degree. But even at the end of the season I saw you do things wanting in the art of horsemanship. Do you remember riding 'Pugilist' near Braunston on the ridge between the gully from Leicester lane? You wanted to jump a big fence near an oak tree. You never gave the horse a chance; he fell and has never been the same horse since you hurt his back. It was a very big fence and people were standing all around. I saw your intention but you never conveyed your idea to 'Pugilist', he half stopped and could not get up, he silpped down on his quarters and you proceeded further. But it was bad riding, very bad. Then do you remember riding 'Downcharge' jumping into the land at Oustown Village? You never gave him a chance. You rode at a fence into the land with a wide ditch; you trotted at it, he dropped his hind legs for no horse could have covered the distance at that pace and he has never hunted since—and I could mention many many times of similar conditions and horses lamed. But I know you do your best. You have a capital nerve, you have a quick eye and mean getting over the country. So you will, and just try to remember there are three rules: 1st. Convey to your horse what you mean and require him to do. 2nd. Judge the speed that will carry you over. 3rd. Never try to jump a fence you don't think your horse can jump, for you will lose his confidence and he will fail you in an emergency. Watch the last two strides, that is the crucial moment for speed or walk.

You ride well, very well, and like myself and many others can improve vastly. I never blame you for anything but want of thought and *discretion*. You had many falls this year almost invariably your own fault, but your horses were new, and new to the country, nor do I think anything of the numerous falls and am only too glad you were not hurt. As you know, if you want a horse, you can ask. If you don't like it I am only too glad to do what I can. 'Lentonius' I think nothing of, for though a magnificent hunter *following* he will not go first, and no one can make him. You shall have him no more for the regular or cubhunting season. This ends the riding criticism, and that I am not dissatisfied. Your remarkable improvement and good riding at the end of the season showed it was experience and practice over Leicester-shire that was wanted, and with the hints that I have now offered to you I feel sure that all will be well.

(c) *Hound Work*. Now for hound work and the system of proving hounds and hunting a fox. I am no artist, nor do I pretend to be, but I know what I want and what I like, and the man that pays the piper has a right to call the tune. I am equally aware that opinions differ on nearly all points as they are, and must be merely opinions, for there is really no way of proving. 'A' may think one thing, 'B' another, they may both be right on certain casts, or fancies or ideas. You cannot argue, and if you do you cannot prove what is fact, and therefore what is right. But there are certain facts that can be argued and proved, and they are 'practice' that comes from practice and observation, which are well to bear in mind, and it is to these that I refer, fully admitting that I may be wrong, but still I wish my ideas carried out. I will take a day as it comes. You choose your pack, draw them into the Hounds. Never have more than 15½ to 16 couples out the crowded side, Tuesday, Saturday. More get in the way and are liable to be hurt, more likely to stray, take more counting and longer to get through the fences. Always try and draw a pack with nothing (unless a remarkable animal) over three years or under one season, if possible: they run better together, come handier, but it is difficult to do. Never get a hound out that cannot keep up, no matter the age. Keep all the rest for the other side and gradually pick your fastest (I mean of course before the bitches come on, for after that you have to make the best pack you can). If a pack is properly managed no hound over five should be in the list. They do not produce the best whelps, and are very apt to hang the pack up at moments of emergency. This all takes time and luck, and I know there are exceptions to every rule, but that is my principle and my experience is that young hounds give better sport, faster by far and become wonderful hunters *as a pack*, which means the best *sport* our only object, and they kill more foxes. You start with your pack next from the kennels and I should like to see you a little more demonstrative and to converse to your hounds on the way to covert. Note that you are a professional receiving a salary for hunting them, but that you are glad and pleased and delighted to see them, talking to them as you go to the meet, and showing each one that you take a personal interest in him or her. *Speak* to them, *whistle* to them, and let them understand every word and sign. If you are at exercise canter along and stop short giving some sign by mouth or whistle, and make friends of them and get off and pat them when they are doing what you want—more can be done this way than in any other, and if you do it continually no whips are needed—pointers, sheep-dogs, retrievers —all animals—are the same—they are all amenable to sound, providing that it is always the same sound or signal.

Casting hounds: to my mind this is a very weak point in your personal art—I have heard you blame the Whips when you were at fault, not the Whips. You held your hounds down a field (say for argument) to a fence down a ridge; as soon as you see the leading casting hound near the fence you turn round, canter off, and blow your horn, whereas you should not use your horn at all at such a moment. You cannot convey variations in casting on the horn—you should speak or whistle to the leading hounds and not attempt to canter back until the hound furthest from you understands—if you do, half the pack, those nearest to you, follow you, the others get cut off, and lose sight of you, and to attempt to drive a hound to a huntsman when it has lost sight of him is *fatal* and very wrong.

Then, again, you canter or gallop off blowing your horn sometimes and sometimes making no sound whatever—absolutely wrong and foolish—you should look back and see what you have got behind you minding that if the extreme hound can see or hear you they will travel quicker and not be disappointed. This was one of your greatest faults last year: you never *spoke* or *whistled* before you turned your horse round, and you seemed to forget that when your head was turned away from hounds they could not hear you. You must talk to your hounds with your mouth inclined towards them, not the back of your head, for your speed through the air reduces the sound by half, so please remember my wish when casting: always wait before cantering away, until your hounds realize that you are about to be off; convey some private signal that they will understand; never the horn unless absolutely necessary, for a fox will hear the horn and won't notice a whistle or voice; never get ahead of your hounds casting; cast them in front of you—this is easily taught by signal or sound in five minutes. If you do not quite understand I will come out and show you at exercise; do not hesitate in telling me if you do not understand—I will gladly demonstrate my meaning with your own pack.

As regards the line of a fox: I think you have a capital system, though not altogether devoid of fault. You hang on the same direction too long, and although everyone (especially those who know nothing about it) talk of a forward cast, you must remember that a forward cast does not mean holding the hounds continually in one direction. If you take nearby ploughed land, or plough at all on a moderate scenting day, or sheep or cattle or nearby harrowed land, or grass, then make that good, but remember a fox seldom crosses it straight. If, therefore, you take an angle downwind and work up you are more likely to save time although idiots may not realize it.

Take, for instance, a field.

The fox has entered the field and turns.

If you hold the hounds downwind from Point A, make from B to C and C to D then D to E. You will hit the line off far quicker than by walking slowly across the field ride. But often you adopt the whole line crossing the same line continuously, losing time. It is utter rubbish to say 'give a fox the credit for going straight'. *Rubbish*—if the fox had gone straight the hounds would have gone too. It is the turn of the fox that creates the check. It is true that if you look forward and see some sign of sheep or cattle or birds ahead, *that* you may cast on, but not on the dead line—a good fox will make his nearly always, but remember you never know when that *point ends*. If ordinary weather, make your downwind side the commencement of your widecast forward; if stormy, hold your hounds upwind, for on a stormy (windy) day there is often a fair scent and hounds will never run from 50 to 200 yards below the real line of a fox, and if the fox travels higher ground, say the side of a hill, the scent drifts down over the pack. Have them upwind and you will soon discover the line—and few have noticed it.

There is one thing I give you great credit for, and that is that you are never afraid or ashamed to say when you have lost your fox—nobody but a fool would be otherwise (there are a large number of fools about), for they lose the confidence of the hounds and get no credit. I have heard huntsmen go into all sorts of details as to what had become of the fox—if they knew all that, why did they not go and catch it? It's silly and I am glad to say I have never seen or heard you attempt to do it. But I think you are a little slow at observing the movements of cattle, sheep, and more especially birds. The latter are the most important, and tell one a great deal by their flight. *Watch this.*

I think you override your hounds continually, and do not see quick enough when a check is about to take place and go too far—you find your Whips naturally follow, and I saw you do this not on one but on nine different occasions—it's a great fault and wanting in observation. *Watch this.*

I do not think you are very quick at knowing where you are in a wood. That is a gift, and want of it not a fault. But remember you can always tell which way you are going in a wood either by the sun or by the shade and back of the trees, no matter how the rides run, and I have often seen you start to draw from *East* to *West* and in a short space of time turn down *South* and back once or twice *before hounds find.* After that it is obviously a question of sound and watching birds, etc., and then it's difficult; but drawing you should always work on some system keeping your hounds *downwind* of you. *Never* let them get upwind of you—you cannot get them when you want them for they cannot hear—and always keep as straight as possible; do *not* turn about the rides—hounds have good eyes, but, I think, they watch you instead of drawing *properly and wide*; and do not keep blowing your horn in a covert—if you do hounds begin to ignore it and soon get tricky. I should be inclined to draw downwind when possible. If you draw upwind the fox turns at the first opportunity; the state of scent is good upwind, and when the check comes the scent has deteriorated, with the result that you lose time; added to this, a good fox goes off downwind, and is more likely to make his point, and the nearer you get to him in the second and third, etc., phase of scent the nearer and better the huntsmen hunt, and the whole thing—fox and pack—are in front of you, and you have less ground to cover, and it is easier to cast and still more easy to regain the line when he turns, for it must be upwind or sidewind which is stronger and hounds draw to it at once.

This all sounds very well, and so it is as far as it goes, but after all is said and done in a year like this absolutely (with few exceptional days) devoid of scent, no one can do anything, and you did the wisest and best thing you could and killed more foxes than have been killed for years—double what Thatcher ever killed and all credit to you. I shall look forward to next season feeling all confidence of a good season and I feel sure you will make the most of it. I know people crab. What are they? Who are they? Remember those who know don't ever crab; those that know nothing always crab, and no one pays any attention. No man is perfect, and no man can make scent any more than he can control the weather. You have done what was possible—your *best*—and no man can do more.

I hope you will forgive my writing so long a letter, and you are not obliged to agree with all I have written. But, anyhow, I hope it may interest you and give you some food for consideration.

I hope your wife and family are well, and that next season you may have the best of health, the best of sport and no accidents.

Yours very truly,

(*Signed*) LONSDALE.

APPENDIX III

*Hugh Lonsdale's Philosophy on Foxhunting**

Why have you selected me, of all people in the hunting world, to divulge my secret views on a subject that I am utterly incapable of criticizing? There are older men better versed in the art of hunting the fox, and also of riding to hounds than your humble servant.

However, if it can be of any interest to the younger and less experienced than myself, for what it may be worth I give my view, knowing that it can be broken up by critics as a pack of hounds breaks up a fox.

The first point is the fox. What can I say that is not already known about the fox? People ask me what do I know about mange? This is a very serious subject. A mangy fox, when hunted by hounds, seems to have a different scent, and it is difficult to get hounds to hunt it—and if they do they become wild and run hare at once. Many years ago as a boy hunting with the Fitzwilliam, I was taken out by my father to learn from old George Castor all he chose to tell me, and what I could learn by myself. I was standing in a wood on a pony and to my great delight I saw a fox come into the ride. I hallooed, and old George came evidently doubting my experience of what a fox was. He asked: 'What was it, Mr. Hugh?' 'A fox I saw and he is so dirty, all over mud.' 'Mud be d——d,' he answered. 'What do you want to halloa us on to a mangy fox for? Hounds won't run that, and if they do they will be upset all day.' My pride went to the depths of my boots; I had received a severe rebuff that would for ever after be imprinted on my mind.

However the hounds killed it in a few seconds, and I got off to look at it. 'Mud you calls it! I calls it mange! ' said old George. 'Only fit to be shot, but you will learn in time.'. . . (Hugh goes on to describe in detail three different kinds of mange with veterinary precision.)

. . . They say that foxes are the enemy of keepers, but I do not believe that a really good keeper cannot produce both game and foxes. I once asked an old keeper how he managed to keep foxes out of the woods when they were going to start to shoot. His reply was this: 'I always put my netting sticks down the night before all along the ride. Foxes are suspicious and won't go back into that part of the wood, and those

* Written for the *Sporting Chronicle* but not published.

254

inside stop there, those that go out of it won't cross that ride again.' When pheasants are being reared, fix a tarred rope round the crops. The keeper has only to walk round just before dark and run his hand all round the string and no fox will trespass inside it.

After the fox come the hounds, and to comment on the present breed of hounds would be a task not of minutes but of years. There is, however, one point worthy of notice; Peterborough and other hound shows are not an advantage to breeding foxhounds. I have seen animals win prizes at Peterborough that out hunting are absolutely worthless, and have no more right to the 'S' opposite to their names than I have to affix a V.C. to mine. It is only an encouragement to owners and huntsmen to keep good-looking animals, irrespective of their worth.

I remember once being out and seeing a hound hit off the line in a ploughed field. I watched the dog and I never heard him throw his tongue once. I saw him do everything that to my mind proved he was wanting in sagacity and foxhound merit. Next day I pointed out the dog to the huntsman and asked his opinion of it. 'Oh,' he said, 'that's the best foxhound I ever saw. Why, he got first prize at Peterborough!'

A real stallion hound is a very rare thing. A hound that is really straight, beautiful neck and shoulders, depth of girth, bone, feet, has that quality of muscle that should exist, refinement of skin and back quarters like a horse, to which you must then add the whole and only value of the hound, sagacity out hunting, plus quick hearing (this is a point few people ever think of, and call a hound obstinate, when really he is deaf). An animal that throws his very soul into the chase from the moment he enters the cover, that will draw well and steady and get far enough from the huntsman to show he has confidence both in his nose and in his hearing, an animal that will drive to cry, and not be satisfied till he gets to the head of the pack, and when there, turn quickly and not run on from jealousy, and yet have drive enough to take him far and wide. One of the most beautiful points of a foxhound is his wide and deliberate swing when off the line, and there is no other class of hound that possesses this swing except the foxhound. When once you overbreak your hounds and have them whipped up to the huntsman, because he is afraid to trust them, you destroy the natural sagacity which is the essence of perfection in a foxhound. Then, lastly, you want to see your hounds come home, and see that each is a good feeder, after a hard day's work. . . .

. . . I often thing that if the general public knew the value of a hound they would be more thoughtful. No wonder that masters and owners make some remarks to a gentleman whose horse kicks a hound, or to the member of the field who thinks he can clear a fence, the hounds and all, and ends up by clearing nothing, and killing the hound.

Many people who go out hunting do not realize the difficulty of breeding hounds; otherwise they would not go trying a new horse to see if he kicks, and stand in a ride where his horse cannot possibly miss the hounds if he does kick, or race the hounds for a gap in a fence, ending in a dead heat, in which the hounds come off second best; and if in the process a hound gets killed or lamed they do not have the honesty to say so.

If they would only say what had happened the huntsman would know what to do, whereas knowing nothing and with no mark of injury, he feeds his hounds at night, and if a particular hound is off his feed no one knows why. Had he but known he would treat the hound differently and save the poor beast much suffering, and often death. . . .

Talking of the merits of various packs of hounds:

(a) The Badminton Hounds are in my opinion the best pack in existence, but with many apologies to my best friend the Marquis of Worcester I don't think the hounds are in the best condition at all times.

(b) Brocklesby, first class, but look to knees and ankles.

(c) The Belvoir, beautiful animals, but see hounds at work before you decide.

(d) I look upon Mr. Chaplin, Mr. Langham and Lord Worcester as the greatest authorities on foxhounds at this time.

(e) Lord Willoughby's or the Warwickshire are one of the best packs in existence, and with men like Lord Willoughby you only have to ask a question and you get an honest answer. The breeding of a hound is the one thing he dearly loves.

(f) The Cottesmore, I leave others to judge. . . .

. . . Let me end my remarks about hounds, and now about huntsmen: I have no hesitation in saying that during my life I have seen but few gentlemen hunt hounds who had the slightest right to be called huntsmen, or who were educated in the ordinary handling of a pack apart from the science of hunting or of animal instinct. The only exceptions were Lord Worcester, Mr. Rolleston and Lord Willoughby. But the gentlemen who do what they choose to call hunt their own hounds have no idea of the knowledge that was instilled into me since I was a child and that I had to hear from Mr. Chaplin, Mr. Langham and Lord Worcester.

I have always come to the conclusion when I attempt to hunt hounds myself that it would be far wiser to leave it to a professional huntsman, though to a man like myself no one can realize the pleasure of trying to hunt hounds himself, however badly he may do it.

The reason why there are no really first-class huntsmen is because whippers-in are brought up under men who are amateurs, who do not understand the rudiments of the game—and so they only make bad, very bad huntsmen.

A Master should ride home with his huntsman and at leisure discuss every detail, if the Master knows his huntsman's value, but if a huntsman sees the Master knows nothing but ordinary observation (which is usually wrong), the conversation has no value.

There is nothing a huntsman likes more than discussing the various situations of the day, getting praise for right and proof where he is wrong.

If gentlemen continue to hunt hounds to the same extent and with the same result as they do now there will soon be no huntsmen left. In 1865 the first year I was allowed to hunt a fox there were:

Packs of Foxhounds
Gentlemen huntsmen
Professional huntsmen.

Now there are only:

Packs of Foxhounds.

I do not say there are no first-class gentlemen huntsmen, I only speak from what I have seen, and I have hunted with forty-five different packs, but to be a huntsman a man should begin as a child, as I did, in the kennel, learn to dress hounds and walk them out and know every detail in the kennel, and the amateur huntsman lacks the detailed knowledge that makes a first-class huntsman.

Acknowledgements

My grateful thanks are due to the Earl of Lonsdale not only for writing the Preface but for giving me full access to the family papers and for many other kindnesses.

I would also like to thank many other people closely associated with the Lowther Estates who have given me valuable assistance. Mr. Derek Pattinson, Mr. John Peel and Miss D. Ravey in particular have done much to lighten my task. Miss S. E. Bailey, with her long association with the Lowther Estate office, was an invaluable guide through the mass of available material and I was glad to take her advice on many points.

Others, like Sir Gordon Richards, Mr. Dick Steel and Mr. Charlie Haines, have told me much that has been useful, whilst yet others, such as the Lady Barbara Lowther, the Earl of Carlisle, Mr. Denzil Batchelor and Mrs. Shirley Shea, have helped with criticism or with expert knowledge.

Finally I would like to tender my most grateful thanks to Muriel, Viscountess Lowther, who has been closely associated with me in the writing of this book and who has contributed much to it. It is to her that this book is affectionately dedicated.

*

The main source of material for the book has been the letters, Press cuttings and other documents kept in the Lowther archives. Where I have not acknowledged the source it is because the cutting has been preserved but not the name of the paper. Considerable use has been made of the life story Lord Lonsdale himself wrote in *The People*, and the official biography written by Captain Lionel Dawson, R.N., during Lord Lonsdale's lifetime.

Of the many other books that have been consulted, the principal have been: Sir Shane Leslie *Studies in Sublime Failure* (Leslie Benn, 1932), Lady Augusta Fane *Chit Chat* (Thornton Butterworth, 1926), Sir John Astley *Fifty Years of My Life* (Hurst & Blackett), Mari Sandoz *The Cattlemen* (Eyre and Spottiswoode, 1961), Charles Towne and Edward Wentworth *Cattle and Men* (University of Oklahoma Press, 1955), Richard Ferguson *M.P.'s of Cumberland and Westmorland* (Bell and Daldy, 1871), Guy Deghy *Noble and Manly* (Hutchinson, 1956), Von Bülow *Imperial Germany* (Cassell, 1914),

ACKNOWLEDGEMENTS

Colin Ellis *Leicestershire and the Quorn Hunt* (George Gibbons),
Cuthbert Bradley *Foxhunting from Shire to Shire* (Routledge & Kegan
Paul), Denzil Batchelor *Jack Johnson, his Life and Times* (Sportsman's
Book Club, 1957), Jem Mace *In Fair Fight* (V. & R. Chambers,
1956), P. Sichel *The Jersey Lily* (W. H. Allen, 1958).

DOUGLAS SUTHERLAND

Index

'Abingdon, Squire' (George Baird): 52–4, 57, 63, 75, 95, 96, 109
Agriculture, Ministry of: 188
Alaska: 93
Alexandra, Queen (consort of Edward VII): 38, 166, 168
Ancaster, Lord: *quoted*, 4
Argyll Rooms (London): 21, 110
Ascot: 3, 191, 214
Asfordby (family home of Lowthers): 2, 17, 23 *n.*, 100, 209, 221
Astley, Sir John ('The Mate'): 23, 55, 75, 93, 94, 96, 103
Austria, Empress of: 100
Aylesbury, Marquis of: 53
Aylesford, Earl of ('The Jedge'): 46

Baird, George: see 'Abingdon, Squire'
Baird, Mr., M.F.H. (*not* 'Squire Abingdon'): 158
Barleythorpe (Rutland): 3, 4, 14–16, 28, 30, 63–4, 107, 133, 158, 187, 191, 216
Barry, Jimmy (boxer): 170, 171
Beaconsfield, Earl of (Benjamin Disraeli): 38, 67
Beauchamp, Admiral (nicknamed 'The Swell of the Ocean'): 114
Beaufort, Duke of: 23, 54
Benson, Jubilee Juggins: 31
Bentinck, Lord Henry: 54. *See also* Appendix I
Beresford, Lord Marcus: 75
Berliner Tageblatt (German newspaper): 119–20
Bertram Mills Circus: 233

Bettinson, A. F. ('Peggy'): 96, 98, 170, 171, 176
'Big Horn' (Wyoming): 42, 43
Birch, Mr. (Lonsdale Trustees' solicitor): 65, 66
Birkbeck, General : 186
Bismarck, Prinz Otto von: 119, 121 *n.*
'Black Diamond, The' (boxer): *see* Jackson, Peter
'Boston Strong Boy': *see* Sullivan, John L.
Bouverie, Mark: 100
Boxing: 18, 73–4, 190, 205, 206: Lonsdale *v.* Sullivan, 56–60; golden age of, 74, 173–7, 216–17: Championships, 77, 224; rules of, 77–8, 175–6; Pelican Club (*q.v.*), 92–6; Smith *v.* Jackson, 93–4; Smith *v.* Slavin, 95–6; its nadir, 96; Slavin *v.* McAuliffe, 97; legality of, 98, 172–3, 205; fatalities in, 170–3; Moran *v.* Driscoll, 205
British Boxing Board of Control: 190, 206
Broadwood, 'Swish': 100
Brockhurst, Mrs.: 41
Brooklands motor race track: 169
Brough, Lionel (actor): 57, 75, 80, 81
Bruges: 95, 97, 98
Bryanston Street (London): 61
Buchanan, Jack: 221
'Buffalo Bill' (Col. W. F. Cody): 46
Buffalo herds: 41
Bülow, Prince von: 130, 131, 132, 200